The Intext Series in

SECONDARY EDUCATION

Consulting Editor

JOHN E. SEARLES
The Pennsylvania State University

Learning to Teach
Secondary School
Mathematics

Learning to Teach Secondary School Mathematics

OTTO C. BASSLER

Professor of Mathematics
George Peabody College for Teachers

JOHN R. KOLB

Associate Professor of Mathematics
and Mathematics Education
North Carolina State University

 INTEXT EDUCATIONAL PUBLISHERS
College Division
Scranton   Toronto   London

ISBN 0-7002-2320-7

Library of Congress Catalog Card Number: 70-151637

TO

Bradley
Erich
Timothy

Preface

Experience with training teachers of mathematics has gradually impressed upon us a fundamental principle; that is, prospective teachers learn few teaching skills from reading a textbook pertaining to the teaching of mathematics. Methods books that inspire and aid practicing teachers are often rejected by beginning teachers because the ideas that are presented are too abstract and too remote for them to apply. A lack of concrete teaching experiences causes many beginning teachers to have difficulty in bridging the gap from suggestions and techniques to their application in the classroom. It is felt that since the inexperienced person lacks this background, it must be provided. This book is designed to help the novice teacher bridge this gap by providing a kind of "second-hand" teaching experience.

The heart of the book is a large collection of specific exercises that either simulate aspects of the teaching process or identify recurring problems of content. In each exercise, a situation is given that focuses on one particular facet of mathematics teaching. The student responds to the given information by choosing among alternatives or devising an appropriate course of action. The student is initiated into teaching by simulating the decisions and actions that a practicing teacher must undertake in the instructional process. While this approach does not replace classroom experience or learning under the guidance of a master teacher, it enables the student to acquire some teaching competence vicariously.

Each chapter consists of four main sections: a brief introduction, a collection of exercises, several suggested activities, and a list of additional sources. The introductions are intended to promote agreement on the use of relevant terms and to provide a framework for successful completion of the ensuing exercises. The exercises expand upon this framework and give concreteness to the ideas expressed in the introduction. The suggested activities contain additional in-depth work in the topic through relevant outside readings or study experiences outside of the class. The chapter concludes with a specific list of additional sources pertinent to the chapter topic.

The book is divided into two parts. Part I, consisting of the first fifteen chapters, pertains to general pedagogical issues which must be considered to become an effective teacher of mathematics. Part II deals with specific subjects or mathematics at a particular grade level and the problems that are peculiar to these levels of mathematics teaching.

When examining the chapters, it may seem that the material in any specific chapter does not cover the subject of the chapter deeply enough or comprehensively enough. This, of course, is true and it results from the commitment to very specific exercises. While the entire book provides a broad base of experiences, the exercises selected for each chapter represent only a core of major ideas considered to be most crucial in learning and important ideas of the topic. Through reflective thinking, the student is expected to recall and extend this core to deal effectively with new problems or situations that might arise in the classroom.

We can envision this textbook being used in a variety of ways. The book contains sufficient material around which to organize a course in the teaching of mathematics. It could also be used as a student assignment book in conjunction with a traditional methods book, or as a discussion guide and source book for in-service training of experienced teachers. Different portions of the book have been used by the authors in a sophomore course, entitled "Introduction to Teaching," a senior mathematics methods course, a course for training teachers of collegiate mathematics, and a graduate level course in mathematics education.

The authors are indebted to a great many friends and colleagues who have provided many helpful criticisms and suggestions for the completion of this book. In particular we wish to express our appreciation to Professor Larry Watson for his critical analysis and refinement of many of our first ideas. We also wish to thank Mrs. Fearing and Mrs. King for the seemingly endless job of manuscript typing. Finally, a huge debt of gratitude is extended to the many students and student teachers with whom the authors were privileged to work. These students have provided us with valuable insights and illustrations that are included in this book.

OTTO C. BASSLER
JOHN R. KOLB

Nashville, Tennessee
Raleigh, North Carolina
April, 1971

Contents

Structure of Algebra. Word Problems to Mathematical Sentences. The Content of Algebra. Exercises. Suggested Activities. Additional Sources.

Teaching for Comprehension of Geometric Content. Teaching "Proof Making." Teaching Students to Make and Test Conjectures. Exercises. Suggested Activities. Additional Sources.

Alternatives for Advanced Mathematics. Trigonometry. Advanced Topics. Exercises. Suggested Activities. Additional Sources.

PART I

INTRODUCTION

Effective mathematics instruction can only be accomplished when the teacher is proficient in mathematics and in methods of teaching mathematics. It is the intent of the first portion of this book to consider general pedagogical issues which must be resolved in order to become an effective teacher of secondary school mathematics.

Major areas in the teaching of mathematics are presented so that the novice teacher gains skills in formulating goals and objectives of mathematics learning, in identification of several different instructional sequences which lead to the same end result, in designing activities which utilize various modes of instruction, and in gathering instructional materials that can be used in teaching the lesson. These activities are then molded together to provide experience in planning for effective instruction. Planning alone, however, is not sufficient for becoming a good teacher. The prospective teacher must also be aware of problems that are encountered in teaching the lesson and maintaining a learning atmosphere. Following instruction, there is then a need for assessment and evaluation, both for the teacher and for the student. All of these phases of the instructional process are considered in Part I.

Each step in the instructional process is illustrated by a variety of concrete situations arising in the teaching of secondary school mathematics. Examples are chosen from any part of secondary school mathematics. By identifying other mathematical concepts which illustrate or pertain to the same issue, the prospective teacher can gain a deeper understanding of the techniques and decisions that a practicing teacher must make in the instructional process.

Chapter 1

The Nature of Mathematics

The mathematics courses you have studied were designed to train you in the acquisition of skills, computational ability, capability to produce proofs, and knowledge of principles in the various branches of mathematics. However, a teacher of mathematics needs a somewhat broader prospective of mathematics than merely recall of theorems and their proofs or facility in mathematical operations. It would seem that a teacher will not have a deep-rooted conception of why or how mathematics is taught if he does not first have some notion of what mathematics is. It is hoped that a fuller understanding of "what mathematics is" will yield a clearer conception of what is required of you in your role as a teacher of mathematics.

MATHEMATICS AND THE PHYSICAL WORLD

Perhaps the major realization required by a person who wishes to understand mathematics is that mathematics, unlike the other sciences, does not deal directly with any physical objects that we can feel, taste, smell, hear, or even see. Rather the "things" of mathematics are all ideas in our mind and have no existence as physical objects. A helpful way of thinking about mathematics is to imagine "two worlds" or two levels of existence.[1] One world is our universe of physical objects—the things we can feel, smell, taste, or in some way observe directly or indirectly. We will call this the physical world. We also can postulate a second world—a world of ideas. It is here that the mathematical entities such as planes and points exist; that is, planes and points are not themselves physical objects but are idealizations of objects such as a flat piece of paper or the sharp tip of a pencil.

---

[1] The description of two worlds given here is not intended as a truism for an actual state of affairs. It is offered only as a convenient model or context within which to discuss certain types of mathematical activities that in turn have a bearing upon the goals of mathematics teaching. The authors make no attempt to judge the "truth" of this view; rather we simply regard it as a useful device to clarify the nature of mathematical activity.

The interaction between these two worlds can be seen from the nature of the activities performed by mathematicians.

1. Situations and problems arising in the physical world are examined to identify the important physical objects and relationships among these objects.
2. The characteristics and relationships between the components of the physical situation are translated into idealizations in the idea world. It is sometimes said that the physical situation is mathematized, or relationships in the physical situations are abstracted into statements that are in mathematical language.
3. The set of mathematical statements are examined and explored by mathematical techniques. The content and methods of one or more branches of mathematics may be applied to the statements to derive new statements of relationships. The validity of the statements is tested by resorting to logical proof. The entire set of mathematical terms and statements is called a *mathematical model* of the physical problem.
4. The mathematical entities and statements in the mathematical model are interpreted as specific objects and relationships in the physical world and applied to the solution of physical problems.
5. The solutions and predictions that are derived from the mathematical model are tested in the physical situation to determine if they are sensible and to see if they work.[2]

The relation of mathematics and the physical world is shown diagrammatically in Fig. 1-1.

If you have examined Fig. 1-1, you will notice the "two worlds" indicated; you should also notice the interrelation between them in processes 1 and 3. Here is where mathematics relates to our physical world. It should be noted that the relationship is in both directions.

Physical situations give rise to idealized reflections in the idea world, like a mirror that takes somewhat imperfect objects and improves their image. However, the process of abstracting to the mathematical world may distort the original situation so that the mathematical model may be elegant from a mathematical standpoint yet not be a faithful image or characterization of the physical problem.

In the same way, in process 3, when a mathematical model is chosen and translated to the physical world, we may find that the reinterpreted mathematical model does not yield a "good fit" for

[2] The procedure described above has been summarized succinctly in *The American Mathematical Monthly* (October 1961), p. 799, as follows: "The use of applied mathematics in its relation to a physical problem involves three stages: (1) a dive from the world of reality into the world of mathematics; (2) a swim in the world of mathematics; (3) a climb from the world of mathematics back into the world of reality, carrying a prediction in our teeth."

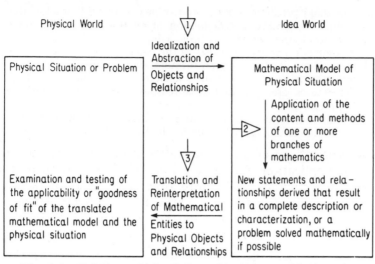

Fig. 1-1. Relation of physical world to the world of mathematics. The processes involved in going from one stage to another are indicated by the arrows.

the physical situation. Another mathematical model must then be found that when applied to the physical problem produces solutions or predictions that are in more accord with observations.

Unlike processes 1 and 3 that deal with the interaction between the idea world and the physical world, the activities of process 2 are conducted entirely in the idea world. Mathematics, as a body of knowledge, consists solely of relationships between certain specified entities in the idea world. Usually these relationships are organized into a deductive structure. The validity of any statement in the deductive structure is established by means of deduction from stated assumptions called *axioms*. Mathematicians must employ logical inference and computation in establishing assertions, not experimentation, since it is impossible to physically manipulate ideas such as points, lines, or numbers that do not physically exist.

The formulation of mathematical models and their application do not occur solely between physical situations and the idea world. Mathematicians formulate mathematical models that are themselves abstractions from other mathematical entities and relationships. Thus, through a utilization of the 5 activities listed on page 4 applied to situations in the idea world, hierarchies of more inclusive and more abstract (that is, more removed from physical interpretations) mathematical models are formed.

As a result of the preceding discussion and Fig. 1-1, we are able to make a distinction between mathematical activity and mathematics as a discipline or body of knowledge.

Mathematics as a body of knowledge is comprised of consistent collections of statements called *mathematical models*. The statements of any model, when the terms are interpreted either qualitatively or spatially, may be applied to systematically order, manipu-

late, and make predictions in our known physical world, or allow the
intellectual conception and deduction of relationships in unknown
parts of our physical world or in an imaginary world.[3]
   Mathematical activity consists of the behaviors of
(a) abstraction, idealization, and formulation of process 1,
(b) inductive reasoning (guessing, analogy, generalization, testing
     conjectures, etc.) and deductive reasoning (proof, computation)
     in process 2,
(c) translation, reinterpretation, and examination of the relevance
     of the model to a specific situation in process 3.

The descriptions of mathematical activity and of mathematics
have clear implications for the teaching of mathematics. It is not
sufficient for students to acquire only knowledge of facts and
principles contained in finished mathematical models. They must
also learn some of the know-how that is a part of mathematical
activity.

ASSUMPTIONS ABOUT MATHEMATICS AND MATHEMATICAL ACTIVITY

Underlying all mathematics and mathematical activity are several widely accepted assumptions or principles. These may be useful in guiding your thinking about mathematics teaching and the
activities of your students.

1. *Principle of Abstraction.* Mathematics does not deal directly with any physical object or physical laws but only
   with concepts that are idealized from physical objects or
   prior mathematical abstractions. For example, three men,
   three stars, or a set containing a pen, pencil, and a ruler
   may suggest the mathematical concept of "three". Yet
   mathematical operations with three involve only the concept of "threeness" without regard to any characteristic
   of the particular objects comprising the set.
2. *Principle of Selective Abstraction.* Only certain kinds of
   properties and relations are abstracted mathematically
   from physical objects. Shape, size, numerosity, or position
   are properties that can be abstracted for mathematical
   analysis, whereas color, mass, or states of matter are not
   abstractions that are included in the realm of mathematical objects.
3. *Principle of Levels of Abstractions.* Mathematics consists
   of increasing levels of abstractions. Mathematical concepts
   or relationships are grouped together on the basis of one
   or more common attributes to form a new mathematical
   abstraction or generalization.
4. *Principle of Mathematical Freedom.* The separation of
   mathematical ideas from the physical world permits idea-

---

[3] These statements are intended as descriptions for the purposes of distinguishing between the two concepts. It should not be inferred that they are
inclusive and exclusive definitions of mathematics and mathematical activity.
Throughout the text, when a term is used and a certain meaning is to be
attached to that term, the term and its description will be set apart.

tions and conceptions unrelated to any physical experience or physical limitations. Mathematical thought goes beyond the limit of physical experience and considers ideas such as n-dimensional geometries, transfinite numbers, and the infinite.

5. *Principle of Deductive Nature of Mathematics.* Sections of mathematics can be organized into a deductive structure in which all technical words are specified either as undefined terms or defined terms, and the statements can be logically deduced from a set of initial assumptions called *axioms.*

6. *Principle of Order of Axiomization.* The axiomization of a section of mathematics is not the starting point, but the terse finished product that results from much inductive and deductive thinking applied to the development of the theory. Selection of an appropriate axiom set is preceded by an intimate knowledge of the statements of the theory that are to be included in the deductive system.

7. *Principle of Variety of Axiomization.* Distinct axiom sets may be possible for the same body of statements. As long as the axioms are consistent (noncontradictory), they will serve the purpose of providing a framework within which to logically deduce statements and thus test the validity of the inferences.

8. *Principle of Variable Rigor.* The logical rigor of mathematical proofs is not absolute, but is in a process of development along with all of mathematics. A mathematical demonstration that is unquestioned in one age may not be considered rigorous enough in a later time. However, mathematical proofs are subject to scrupulous rules with the view of making the results incontestable within the rules of deduction.

9. *Principle of Economy of Effort.* The abstraction of physical situations reveals the basic mathematical structure and relationships that hold in general. When the mathematical model has been investigated (solved, proved), all "true interpretations" of the model are solved. The economy of abstraction is that when something is done in general, it is done for all possible special cases. The more general and abstract a formulation is, the more applications can be found to fit it; hence an economy of effort is the result.

10. *Principle of "Goodness of Fit."* When a mathematical model is being interpreted into a physical problem, care must be exercised to insure that the assumptions and limiting conditions of the mathematical model are satisfied. In the mathematical model of the rational numbers, $3/5 + 4/5 = 7/5$. However, if a boy throws darts and gets 3 hits out of 5 on one trial and 4 hits out of 5 on another, then clearly $3/5 + 4/5 = 7/10$, which relates his combined proficiency for both trials.

11. *Principle of Choice of Mathematics.* In applying mathematics, mathematicians can choose, from the repertoire of mathematical models or descriptions, those that yield the closest fit to data gathered experimentally or given by the physical problem. For example, in fitting a curve to plotted data, there may be several functions that would yield a reasonably good fit for the limited range of the data.

12. *Principle of Interaction.* There is continual interaction between the idea world of mathematics and the physical world. The physical world gives rise to idealizations in the mathematical world and abstractions constructed in mathematics, without motivation from the physical world, find fruitful physical interpretations.

13. *Principle of Growth and Evolution.* Mathematics has grown as society has grown and demanded its benefits. As mathematics has expanded in subject matter and range of application, there has been an evolution of thought concerning the nature of mathematics and axiomatics.

14. *Principle of Mathematical Reasoning.* Mathematics requires the use of inductive and deductive reasoning. The production of abstract concepts and the discovery of relationships and proofs is aided by the use of models, pictorial representations, and physical analogies.

1-1. The principle of abstraction states that the "things" of mathematics have no physical existence other than in our minds. The principle of selective abstraction states that of all the abstractions that might be extracted from any physical object or situation, only certain kinds of attributes are idealized for mathematical treatment. The following activities are intended to help you understand these two assumptions.

Imagine you have before you three sets, A, B, and C that contain objects as follows:

$$A = \{book, pencil, pen\} \quad B = \{pipe, wagon, dog\}$$
$$C = \{box, candle, cup, radio\}$$

1. What property *is* shared by Set A and Set B that *is not* possessed by Set C?
2. Could the property shared by Set A and Set B and *not* possessed by Set C be distinguished by you if your native language were Chinese, Eskimo, Spanish, or Cherokee?
3. Suppose you could talk over a telephone to a learner and you wished to help him get the concept you have attained of the property shared by Set A and Set B. Assuming the learner cannot count, how would you describe this property to him?
4. State whether the property shared by Set A and Set B but *not* possessed by Set C depends on:
   (a) the type of objects in the set
   (b) the material comprising the objects
   (c) the weight of the objects
   (d) the shape of the objects
   (e) any physical property of the objects in the sets

1-2. You may feel that while arithmetic and algebra deal with abstract ideas, geometry is concrete and treats objects in our physical world, such as lines, planes, circles, and squares. A little reflection will convince you that no physical object can satisfy the requirements of mathematical figures. For example, any flat object you might choose to be a plane will be finite with three dimensions and hence will not suffice as a geometric plane.

1. In what ways are the following physical entities inadequate representations of the geometric figures they suggest?

	Physical Object		Geometric Figure
(a)	Edge of a razor blade	(a')	line
(b)	A molecule	(b')	point
(c)	A die	(c')	cube
(d)	A pane of glass	(d')	rectangular region
(e)	A tin can	(e')	right circular cylinder

2. What difficulty is a student encountering who shows you two sheets of paper positioned like those in the illustration below and says: "One of our theorems is wrong. It says two distinct planes either intersect in a line or not at all. I can show that they intersect in a point. See!"

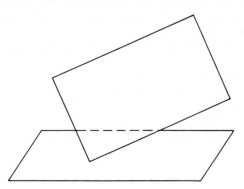

1-3. The concept of "What is geometry?" has been changing since the beginning of history. Each statement below contains a different historical concept of geometry.

(a) Geometry is the study of spatial figures and relations in a logical, deductive fashion.

(b) A geometry is the study of the properties of the elements of a set that are invariant under a group of transformations on the set.

(c) Geometry is a collection of practical rules for making earth measurements.

(d) There are several quite different but valid geometries depending upon the axioms chosen. Hence geometry goes beyond a study of physical entities.

(e) Geometry is the study of figures and relations in our physical world, deductively, either in terms of their algebraic representation by equations or the study of the figures directly, without the use of their algebraic representations.

1. What is the correct historical order, oldest to most recent, in which to list these statements?

2. Which statement about geometry probably best expresses the concept of geometry held by (a) Early Egyptians, (b) René Descartes, (c) Euclid, (d) Felix Klein, (e) Nikolai Lobachevski?

3. The changing concept of geometry discussed above supports which of the assumptions about mathematics at the end of the chapter?

1-4. The interaction between the physical world and the world of mathematics is outlined in five steps in the textbook. These five steps are illustrated in this exercise with an example.

1. Suppose a mathematician is confronted with the physical problem of determining the elevation from sea level at any time of an object tossed into the air. Which of the following variables seems relevant in this problem? (a) Direction of the toss; (b) weight of the object; (c) shape of the object; (d) earth's gravity; (e) elevation of site of toss; (f) initial velocity of the toss.

2. The mathematician decides to limit and idealize the problem by ignoring any effects due to wind or air resistance. The mathematical model he chooses for this problem is: The altitude h of an object t seconds after being thrown upward vertically with a starting speed of r ft per second from an altitude of k ft is given by: $h = rt\ {}^-16t^2 + k$. Which parts of the original problem are ignored, which are limited, and which are fully considered in this mathematical model of the physical situation?

3. Using that part of mathematics that deals with quadratic functions, verify that the following statements can be derived from the mathematical model.
    (a) Increases in r produce increases in h when k is constant
    (b) h is maximum when $t = r/32$
    (c) When k and r are positive and constant, there must be a value of $t > 0$ when $h = 0$

4. Interpretations of the statements derived in part (3) can be made to the physical situation. For example, the fact that h is maximum at $t = r/32$ implies that the object rises until $t = r/32$ and is falling after that. How would you interpret the other two statements derived above?

5. The mathematical model gives values of h for all values of t. Obviously, in the physical problem, those values of t before the object is tossed and after it returns to the ground are not sensible in the problem. The predictions from the model are ignored outside of the limited domain of t for which it sensibly applies in the problem. For what domain of values of t does the model apply to the physical problem?

1-5. When a mathematical model is formulated, there are always some tacit assumptions made in order to idealize and abstract to the world of mathematics (process 1). Hence, when a mathematical model is selected and applied to a physical problem (process 3), the predictions it yields must be compared to the physical realities to determine the extent to which they agree.

Using the same model as in the previous exercise, $h = rt - 16t^2 + k$, consider the following:

1. Suppose you threw a baseball upward vertically where $r = 48$ ft per second and $k = 300$ ft. Suppose, also, you threw a feather upward vertically where $r = 48$ ft per second and $k = 300$ ft. According to the mathematical model, what would be the maximum height attained by the baseball? The feather? According to the mathematical model, would both objects require the same amount of time to acquire $h = 0$? Do you think that the predictions of the model would much more closely approximate the physical situation with one object than with another? Why?

2. The mathematical model predicts that for all positive values of r and k there must be a value of t when the object hits the ground. Why? Yet some space probes leave the earth never to return.

   (a) What causes the contradiction between the prediction of this mathematical model and the fact that some space probes do not return? Does that mean the model is wrong and hence should be avoided?

   (b) Suppose a gun could be made to propel upward a bullet at any initial velocity you may choose. Could r be increased to the point where the bullet would not return? Why or why not?

3. Which of the principles in the list given at the end of this chapter does this exercise illustrate?

1-6. When confronted with a new problem, we usually do not have to create a new mathematical model. Instead, using clues from the problem situation, we search the mathematics we already know in an effort to find one or more mathematical models that may be applied. Often, a known mathematical model cannot be used unchanged, but it can be modified and applied to the new situation.

Write the mathematical model you would choose to represent each of these situations:

1. Determine the height h in feet at any time t of a ball dropped with no initial velocity from a platform 300 ft high?

2. A sandbag is thrown directly downward from a stationary balloon at an altitude of 720 ft with an initial velocity of r ft per second. Determine the height h in feet of the sandbag at any time t.

3. Determine the height h in feet at any time t of a ball thrown upward from a platform k ft above the ground at an angle of 30 degrees to the horizontal.

1-7. Here is another problem much like those considered previously. An airplane is flying horizontally k ft above the ground at a constant speed when an object is dropped from the plane.

Suppose you wanted your class to derive a mathematical model relating the height and time of drop of the object.

1. Make a list of the factors the students may think will influence the height and time of drop of the object.
2. Looking at your list, what could you do to enable the students to identify important factors, and either ignore or idealize them?
3. Devise a procedure to help the students construct a mathematical model for this problem.
4. List some additional questions that could be investigated in this problem such as, What kind of curve is the path of the dropping object? (Can you prove your conjecture?)
5. What are some of the limitations of the model constructed for this problem and how would you illustrate these limitations for your students? [*Hint*: If you have difficulty with this problem you might get a start by consulting Kline (1953), p. 195.[4]]

---

[4] References will be indicated by the last name of the principal author followed by date of publication. Full bibliographical information is listed at the end of each chapter.

1-8. A different kind of mathematical model from that considered in the previous exercises is a deductive system. Consider this example of a deductive system:

Let S be a set of elements and F a relation satisfying the following axioms:

P_1: If a and b are distinct elements of S and
if bFa, then aFb cannot hold.

P_2: If a is an element of S, then there is at
least one element b of S such that bFa.

P_3: If a, b, c, are elements of S such that
bFa and cFb, then cFa.

State which of the three processes of mathematical activity shown in Fig. 1-1 a person would be engaged in if

1. He proved the theorem: If x is an element of S, then there are at least two elements, y, z, of S such that yFx and zFx

2. He noticed that the elements in S could be the positive integers and the relation F could be thought of as the words: "is a multiple of?"

3. He formulated this deductive system by observing the relation ">" on the set of real numbers and generalized its properties

ADDITIONAL SOURCES

Bunt, Lucas N. H. "Equivalent Forms of the Parallel Axiom," *Mathematics Teacher*, 60 (October 1967), pp. 641–652.

Denbow, Carl. "To Teach Modern Algebra," *Mathematics Teacher*, 7 (March 1959), pp. 162–170.

Kline, Morris. *Mathematics in Western Culture*. New York: Oxford University Press, 1953.

Manheim, Jerome H. *Mathematics in the Petroleum Industry*. American Petroleum Institute, 1271 Avenue of the Americas, New York, N. Y. 10020.

Tuller, Anita. *A Modern Introduction to Geometries*. New York: Van Nostrand Reinhold Company, 1967.

Chapter 2

Mathematics Learning

TEACHING AND LEARNING

Teaching and learning are central to education, yet there is often much confusion between these two activities. There are distinct differences between these two processes that need to be understood. If these distinctions are accepted in the general case we can then give a description of mathematics learning and mathematics teaching as special situations.

Learning as used here is the process or act by an individual of acquiring new behavior. It should be stressed that, in this view, learning is an activity in which the learner engages. We may observe some of the activities or movements in which an individual engages when he is learning, such as moving objects, writing symbols, or talking aloud. However, much of the learning act consists of processes that occur inside the learner. These processes are hidden from an observer and possibly from the learner himself.

We say that an individual has learned when he has acquired new behavior, i.e., when he is able to do something he could not do before. Usually, for school-related learning, we are more specific about the behavior that we expect the learner to acquire so we establish objectives that are expected to be learned by the individual. Thus mathematics learning might be described as the process of acquiring the behaviors included in the description of mathematics and mathematical activity in Chapter 1.

Teaching may be conceived as the structuring of materials, stimuli, and conditions for the learner. The purpose of the teaching process is to motivate and aid the learner in acquiring desired behaviors. Structuring of conditions that will facilitate learning may be accomplished by the learner alone—i.e., he may teach himself, another person ("teacher" or "student"), a programmed textbook, or a machine. Obviously, mathematics teaching is the structuring of materials, conditions and stimuli so that the student is more likely to learn mathematical behaviors.

Several conclusions can be drawn immediately from the description of teaching and learning. A learner must acquire *his* behavior himself. His learning cannot be accomplished for him by another person nor will his observation of another person engaging in the desired behavior guarantee his attainment of the task. A teacher must structure conditions for the learner so that he is given the time and opportunity to try to exhibit the desired behavior. To summarize the last several sentences, just because a teacher has taught (structured the conditions or shown the learner the expected behavior) does not insure that the learner has learned (has acquired the expected behavior).

TEACHING MATHEMATICS FOR MAXIMUM LEARNING

The set of behaviors that are expected as a result of teaching and the set of behaviors that are learned by the students in a mathematics classroom are not equal sets. A possible picture of these two sets appears in Fig. 2-1.

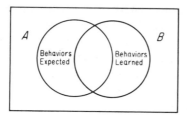

Fig. 2.1. Relationship between expected and learned behaviors.

The central problem in teaching is to structure conditions so that the students are able to learn the expected behaviors. In fact, one measure of the success of any lesson is to assess the extent of $A \cap B$, the intersection of the two sets. It is not enough, however, to assess the extent of success; we must also be concerned with the extent of failure, that is, $A \cap B'$ (B' is the complement of set B) and $A' \cap B$. An analysis of the set of behaviors in $A \cap B'$ will yield an indication of the teaching techniques that were used that were not effective. The set of behaviors in $A' \cap B$ is a set of unexpected behaviors. This would include erroneous or unwanted behaviors as well as desired behaviors such as a novel but unexpected solution to a problem.

If teaching is the structuring of conditions for the learner so that he will be aided in acquiring the behaviors expected of him, how do we as teachers create or select the best way to structure the conditions to insure maximum learning? The answer is that teachers use a combination of intuition, past experience, and creative insight into the task to be learned, plus hard work and a few assumptions about conditions that seem to facilitate learning. It is the purpose of the next section to state some of these assumptions. It is the purpose of the entire book to give you the opportunity to develop the other necessary characteristics of a good teacher.

ASSUMPTIONS ABOUT CONDITIONS FOR LEARNING

Since the teaching process and the learning process are distinct but related processes, a theory of learning would have many implications for a theory of teaching. If we knew exactly how people learn mathematics, the choices and decisions in structuring the conditions for learning a mathematics task would be easier to make. However, at present there is no theory of mathematical learning nor is there a theory of mathematics teaching. In other words, no one knows exactly what to do to a learner to make him learn any particular mathematical task, since no one knows exactly what conditions external to the learner cause mechanisms, internal to the learner to produce learning. As a result we cannot make any list of statements about learning or teaching that would comprise either a theory of learning or a theory of teaching.

The guidelines that we will list consist of assumptions that have been found to be useful and certain empirical statements that have sometimes been found in practice to enhance mathematical learning. The statements (with the exception of the first) are not assumptions about how learning occurs but are descriptions of certain sets of conditions whose presence is presumed to aid the student in acquiring, retaining, and transferring mathematical behavior. The assumptions listed are offered only as guidelines; there has been no attempt in this formulation to be either mutually exclusive or exhaustive.

1. *An individual learns all new behavior as a result of his interaction with his total environment.*

We assume that how an individual learns and what an individual learns is shaped solely by the activities and experiences in which he has engaged within the two parts of his total environment. The one part of his environment consists of the forces and objects external to him that either act upon him or upon which he acts. The second part of his environment is within him and includes his view of himself and the world, his stored knowledge and ways of handling knowledge, and his feelings. This also implies that no new learning could occur if somehow an individual's total environment were removed from him and he were left in a void.

This assumption has already been used as a premise in this chapter to arrive at a conception of teaching. By assuming that all learning is produced and shaped solely by the individual's total environment, we conclude that we can intervene in the learner's total environment and structure one part of it so that what he learns and how he learns is affected by our action. This in turn permits teaching to be conceived as the structuring of a part of the environment so that the learning of desired outcomes is facilitated. Thus the assumption that the process of learning can be influenced by someone other than the learner justifies the existence of the profession of teaching.

The remaining statements describe conditions or states of affairs within and surrounding the learner. We assume that the presence of these conditions facilitate the learner in acquiring, retaining, and applying desired mathematical behavior. The statements describing conditions within the learner belong in the learning domain and only imply conditions for teaching, while statements describing conditions outside of the learner belong to the teaching domain.

2. *Learning is facilitated if the behavior to be learned is consistent with the learner's view of the world and his view of himself and his role in the world.*

This assumption would imply that if a person views himself as a mathematician, he will engage in behaviors which reflect this view; if a person aspires to be an auto mechanic, he will often be found tinkering with automobiles; or if he plans to go to college, he will enroll in a college preparatory curriculum. There are many implications of this assumption for school-related learning, for if an individual has convinced himself that he cannot learn mathematics, it becomes necessary to change his view of himself. Individuals of this type must first be convinced that they can do mathematics by providing them with mathematics they can do,— that is, provide them with a successful experience in mathematics. The maxim, "Nothing succeeds like success," has been demonstrated to be true all too often to ignore the effect of success in changing attitudes from negative to positive. If we are to successfully teach mathematics we must make sure that each student has a view of himself that will make him receptive to mathematics learning.

Although a person's view of the world is undoubtedly an outgrowth of his view of himself, his conception of his external environment is probably an important variable in his success in acquiring a new behavior. When the learner can perceive the contribution that new behavior, such as mathematics, might make to his world, he may be more motivated to learn the behavior.

3. *Learning is facilitated if the learner perceives the task as being meaningful and applicable.*

This assumption implies that if information is perceived as useful to the individual then it will have a greater effect and be retained longer than if the information does not seem to be useful to the individual. It is well to recall that learning is used for the solution of real or contrived problems. If information is used in solving real problems, it is meaningful. On the other hand, if the *only* use of the information seems to be in the solution of contrived problems, much of its meaningfulness may be lost. For this reason we as mathematics teachers should strive to find real and meaningful illustrations of the content that is being taught. When the application must be contrived, the least we can do is to phrase the problem in an interesting context.

4. *Learning is facilitated when the learner has previously attained and can recall all the prerequisite knowledge necessary for learning a specified behavior.*

Learning mathematics is not happenstance; it is based on a carefully structured sequence of activities. Since much of mathematics is cumulative in nature, i.e., one concept utilizes preceding concepts, a carefully prescribed sequence of instruction must be followed. This sequence would teach lower-level skills or concepts first and continue to build on these. Then the next higher-level skills or concepts would be taught and so on. This assumption means that the learning of a new behavior is not possible if the preceding prerequisite behaviors have not been learned.

The major task of any teacher is to structure conditions outside of the learner so that learning is facilitated. Some of the below assumptions have already been implied from assumptions about conditions that are assumed to aid learning and operate inside the learner.

5. *Learning is facilitated when the goal or outcome of the task to be learned is known to the learner.*

We have already assumed that the learner must perceive the task as meaningful and applicable. This perception for most school-related tasks is a consequence of knowing about the purpose of the task to be learned and how it fits into the overall mathematics program for the learner. This does not mean that the learner must know or be informed of every aspect of that which is to be learned. Rather, the pupil needs to have some sort of a general idea or conception of the direction in which his activities are being guided.

6. *Learning is facilitated when the learner actively participates in the performance of the task to be learned rather than passively receives information.*

Since learning is an individual act, it seems obvious that the learner must be an active participant in achieving any new behaviors. Thus the teacher must structure the learning situation to provide student activities and involvement at the initial stage of learning as well as a variety of recurring experiences. The experiences should certainly permit the learner to use several senses simultaneously. One of the most neglected aspects in school learning is the use of the sense of touch and the resulting feelings of manipulating, positioning, measuring, drawing, sequencing, and experimenting with cause and effect relationships. These types of activities will insure that the learner has an active role in the instructional process. The statement that the only way to learn mathematics is to do mathematics may be considered as a restatement of this assumption.

A second implication of this assumption along with assumption 4 is that the involvement of the learner must begin at a level that is within the learner's experience and then extends this level by numerous concrete examples so that the student makes generalizations to more abstract levels. In other words, instructions and experiences must be within the grasp of the learner; then through varied experiences the learner should be led to apply the behavior to more general and higher-level behaviors.

7. *Learning is facilitated when erroneous behaviors are eliminated and when the learner can distinguish between behaviors which may be confused with the behavior to be learned.*

It is entirely possible for erroneous behavior or incompatible behavior to prohibit the acquisition of new behaviors. Also, if the learner is not shown how to discriminate between old behaviors and the new behavior to be learned, he may acquire and practice behavior which is not applicable to the given situation. It is much more difficult to teach or learn when erroneous behavior must first be eliminated; therefore, in our teaching every effort should be made to prevent erroneous behavior from occuring.

8. *Learning is facilitated when the learner is informed of his progress in relation to the goal to be attained.*

We all like to know things that we do well and correctly; however, we should also be informed of our shortcomings and errors in order to improve. Feedback relating to individual responses should be provided so that incorrect behavior is not practiced and not learned. The learner should also be provided with some knowledge about the overall progress that he is making with respect to a unit of work or an entire course. One manifestation of this assumption in education is the assignment of letter grades to indicate student performance.

9. *Learning is facilitated when a planned program of spaced continuous development of the behavior is provided.*

This assumption would imply that complete mastery of new behaviors is not immediately demanded or expected of the learner. Mastery of a task requires repeated practice in performing the task, and it requires time to assimilate the new performance into the existing structure of knowledge of the learner. Thus a program of spaced practice not only aids in mastery of new behavior but also facilitates retention of existing behavior in the learner's repertoire.

10. *Learning is facilitated when the learner has the opportunity to practice the task with a wide variety of problems in many contexts different from that in which behavior was learned.*

This assumption might be thought of like the ripple effect that results from a stone dropped in water. The learner cannot be expected to perceive all of the implications of a task that he has successfully exhibited only one time. New situations must be planned that will include extreme cases, more general or broader results and applications. The learner should have the opportunity to see the broader aspects of the behavior and hence proceed to the edge or limits of the behavior's domain.

11. *Learning is facilitated when the learner has the opportunity to see relationships of the new behavior to old behavior or knows how the new behavior is part of some larger plan or recurring technique.*

This is probably the condition that a human teacher can best implement. A learner may easily learn many facts and skills efficiently without a teacher. Yet he will probably not be able to reorganize or restate these facts in ways that will make it more useful for specific purposes. He will not understand that what he is learning is one example of a more general situation or recurring pattern. In a sense, learning some complex task is more than learning the sum of all of its constituent parts.

2-1. When we teach by the lecture method, the teacher is the active participant in the teaching-learning process. This type of teaching permits limited interaction between the student and teacher and even less interaction between the student and other components of his environment. If an individual learns all new behavior as a result of his interaction with this total environment, the lecture itself provides little opportunity for the student to interact with more than one component of his environment.

There are a variety of opportunities even within a lecture to structure conditions with which the students might interact. The most obvious of these is to write pertinent points, such as a topical outline on the chalkboard or overhead projector. Another would be to illustrate the concepts in the lecture by means of a model, either physical or pictorial. Following the lecture, there should also be follow-up activities which provide further opportunities for the student to interact with his environment.

1. What learning assumption is violated when students have little opportunity to interact with conditions in their environment?
2. List several other techniques that could be used to enrich the environment in a lecture lesson —that is, alternative conditions with which the students might interact.

2-2. The learning assumptions stated in this chapter have implications for the organization and sequencing of activities in the development of a concept or a skill. Listed below are a variety of conditions to which the teacher must attend in order to develop a concept. Sequence these in an acceptable order and state which learning assumption(s) is (are) being used.

(a) Provide practice work.

(b) Motivate the need for learning.

(c) Review prerequisites.

(d) Convince the learner he can perform the task.

(e) Give an example of the task.

(f) Correct student errors.

(g) Provide multisensory aids for initial learning.

(h) Structure learning activities.

(i) Provide a wide range of applications.

(j) Structure conditions to assess the effects of instruction.

(k) Summarize what has been learned and permit students to see the whole picture.

2-3. What learning or teaching assumptions are being used in the following situations?

(a) When a student has just completed a task for the first time, the teacher pauses at his desk and says, "That's a good piece of work, John."

(b) In order to illustrate the binomial probability distribution, the teacher asks each student to flip three coins 100 times. Each student is also asked to tabulate the number of times 0 heads appeared, 1 head appeared, and so on, and to record this data in a bar graph.

(c) When developing the system of integers, the teacher says. "One of the reasons for extending the number system is to obtain a system in which subtraction is always possible."

(d) After talking about the graph of $y = ax^2 + bx + c$ in class, the teacher asked the students to find examples of this type of curve in the physical world. (What types of examples might be found?)

2-4. Textbooks in mathematics are often constructed so that practice on a particular concept immediately follows the development of that concept. In using a textbook of this sort a teacher might follow the procedure below:

Day 1   Develop factoring of a binomial or trinomial with a common monomial factor. Assign factoring exercises of the form $ax + ay$ or $bx + by + bz$.

Day 2   Develop factoring of perfect squares. Assign factoring exercises of the form $a^2 + 2ab + b^2$.

Day 3   Develop factoring of the difference of two squares. Assign factoring exercises of the form $a^2 - b^2$.

Day 4   Develop factoring of $x^2 + ax + b$ into the product of two binomials. Assign factoring exercises of the form $x^2 + ax + b$.

The students all did reasonably well on the assignments so the teacher decided to evaluate the effects of instruction with a quiz that contained all four types of factoring. The results of the quiz would probably indicate a much lower performance than the results of the homework.

1. Why?
2. What learning assumptions were not followed?
3. How might the conditons of learning and practice described above be modified so that the learning assumptions you identified would not have been violated?

2-5. Often teachers will be heard to say such things as:

Most of the students in this class shouldn't even be taking algebra. They can't really do the work, but their parents insisted that they take algebra.

Any one of the statements below may convey the meaning of the teacher's remark.

(a) These students are so stupid that they can't learn algebra, they can only learn general mathematics.

(b) Algebra is a subject that can only be learned by an intellectual elite and cannot be watered down for the masses without damaging its integrity.

(c) These students work slowly in algebra since they do not possess all of the prerequisite skills. Hence these students cannot keep up with me and do well when I adhere strictly to the syllabus and time schedule.

(d) While these students can eventually learn algebra, the capabilities and mathematical know-how they will acquire from algebra are not the most worthwhile goals for them to attain. They should spend their time learning something that is more relevant and worthwhile for them.

1. State your reaction to each of the four interpretations.

2. Which of these interpretations can be justified on the basis of one or more learning assumptions?

2-6. Some of the conditions of learning stated in this chapter could be implemented by a machine as well as or better than a teacher. Thus, for example, a machine can be programmed to implement assumption 4 by recalling prerequisite knowledges for a specified behavior. A machine can also implement assumption 9 by being programmed to provide short, spaced practice on a variety of topics. Finally, a machine can provide feedback regarding the correctness of response more rapidly and more accurately than a teacher. This would imply that the learner is almost continuously informed of his progress, and hence assumption 8 is partially fulfilled.

1. For each of the learning assumptions in this chapter, determine if a machine or a teacher could better implement the implied conditions of learning.
2. From your responses to the above, do you feel that machines will replace teachers? Discuss.
3. Can you learn from a room, a street scene, or a dinner?

2-7. An often-heard student comment is, "I never did like mathematics and know that I can't learn it." This attitude may have evolved from a parent who has a similar attitude toward mathematics or from a previous teacher who did not have a positive attitude toward mathematics. Observable behaviors that may be exhibited by this type of student may be (a) the student exhibits an unwillingness to respond in class. (b) the student does not complete assignments.

1. List three other student behaviors that might be exhibited by this student.
2. Compare your responses with another student who has completed this exercise.
3. The student comment reflects which learning assumption?

2-8. In the preceding exercise a student with a negative attitude toward mathematics was described. One behavior that this student might exhibit was stated as an unwillingness to respond in class. It is the teacher's responsibility to help the student to change his negative attitude to a more positive one. In order to change an attitude of dislike for mathematics, the teacher must convince the student that he can do some mathematics and appreciate the uses of mathematics.

To combat the specific behavior, unwillingness to respond, the teacher may ask the student a question which he can answer. When he answers correctly, this should be made evident to him. Through a series of such questions it is possible to build confidence and possibly lead the student to a place where he will willingly respond.

1. What specific technique might be used to get the student to complete assignments?
2. What could you do to combat the three student behaviors that you stated in the last exercise?

2-9. In a seventh-grade class the students were learning to find the degree measure for various angles. The beginning instruction recalled the definitions of right angles, obtuse angles, and acute angles.

1. What learning assumption was used here?

> The teacher had a small protractor which she showed to the class and explained: "You put the arrow of the protractor on the vertex of the angle and the edge of the protractor on a side of the angle. Then if the angle is acute you read the scale with a number between 0 and 90; if the angle is obtuse, use the scale with numbers between 90 and 180." The teacher then went on, "Everyone measure the first angle on page 184." After this explanation, a helper distributed protractors to the class. To be sure, this description is very much abbreviated from the actual lesson; however, the complete gist of the lesson is given.

2. How could this lesson have been improved by implementing learning assumption 6?
3. What other learning assumptions are positively applied in this lesson?
4. Do you think the students have learned the stated task with this instruction?
5. How could this lesson have been improved using an overhead projector?

2-10. At times it is difficult to observe a learner's behavior and from it infer that he has learned what we want him to learn. As an example, consider an instructor teaching a student the definition of an angle.

Definition: An angle is the set of points in the union of two noncollinear rays with a common endpoint.

1. One level of learning is the verbal level where the students learn to say the correct words in the right order. What question could the teacher use to determine if the student knows the definition verbally?
2. To make sure that the student understands what the words mean, the teacher would probably ask the students to determine which of the following are angles and to justify their decisions. Which of the following are not angles, and why?

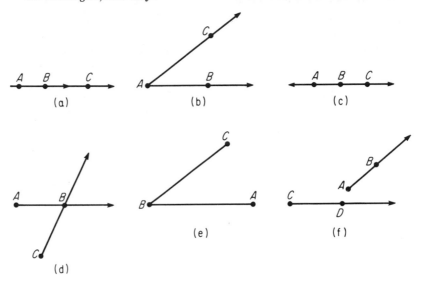

If a student successfully chooses (b) and rejects the other examples, can we conclude that he has learned the concept of angle? Consider this question and fill in the blank with the correct answer.

$\angle ABC \cup \angle CBD = \underline{\ ?\ }$

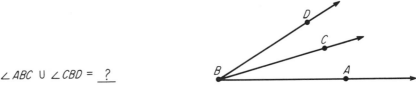

4. Here are two different responses, one right and one wrong.

     Child A: $\angle ABD$ $\longrightarrow$
     Child B: $\angle ABD \cup \overrightarrow{BC}$

Which child has the correct concept of angle stated in the definition?

5. What does this exercise suggest about the level of learning of the concept of angle?

2-11. It should be clear from the last exercise that there are different levels of learning for the same mathematical topic. Choose from the list of descriptions the minimum level of performance you would expect of a seventh-grade, a ninth-grade, and an eleventh-grade student in order to infer that he has learned the distributive property.

(a) The student can say "a times the quantity b plus c equals a times b plus a times c" when asked to state the distributive property.

(b) The student can write "$a \cdot b + a \cdot c$" when asked to restate $a \cdot (b + c)$ by applying the distributive property and vice versa.

(c) The student will point to $a \cdot b + a \cdot c = a \cdot (b + c)$ when asked to point to the distributive property and shown the following statements:

 (i) $a + b = b + a$ (iii) $a \cdot b + a \cdot c = a \cdot (b + c)$
 (ii) $a \cdot (b \cdot c) = (a \cdot b) \cdot c$ (iv) $(a + b) + c = a + (b + c)$

(d) Given three unfamiliar symbols $\square$, $\triangle$, 0 and two unfamiliar operations symbols $\wedge$, $\vee$, the student can write statements such as "$\square \wedge (\triangle \vee 0) = (\square \wedge \triangle) \vee (\square \wedge 0)$" when told: Illustrate the distributive property of $\wedge$ over $\vee$, where $\square$ is the element distributed."

(e) The student can state the reason for each step in the multiplication: $(x + y) \cdot (u + v) = (x + y)u + (x + y)v = x \cdot u + y \cdot u + x \cdot v + y \cdot v$.

(f) The student can factor $x^2 - 10x + 21$ by writing $x^2 - 10x + 21 = x^2 + (^-7 + ^-3)x + 21 = x^2 - 7x - 3x + 21 = x(x - 7) - 3(x - 7) = (x - 3) \cdot (x - 7)$.

(g) The student can use the distributive property to develop the rule of signs for multiplication of integers.

SUGGESTED ACTIVITIES

2-12. One view of learning mathematics is to ask: How did great mathematicians such as Gauss, Poincaré, or Riemann make their discoveries? When students solve new problems, do they act like these mathematicians did when they made their discoveries? For a discussion of how mathematicians think and discover, see Hadamard (1945), pp. 100–115.

2-13. For an alternative discussion of mathematics learning, see Fremont (1969), pp. 44–51. A good treatment of the theories of several well known psychologists is included in this source.

2-14. Gagné's book (1970) dealt explicitly with a classification system for types of learning. Capsule explanations for each type are provided on pp. 33–60. A worthwhile activity would be to examine each task listed in Exercise 2-11 and relate it to an appropriate learning type in Gagné's classification system.

2-15. A comparison of several instructional approaches is given by Shulman (1968). In this article some of the views stated by Deines, Gagné, Bruner, and Piaget are compared and contrasted with reference to such topics as discovery learning, readiness, sequence of the curriculum and transfer of training.

2-16. A concise summary of the conditions of learning that mathematics teachers have found to facilitate learning can be found in Lankford (1959), p. 429. The statements summarized are amply illustrated with examples and, in addition, the implications for teaching are explored.

ADDITIONAL SOURCES

Fremont, Herbert. *How to Teach Mathematics in Secondary Schools*. Philadelphia: W. B. Saunders Company, 1969.

Gagné, Robert M. *The Conditions of Learning* 2d ed. New York: Holt, Rinehart and Winston, Inc., 1970.

Hadamard, Jacques. *The Psychology of Invention in the Mathematical Field*. Princeton, N. J.: Princeton University Press, 1945. (Dover edition, 1954.)

Lankford, Francis G., Jr. "Implications of the Psychology of Learning for the Teaching of Mathematics," *The Growth of Mathematical Ideas, Grades K-12*, 24th Yearbook, Washington, D.C.: National Council of Teachers of Mathematics, 1959, pp. 405–430.

Shulman, Lee S. "Psychological Controversies in the Teaching of Science and Mathematics," *Science Teacher*, September 1968, pp. 34ff.

Chapter **3**

Goals of Mathematics Instruction

The two previous chapters have concentrated on two questions: What is mathematics? What are the conditions that facilitate the learning of mathematics? The chapters after this one will focus on the many specific techniques and details stemming from the query: How do you teach mathematics? Before we get too involved in *how* to teach mathematics, a more basic question must first be considered—"Why should mathematics be taught?"

Like many mathematics teachers, you may feel that there is little need to justify the teaching of mathematics. For the remainder of this chapter, imagine yourself confronted with a hostile student, or a concerned parent, or an administrator, or a fellow teacher who advocates eliminating mathematics from the curriculum to make room for some other subject. You have to answer convincingly the question: Why should students have to spend time studying mathematics after elementary school? Your ability to formulate, implement, and defend a response to this question will be influential in your success as a teacher. In fact, it will pervade everything you do and every decision and judgment you make.

MATHEMATICS CONTRIBUTES TO INDIVIDUALS AND SOCIETY

A partial reason can readily be given to justify the importance of mathematics instruction. Quite simply, mathematics is studied because it contributes to the life of the individual and through the individual to the society in which he lives. Mathematics contributes in varying degrees to each of four overlapping areas of an individual's life: vocational, utilitarian, recreational, and cultural. Different people will require differing degrees of mathematical competence in each category, but all will need some minimum attainment of knowledge, mathematical know-how, appreciation, and attitudes. A partial description of the ways mathematics contributes in each area follows:

1. *Vocational or Professional*. Mathematical competence in this area includes that which is essential to function in the work an individual does or aspires to do. It also must include the mathematical competence necessary to permit the individual to retrain for another kind of work or a change in mathematical competence required in his own field of work.

2. *Utilitarian Aspect of Daily Living*. The mathematical competence that is necessary to function and live independently in society and includes ability to count, measure, handle money, and conceptualize spatial properties.

3. *Recreational*. The mathematical competence needed to engage in hobbies, games, and leisure time pursuits that add enjoyment to living.

4. *Cultural*. The mathematical competence necessary for knowledge and awareness as a voting citizen and the ability to process information that uses some mathematics. This would also include an appreciation and reception of mathematical ideas as well as trust and belief in results based upon mathematics.

The imaginary adversary whom you are to persuade that mathematics instruction is important will not be convinced solely by the argument that mathematics contributes to each person's life. He will wish to know what it is that mathematics contributes to his life and if this contribution is worthwhile. Consideration of these questions inevitably leads back to the nature of mathematics and mathematical activity explored in the first chapter. Before considering these contributions, it will be helpful to introduce an agreement about the words "goals of mathematics instruction."

> A *goal of mathematics instruction* is defined by an explicit answer to the question: "What does the study of mathematics contribute to a learner?"

CONTRIBUTIONS OF THE STUDY OF MATHEMATICS AND MATHEMATICAL ACTIVITY

The benefits of studying mathematics appear to be divided into three categories: content goals, process goals, and affective goals. These roughly correspond to knowledge of mathematics, acquisition of mathematical modes of thought or the methods of mathematical know-how, and appreciation of mathematics.

A. *Content Goals*. The study of mathematics results in the acquisition of
1. Knowledge of mathematical models that permit manipulation and understanding of the learner's environment, both physical and intellectual.
2. Skill in manipulation and computation of the operations and relations in mathematical models that are useful in the learner's environment, both intellectual and physical.

      3. A language to clearly communicate with precision ideas about mathematical models that are useful in the learner's environment, both intellectual and physical.

   B. *Process Goals.* The acquisition of the behaviors of mathematical activity results in the capability

      1. To reinterpret, apply, and examine the relevance of using a specific mathematical model in a situation from the physical or intellectual environment.

      2. To abstract, idealize, and formulate a mathematical model from a situation in the physical or intellectual environment.

      3. To discover new relationships or deduce new abstractions in an existing mathematical model and test its validity by logical inference.

      4. To transfer to other disciplines and successfully apply a repertoire of behaviors such as abstraction, formulation, induction, deductive proof, analysis, synthesis, and application of models.

   C. *Affective Goals.* The study of mathematics and the exposure to mathematical activity should result in valuing

      1. The ability of human intelligence to invent and discover relationships whose application permits man to influence and order his environment.

      2. The ability of human intelligence to go beyond the known and observable part of its physical environment and engage in imaginative thinking.

      3. The enjoyment that can result from intellectual pursuit and a love of knowledge.

      4. Mathematics and mathematical activity as a substantial part of the cultural heritage of the human race that deserves the support and encouragement of society.

Mathematics teachers and mathematics textbooks have concentrated their primary attention and energy in achieving content goals. Knowledge of mathematical terms and principles have been emphasized in teaching and in testing as well as proficiency in computational skills. Teaching for process and affective goals is often undertaken *incidentally* to the main emphasis of teaching specific mathematical content. The only exception seems to be the conscious teaching of deductive proof in some mathematical subjects as an aspect of mathematical know-how. While the importance of content objectives should not be downgraded, it would seem that the study of mathematics could be more beneficial for all learners and contribute more to their lives if process goals and affective goals received more emphasis than they now do in teaching and testing.

Process goals include the ways of acquiring knowledge of mathematical content that are a part of the description of mathematical activity found in Chapter 1. Some of these processes are making observations, making guesses and testing them, collecting and systematizing data, using analogies, asking meaningful questions, making definitions, formulating abstractions and generalizations, discovering relationships by analysis and synthesis, recognizing and extending patterns and regularities, using symbols to represent ideas, and testing the relevance of answers in the physical situation. Actively planning, teaching, and testing for these kinds of process behaviors can be accomplished within many mathematical topics presently taught to students. A student who is exposed to and begins to practice these behaviors should find them useful not only in mathematics but also in other fields of endeavor.

Some of the most important and enduring objectives that many students will attain in mathematics are attitudinal in nature. All pupils will have an attitude toward mathematics. For many students these feelings will be positive or neutral, but too often they are negative. A positive attitude is important, both for student achievement and to produce an educated citizenry that feels mathematics is valuable. The values that mathematics can impart are necessary for society and in many cases can be imparted *only* by mathematics.

Most mathematics teachers want their students to like mathematics. Yet they are reluctant to design game activities, show a movie, read a fantasy story, or digress on interesting side trips where the main emphasis is to enable the students to acquire some affective behavior. Teachers feel guilty when they turn their attention from meeting content objectives for any length of time. The importance of affective goals should be more widely recognized and stressed so that their achievement can be pursued without apology.

LEVELS OF GOALS

The goals of mathematics instruction that have just been presented and discussed are very general. They are stated very broadly so that they apply to mathematics instruction from kindergarten through graduate school seminars. In this way they can be used as a framework for stating more specific goals or for giving perspective and proper balance to clusters of narrow objectives. As smaller and smaller portions of mathematics are being focused upon, the goals of instruction become more and more specific.

Consider Fig. 3-1 which shows an example of the relationships between some subcategories within mathematics. Goals could be stated for each level of content shown in the figure. At the level of a specific course, the goals would remain somewhat general, but they would refer to the particular content in the course. The goals become more specific at the level of a unit, quadratic functions, and at the level of a topic, solving quadratic equations. Goals associated with a particular task within a topic will be called *objectives*; they are characterized in the next chapter. The exercises will deal more fully with goals at an intermediate level.

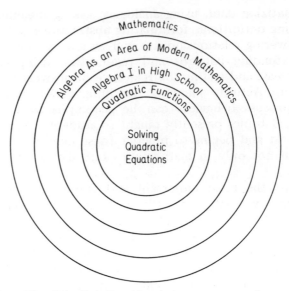

Fig. 3-1. Relationships between some subcategories within mathematics.

IMPORTANCE OF STATED GOALS

Goals of instruction exist whether they are explicitly stated or
are only vague notions in the back of the teacher's mind. Every
teacher has some thoughts concerning the contribution that mathematics should make to a learner's education. Even if these goals
are not given extensive thought and succinctly stated, they will
manifest themselves in various ways. The teacher's conception of
the goals of mathematics instruction will influence every other
aspect of the instructional program. The selection of content, the
choice of instructional activities, the writing of test items, and the
judging of acceptable performance will be determined by the expected outcomes. Aside from anything a teacher says or writes, his
true goals can be determined by extended observations of his
teaching and examining his tests. These will reveal what the
teacher really considers important.

Because goals are so influential in how mathematics is taught
and learned, it behooves mathematics teachers to clearly state
these assumptions. One reason for stating goals is to evaluate the
effectiveness of instruction. The goals provide the benchmark that
both teachers and students must use to measure how closely classroom performance conforms to expected outcomes. Without
written goals there is no fixed and accessible standard against
which behavior can be compared and reliably judged. Secondly,
written goals can be used as guidelines to develop appropriate
instructional activities or they can provide the rationale for deciding between two different alternatives. Finally, and most importantly, when goals remain unstated the result is usually a very
narrow conception of mathematics teaching. Many bad practices

in teaching persist because of a very limited and narrow interpretation of the purpose of mathematics instruction. The goals that are being achieved are often of much less worth than those that are being neglected. When goals are stated and available for scrutiny, narrowness and worthlessness become more obvious and the more important aspects are identified. The activity by an individual of trying to state goals for mathematics instruction can be rewarding and very revealing. One becomes aware of personal biases that influence his thinking and begins to develop an awareness of a personal philosophy of the purpose of teaching mathematics.

We have now stated some goals of mathematics instruction. They are of necessity very broad general statements that naturally reflect the biases of the authors. The exercises at the end of this chapter—and, in fact, the rest of this book—will be devoted to expanding upon the goals stated here and to describing ways of teaching and testing in mathematics that will hopefully optimize the attainment of these goals. Other people may state different goals or give more emphasis to some goals than others, and hence disagree with the goals stated here. That is not important. The important consideration is that the goals of mathematics instruction are carefully considered, thought through, stated, and continually subjected to reexamination and challenge by every mathematics teacher.

EXERCISES

3-1.

1. Listed below are some mathematical activities. Indicate which of the four areas—vocational, utilitarian, recreational, or cultural—you think each activity fits into best. Some may be classified in more than one area.

2. People like to speak of the minimum essentials in mathematics that every citizen must have to survive. Certainly, all people need some mathematics; at the very least to distinguish a set with one object from another set with two objects. The minimum level of mathematical competence required by a free citizen to function and live happily is a very hard boundary to define. The mathematical activities listed below require different levels of competence. For each activity, indicate if it is a mathematical competence you would expect of all citizens as a minimum (A) only a few in society (F), or most people (M).

(a) Ability to interpret a simple sampling opinion poll.

(b) Find the area under the curve of an elementary function by integrating the function.

(c) Figuring the square yards of carpeting needed for a room.

(d) Recognizing why three of a kind will beat a pair in poker.

(e) Read about the ability of computers to perform real-time and analogue computing.

(f) Believe that it is possible to find the distance to the sun without actually traveling to the sun.

(g) Compute gas mileage of an automobile.

(h) Estimate distances visually.

(i) Recognize that a good prediction of a win in an election can be accomplished with a sample of 2 percent of the whole vote.

(j) Ability to interpret graphs in the daily newspaper.

(k) Read a measuring device such as clock or yardstick.

(l) Marveling at the ability to compute the trajectory of a space ship.

(m) Compute the simple forces acting on an airplane in flight in order to determine and fly a course.

(n) Make change and count money.

(o) Prove the Pythagorean theorem.

3-2. A group of prospective teachers were asked the question, "Why should mathematics be taught?" Some of their comments are listed below.

1. Determine whether you agree with their remarks.

2. Decide for each statement whether the writer feels that mathematics contributes most to the vocational, utilitarian, recreational, or cultural side of life.

3. Decide whether their emphasis is content, process, or affective.

   (a) Mathematics is useful in developing an ability to solve everyday problems which do not contain mathematical language or symbols.

   (b) Math trains people to think, plan, and organize their thoughts into a basic direction.

   (c) Mathematics is used as a tool in the physical sciences and in higher education.

   (d) Various occupations require more and more mathematics.

   (e) Mathematics as compared to other subjects appears to have few practical applications.

   (f) Because, in a society which is advancing so fast in technological areas, an understanding of mathematical principles is essential if one is to be acquainted with what is happening in the world.

   (g) With the coming of the computer and universal automation, the only jobs left available will be those dealing with computers and related fields like mathematics.

   (h) Through the study of math, people develop a sense of problem-solving techniques.

   (i) Math is necessary to become an educated person who possesses a mind which can formulate problems and think logically.

   (j) One needs some understanding of mathematics to proceed through the normal transactions of the daily routine.

3-3. You are the chairman of the mathematics department and the principal asks each department chairman to write a paragraph describing the major purpose of instruction in each area. You ask some members of your department to write paragraphs for you and receive examples such as:

(a) To provide the student with the knowledge and patterns of thinking about mathematics that will enable him to pursue a career in mathematics or a related field.

(b) To develop in the student a high degree of competence in the manipulative and computational skills of mathematics that he will need to utilize in his everyday life.

(c) To develop in the student the literacy in mathematical thinking and the functional competence in mathematical computations necessary for his career choice and his future role as an informed citizen.

(d) To train the student in the patterns of rigorous mathematical thinking that will develop mental discipline and exercise his powers of reasoning.

(e) To develop a preference for enjoyment and success resulting from intellectual endeavors and the pursuit of knowledge.

The first one seems too narrow a choice if the majority of your students will probably not choose a career closely related to mathematics or perhaps not attend college at all.

1. Discuss the remaining four choices in terms of the type of school and the kinds of students. What type of instructional program might have each of these as a main objective?

2. Determine which of the five are content goals, which are process goals, and which are affective goals.

3-4. You are to imagine in the introduction to this chapter that you have to defend the place of mathematics in the secondary school curriculum. Listed below are several reasons you might use for justifying the teaching of mathematics in the secondary school curriculum.

   (a) To teach analytical thinking.

   (b) To teach procedures and skills which will be useful to each individual in his later life (social utility).

   (c) To exercise the logical faculty of the brain.

   (d) To teach inductive and deductive reasoning.

   (e) As a service to the other disciplines such as chemistry, physics, etc.

   (f) To provide students with the pleasure of studying mathematics.

1. Discuss each of the above reasons with regard to its meaning, validity, and worth when we are trying to justify mathematics in the secondary school.

2. State the argument you would use on the imaginary person you wished to convince of the value of studying mathematics.

3-5. You are a geometry teacher and you open your morning newspaper to the Letters to the Editor column and find the following letter from one of your students:

LETTER TO THE EDITOR

I am a student in Central High School taking geometry. I need the course to get into college, or I would take something more worthwhile. I plan to go to college and major in journalism; and if I didn't have to take geometry, I would take something more useful like history, English, or typing.

I can understand how arithmetic will be helpful to me in my everyday life and my future work. Even algebra will be useful since I will need it to pass the mathematics course required of all freshmen in college; but I don't see how geometry will be of any value to me.

In our geometry class, we spend all our time writing statements and reasons in proofs. We have to get all the statements in just the right order on the left side of the page and always write some reason for the statement on the right-hand side of the page. We memorize definition after definition for things we already know. We memorize the definitions and proofs for the tests, but the theorems we prove are either things we already know like a line segment has one and only one midpoint or things that are not worth knowing like the perpendicular bisector of a chord of a circle passes through the center.

It seems like all you get out of geometry that is of any value is recognizing and naming a few common figures and learning how to compute the area and volume of a few figures. It does not take all year to learn these things, and we could use the rest of the time more profitably. Courses in home economics or house wiring would seem to be more worthwhile.

I would like to hear your opinion on this matter, Mr. Editor. What did you learn in geometry that was worthwhile to you that could not be learned in some other high school course?

                                                    Chairman, SCAG
                                                    (Student Committee Against Geometry)

1. What passage indicates that the student has a mistaken notion of what proofs prove? Why?
2. If the student's description of the activities in this classroom are accurate, is he justified in his criticism?
3. How would you, as the teacher, answer the last question in the letter?

3-6. After reading the Letter to the Editor you resolve to teach your geometry class so that it will be obvious to your students that much of what they are learning is important, not only for geometry and other mathematics, but is know-how that is useful in other human activities. For example, one of your goals may be making reasonable conjectures, and you say:

"We have been stressing the importance of making intelligent guesses and testing these guesses. We drew pictures of triangles and noticed such things as an exterior angle is greater than either opposite interior angle or the greater side lies in the interior of the greater angle. We then tried more examples with various types of triangles to increase our confidence or revise our hunches, if necessary. Finally, we subjected our conjectures to the final test; could we prove it as theorem.

"A historian also makes guesses and tests them. He may suspect that a certain document written under a fictitious name was written by a famous person. Upon examination, he may find that the person in question held the views expressed in the document and had a similar writing style. He may uncover more indirect evidence of this type that strengthens or weakens his conjecture. Ultimately he may find a reference to the document in the famous person's diary or personal papers that definitely establishes the authorship of the document."

1. What kinds of goals is the teacher trying to emphasize with the class?
2. Would you consider the analogy to the work of a historian a valid one?
3. Two other examples of the manner in which mathematical reasoning is used are listed below along with an occupation. Describe how these are used in geometry and may be applied in the occupation outside of mathematics in the same way as was done for the historian.
   (a) Observation of patterns and relationships to make inferences—physician.
   (b) Using deduction to arrive at a conclusion from certain starting assumptions—lawyer or judge.

3-7. Figure 3-1, as we have seen, shows levels of content within mathematics. The figure was used to indicate that goals may be very narrow and specific or they can be broad and general, depending upon the level of mathematics content being considered.

Another scheme for identifying the specificity of goals would be to find their place in the following descending classification.

Mathematics
    Subject
        Course
            Unit
                Topic
                  Task

Sometimes these categories are not mutually exclusive, but in most cases it serves as a useful model for thinking about yearly goals, unit goals, and goals of the daily lesson.

Listed below are five areas of mathematical content. Some are specific and some are very broad. Match each one to the appropriate level of content it illustrates in the classification scheme given above.

(a) Integral calculus of one real variable
(b) Antiderivatives of rational functions
(c) Rewrite $\int (y^2 + 1)^3 y \, dy$ in the form $\int x^n dx$
(d) Calculus
(e) Antiderivatives of the form $\int x^n dx$

3-8. In Appendix A there are listed some goals of instruction that are written at the level of a unit. More specific goals (called objectives) are found in Appendix B that identify clusters of tasks within some of the unit goals.

1. For each unit goal in Appendix A, determine if it is a content goal, a process goal, or an affective goal.
2. For each task objective in Appendix B, find a unit goal in Appendix A of which it is a particular part.

3-9. One question that a teacher must always be prepared to answer is, "Why do we have to learn this?" Many times this question is varied to be

What good is this?

How can this be applied?

The student is usually asking the question at the level of a task or a topic.

1. Several procedures that might be followed appear below. Discuss each of these procedures with regard to its probable success and the effect it might have on the student or class.

   (a) Answer the question with a question such as, "Why do you want to learn anything?" or "What good is any knowledge," and then discuss the need for any particular knowledge.

   (b) Answer the question with the vague statement that this knowledge will be useful in later studies of mathematics.

   (c) Answer the question with the statement, "It's in the book, and the authors felt it was important enough to include, so we'll cover it."

   (d) Tell the student something specific that he will be able to do as a result of learning the task, such as, "You will be able to solve problems that involve percentage."

   (e) Relate the attainment of the task to the achievement of more general goals in the topic, unit, and eventually the goals for the year in the subject.

2. What do you do with a student who does not "want to achieve" the goals of the course? Who has no general "motivation to achieve" or "motivation to continue learning tasks"?

3. Which of the learning assumptions in Chapter 2 relates to the problems raised in (2)?

3-10. When the question, "Why do we have to learn this?" is asked, what special reason could be given for each of the particular topics below?
  (a) Factoring of expressions such as $ax^2 + bx + c$
  (b) Polynomial division
  (c) Properties of tangents to a circle
  (d) Graphing of the trigonometric functions
  (e) Indirect proof

3-11. Closely related to the overall goals of mathematics instruction is the question of what mathematics should we teach and should all youngsters have the same mathematics training. In a particular case we might say there should be differentiated curricular materials for seventh-grade youngsters because:

(a) The ability levels of the students differ.

(b) The interests of the students differ.

(c) The future careers of the students will differ.

1. Are these valid reasons for a differentiated curriculum?

2. Can you give an instance where each of these might be repudiated?

3. Does this mean there should not be a differentiated curriculum for seventh-grade mathematics? Why or why not?

4. If you argue for a common curriculum at the seventh-grade level, where does this argument fail at the eleventh-grade level?

3-12. Process and affective goals have never received the same emphasis and thought as content goals, although most teachers would agree that they are of equal importance. For a good description of some process goals and affective goals in mathematics, see Kolb (1970).

3-13. For the interested reader, various goals for mathematics as reflected in the history of mathematics education in the United States are briefly discussed in Willoughby (1967).

3-14. Throughout the history of mathematics education in the last three-quarters of a century, many committees and commissions have studied the goals and place of mathematics in the secondary school curriculum. One of the committees that made projections for a mathematics curriculum of the future is the Cambridge Conference on School Mathematics. For a taste of the controversy that has surrounded this report, read Stone (1965).

ADDITIONAL SOURCES

Kolb, John. "Goals of Mathematics Instruction," *High School Journal*, Vol. 53, No. 5 (February 1970), pp. 253–263.

Stone, Marshall H. "Review of Goals for School Mathematics," Report of the Cambridge Conference on School Mathematics, *Mathematics Teacher* (April 1965), pp. 353–360.

Willoughby, Steven. *Contemporary Teaching of Secondary School Mathematics*. New York: John Wiley & Sons, Inc., 1967.

Chapter 4

Objectives

The goals of mathematics instruction represent the broad aims or outcomes that justify the inclusion of mathematics as a body of knowledge worthy of serious study. Each of these stated goals is partitioned into many levels of goals, some of which are very specific and very narrow in scope, but whose totality mesh together to cover all aspects of a higher level goal. Task goals will be called *objectives*.

NEED FOR STATED OBJECTIVES

All too often in teaching, materials are assembled, textbooks selected, learning activities structured, and student progress evaluated without any thought given to the outcomes that are expected at the end of instruction. This is not unlike a man who decides to build a house but has no blueprint or plan. He begins nailing lumber together, saws off ends that seem to be sticking out, tacks on roofing to exposed boards, puts plaster on rough surfaces and generally goes through the motions of building a house. But without any kind of plan, the finished product is likely to be a monstrosity.

Mathematics teachers with a limited conception of their objectives are somewhat like the do-it-yourself carpenter described above. They are going through the motions but they will not make the most advantageous selection of materials and the best disposition of time, effort, and emphasis. Stated objectives serve as a focus for the structuring of materials and provide guidelines for the selection of teaching strategies. In addition, they serve as a standard against which the actual outcomes of instruction can be compared and evaluated.

TEACHER VS. STUDENT OBJECTIVES

A teacher writes a lesson in geometry that is to motivate, develop, prove, and give applications of the Pythagorean theorem.

The teacher writes as the lesson objective: To teach the Pythagorean theorem. The teacher walks into the classroom and lucidly
develops the entire lesson using many visual aids and, in general,
gives a magnificent presentation. There is only one difficulty.
There are no students in the classroom; the presentation was given
to an empty room. The teacher has clearly attained his stated
objective, yet no student learning has taken place. Perhaps the
teacher would not have performed differently if the room had
been filled with students. Under either condition his objective is a
teacher performance rather than an outcome that the students are
expected to exhibit. This is certainly true of teachers who measure
their success in teaching by the sophistication and difficulty level
of their presentations and by the number of students they fail.

How can we measure a successful lesson? One manner is to
observe the behavior of the teacher; a better manner is to assess
the performance the student has learned and can exhibit as a result
of the lesson. It is our belief that the student is the key to measuring the success of a lesson. A lesson is successful to the extent that
the student behaviors conform to the anticipated behaviors as
stated in the objectives. (See Fig. 2-1.) In this view, objectives
should be stated in terms of student performance and not be
descriptions of teacher behaviors. This attitude reflects a very
basic premise about learning. *Learning is done by the learner.* This
means that whatever a teacher does or does not do, he can only
structure materials, conditions, and occasions for students. He cannot *learn for* his student. Each student must do that for himself.
The teacher must focus his attention on the students; he must
know his objectives in terms of what he expects his students to be
able to do. He must observe and "read" his students during the
lesson to determine the success of his techniques in enabling the
student to acquire the behaviors expected of them. No matter how
sterling a teaching performance, it is unsuccessful if the students
cannot exhibit the behavior associated with the objectives they
were expected to attain.

OBSERVABLE BEHAVIORS

When the focus in measuring successful teaching is shifted
from teacher performance to an emphasis on what the student is
able to do, an additional problem presents itself. Consider the
objective: At the conclusion of the lesson the student will understand the Pythagorean theorem. How will the teacher know at the
conclusion of the lesson that this objective has been attained by
the student? The teacher cannot look inside a student's head to
determine if he understands or knows a concept. The only way the
teacher has of assessing the attainment of this objective is by
observing student behavior when the student is confronted with
Pythagorean theorem situations. The student may "know" a great
deal about the Pythagorean theorem but it will remain unknown
to the teacher unless the student exhibits some behavior that can
be observed (i.e., seen or heard) by the teacher. The measurement

of the achievement of an objective is accomplished by observation of the behavior a student exhibits.

BEHAVIORAL OBJECTIVES

One reason for stating objectives behaviorally is to clearly identify the kind of performance that will be accepted as evidence that the learner has achieved the objective. This is helpful in selecting materials and learning activities. It is also useful for the construction of test items that reliably measure the objectives they are intended to measure.

The main criterion of an objective is that it communicates the intent of its composer. One test of the communication ability of an objective is, Can another competent person use the stated objective as a basis to select successful performances by learners so that the objective writer would agree with the selections? While this is a very stringent criterion, behavioral objectives are advocated by many people as more nearly satisfying this criterion than nonbehavioral objectives.

The key to stating any behavioral objective is the verb used to indicate the observable student behaviors. Words such as *write*, *state*, and *point* are relatively unambiguous verbs and produce little confusion when the test given above is applied. However, words that suggest higher-level behavior such as *solve*, *demonstrate*, *interpret*, and *apply* are subject to different interpretations and need further definition in order to communicate effectively. Finally, words such as *understand*, *appreciate*, and *know* possess quite a range of interpretations and are almost useless for technical communication about objectives unless they are decomposed into components that are more amenable to observation. This is not to imply that certain words are not to be used in objectives; rather, for the purposes of effective communication, there should be some agreement and mutual understanding concerning the observable behavior associated with any verb used in a behavioral objective.

There has been some controversy surrounding the use of behavioral objectives for the selection of activities and evaluation of instruction. Critics have maintained that only relatively low-level objectives are represented by behavioral objectives. Opponents believe that only those outcomes that easily lend themselves to direct observation will be stated as objectives. Many important objectives, particularly higher-level ones, in the domain of process goals and affective goals may be ignored in teaching and testing.

Criticism has also been leveled at the idea that it is desirable to have all the objectives of a course stated behaviorally, if that were possible. It is claimed that many important things are learned by students that are unanticipated and unplanned for by the teacher, but rather just happen. They feel that with many goals explicitly stated, the emphasis and activities of the course may focus exclusively on the attainment of the stated objectives to the exclusion of many more important outcomes whose attainment would somehow occur if a less directed approach were taken.

EXERCISES

4-1. For each objective listed, determine if the statement refers to a student performance or to a teacher objective. (i.e., Would you test to see if the objective is met by watching the student or watching the teacher?)

(a) To teach the concept of least common multiple of two algebraic expressions.

(b) To help the students understand word problems.

(c) The student can appreciate the role of proof in mathematics.

(d) Students are able to prove deductively that $(^-x)(^-y) = x \cdot y$.

(e) Given a function defined by $y = x^2 + 4x + c$, the student can describe the changes in the zeros of the function as c takes on integral values from 0 to 5.

(f) To develop the students' ability to apply the rule for determining if a whole number is divisible by nine from its base-ten numeral.

4-2. Objectives can be written with the focus on student behavior and still not fulfill the requirements of a behavioral objective. A behavioral objective must name the act a student can be observed performing when demonstrating that he has achieved the objective.

Determine which of the following objectives are behavioral objectives that specify observable behavior and describe what you would see or hear the student do when he attained it.

(a) The student is able to grasp the significance of the concept of field in mathematics.

(b) Given a natural number, the student can write its prime factorization.

(c) The student is able to construct the graph of a linear equation of the form $y = ax + b$, where a, b are real numbers on rectangular coordinate axes.

(d) Given a quadratic equation of the form $ax^2 + bx + c = 0$ where $a \neq 0$, the student can demonstrate the procedure of completing the square.

(e) The student understands the commutative property of multiplication of integers.

(f) The student knows how to divide, given two rational numbers named by fractional numerals.

(g) Given a right triangle, the student can appreciate the beauty of the Pythagorean theorem.

4-3. Identify the portions of the behavioral objectives below by: (1) underlining the observable student behavior, (2) blocking in the materials given or the condition under which the behavior is performed, and (3) ellipsing the minimum level of acceptable performance.

(a) Given an obtuse angle, a compass, and a straightedge, the student can construct the bisector of the angle. All construction marks must be shown.

(b) Given the equation $3x + 7 = \frac{1}{4} - \frac{1}{8}x$, the student can solve the equation by writing each step involved in producing equivalent equations and can check each solution in the original equation.

(c) Given the length of a chord of a sphere and the distance from the center of the sphere to the chord, the student can state the measure of the radius correct to tenths.

(d) Given the system of inequalities

$$y \leqslant x + 2$$
$$y \geqslant 2x^2 + 4x$$

the student can describe a sequence of steps that when followed by another person will enable that person to graph and shade the appropriate region corresponding to the solution set.

4-4. Stating objectives behaviorally is intended to facilitate the construction of test items to measure achievement. Even when objectives are specified behaviorally, test items are often used that are inappropriate for evaluating whether the objective has been attained.

> *Objective:* Given a linear equation in two variables, the student can construct its graph.

Which of the following test situations are appropriate for evaluating whether this objective has been achieved?

(a) The student is given two ordered pairs of numbers and asked to plot them on the coordinate plane.

(b) The student is asked to state the general form of a linear equation.

(c) Given an equation of the form, $y = ax + b$, where a, b are real numbers, the student is to draw the appropriate line on the coordinate plane using the slope and intercept.

(d) Given an equation of the form $y = ax$, where a is a real number, the student should write the slope and both intercepts.

(e) The student is asked to name the mathematician who invented the coordinate system for graphing linear equations.

(f) The student is given an equation $3x + 5 = y$. He is asked to plot three ordered pairs in the solution set of the given equation and draw the line determined by these points.

(g) Given an inequality of the form, $y \leqslant ax + b$, where a, b are real numbers, the student must shade all points of the coordinate plane corresponding to the elements in the solution set of the given inequality.

(h) The student is given the equation $5x - 7y = 1$. He is to illustrate the solution set of the equation graphically.

(i) Given that the slope of a line is $2/3$ and the coordinates of a point on the line $(4, \ ^-2)$, the student is to state the x-intercept.

(j) Given: $(1, ^-3)$; $(^-2,7)$. Plot each pair of points and draw a line through them. Determine the slope of the line.

4-5. Although many teachers do not write behavioral objectives, they still need to use the idea. One important task of a teacher is to examine a test item and determine exactly what behavior it is measuring and specify exactly what the student would do to complete the item.

For each test item below, (1) identify the action verbs such as name, select, solve, and translate that you would observe the student doing, (2) identify the conditions of performance; and (3) determine the minimum level of acceptable performance.

(a) Solve the equation $5w + 2 = w + 7$, and show all your work.

(b) Graph the equation $3x + 4y = 10$.

(c) The following illustrates the application of what property in mathematics: $a + (b + {}^-b) = a + 0$?

(d) The force of earth's gravity F varies inversely as the square of its distance S from the center of the earth. If $F = 120$ when $S = 60,000$, find F when $S = 40,000$.

(e) Prove $\ {}^-(x + y) = ({}^-x) + ({}^-y)$.

(f) Use a compass and straightedge and divide the given line segment into four congruent segments.

(g) $\cos x < \sin x$ if
    (A) $45 \leqslant x < 90$
    (B) $45 < x \leqslant 90$
    (C) $0 < x < 90$
    (D) $0 < x < 45$
    (E) $0 < x \leqslant 45$

4-6. In preparing to teach a unit on "quadratics," you turn to the teacher's guide for your textbook, and you find the following objectives:

"As a result of this unit, the student should

(a) Understand quadratic polynomials, quadratic functions, quadratic equations, and quadratic inequalities.

(b) Be able to solve quadratic equations or inequalities and draw graphs.

(c) Be able to determine the nature of the roots of a quadratic equation.

(d) Be able to solve word problems."

1. Suppose that other teachers in your school turned to the above objectives in the teacher's guide. Do you suppose their interpretation of the objectives would be the same as yours or different from yours?

2. Write several well-formulated behavioral objectives that detail the exact behavior expected of a student who can solve quadratic equations.

3. For each objective you write, apply the test: Can another competent person use only your stated objective as a basis to look at the behavior of the students and select those who have successfully exhibited the expected performance so that you would agree with the selections?

4. Show your objectives to a classmate and ask him what he would expect a student to be able to do who has successfully met the objectives you wrote. Ask him to state a test item he would use to measure the attainment of your objectives. Is his test item appropriate for the behavior you intended to communicate?

4-7. Teachers are continually testing and evaluating students, but are themselves very infrequently evaluated or held accountable for their own efforts by their supervisors or principals.

Suppose a supervisor or principal came into your class every week and asked for the list of behavioral objectives the students were expected to achieve as a result of the lessons during that week. Assume that he would use the stated objectives as a basis to test a random sample of students to determine the number of behaviors these students were able to successfully exhibit. You would then be paid on the basis of the student performance as measured by your supervisor.

1. Would this be a fair way to determine teacher effectiveness?
2. Would teachers be more aware of what the students are actually learning rather than going their own way and assuming the students are deficient and can't learn what is being taught when they eventually can't pass a unit test?
3. Would teachers select only low-level objectives that are easy to attain and easy to measure rather than more worthwhile but higher-level capabilities?
4. Would teachers be more likely to search for more effective teaching methods and materials to make sure the students learned?
5. Would student achievement be greater under such an arrangement?
6. Would you be willing to teach in a situation like the one described?
7. Do you believe that teachers should be evaluated on their teaching ability? If yes, by whom? The department head, the supervisor, the principal, other teachers, the students, standardized achievement tests, or a professional organization of mathematics teachers?

Actually, knowledge implies no understanding, since all that is presumed is recall or reproduction of previously related facts. That is, however, an essential ingredient for understanding. Comprehension is then the lowest level of understanding. The meaning of comprehension as a level of understanding is that the student can translate or interpret ideas. Given a definition of an exponent, the student can comprehend this definition when he can restate the definition using his own words. Interpretation questions are slightly different than translation in that the student is expected to use or compare certain stated ideas which have previously been studied. It is unfortunate that the vast majority of test items and objectives that are established for our students are classified as knowledge or comprehension. In this regard we view the students as repositories of knowledge with little or no understanding.

There is so much more to understanding, however, and we should strive to include the categories of application, analysis, synthesis, and evaluation in our objectives and test items. Application is similar to interpretation in that the student is expected to use certain ideas which have been previously studied; however, the needed concepts must be recalled by the student in application questions. Analysis is an emphasis on and study of the relationship of the constituent parts of an idea or argument. In this case the student should consciously observe valid mathematical reasoning processes such as induction and deduction. In synthesis the student is asked to create something; it is the process of taking ideas and combining them in such a way that a pattern is formed which was not there before. Finally, evaluation is the process of judging the worth of some aspect of the content under consideration.

Depending on preceding conditions, the same question or objective may illustrate different levels of understanding. For example, asking a student the meaning of the statement, "The sides opposite equal angles in a triangle are equal" may be either knowledge, if this has been considered before, or comprehension if it has not been previously taught. Illustrations of questions for each level of understanding are included in the exercises.

TYPES OF TESTS

We can also establish a classification system for tests that have particular uses. The three types of tests to be discussed are *diagnostic*, *achievement*, and *transfer*, and they bear a strong relation to the levels of understanding previously described. Further, the reader should be aware that these tests are rarely used in isolation—that is, a good test would usually have subtests that could be classified as one of the types of test.

Diagnostic tests are tests used to identify and recognize the various strengths and weaknesses of the students. A diagnostic test may be used as a pretest in an attempt to ascertain the level at which to begin instruction or as a posttest to evaluate the instruction that was provided or the learning that has occurred. In either case the items used on a diagnostic test should be the simplest of a type of item so that an error can be traced to the particular behavior that is lacking. In general, the questions that would appear on a diagnostic test would measure knowledge, comprehension, or application. The reason that the items would be limited to these categories is that higher levels of understanding would sample multiple concept items, and it would be difficult if not impossible to identify concepts or behaviors which the student does not have.

Achievement tests are usually used to evaluate a student's progress over a relatively large number of concepts. Achievement tests are also referred to as *performance tests*. This type of test is comprehensive in its coverage, should include some diagnostic items, but should also go beyond this to test analysis-type questions. Some of the items on this type of a test would consist of the solution of problems which require critical thinking, a knowledge of several concepts and applications of inductive or deductive reasoning.

Transfer tests consist of items that are drawn from the application, analysis, synthesis, or evaluation levels of knowledge. It is sometimes convenient to think of levels of transfer. Application of a mathematical model to a physical situation, as explained in Chapter 1 is one type of transfer. Usually the problem is presented as a phenomenon from the physical world. This situation must be abstracted to a mathematical model, solved within this abstract model and then interpreted in the physical setting. Thus the problem itself requires interpretation, application, and analysis, but these levels of knowledge are welded together to form a synthesis type question. Failure of some students to achieve this type of transfer is heard when the physics or chemistry teacher states that the students who have completed algebra cannot solve linear equations that arise in a physical context.

A second type of transfer problem may be illustrated by an original proof of a stated theorem. The student must interpret the meaning of the theorem, and then apply previously learned concepts or facts in a deductive manner to create a proof of the theorem. Usually the student is not asked to extend the mathematical model but is expected to provide original thinking in verifying a fact in the system. If on the other hand the student is asked to extend the mathematical model by first developing the statement to be considered and then proving or disproving this statement, a higher level of transfer is required. This second type of transfer is very worthwhile and a level of understanding for which we should strive; it is, however, a level that may not be attained by all students.

Finally, an evaluation of the worth of a mathematical model in terms of its utility, beauty, consistency, or applicability to physical models is also a type of transfer. Although this evaluation can be accomplished only in a limited sense in the secondary school, every good teacher should nevertheless strive to provide simple for different situations demand different content approaches. Factors to be considered in these decisions are the goals and objectives, the students, and the teacher. For example, the approach to a mathematical topic will differ depending on whether the main emphasis is to be placed on content goals, affective goals, or process goals. In the same way, one instructional strategy may serve well to develop a concept, a different one may be necessary for reteaching it, and a third one may be best for review or generalizing the concept. Perhaps the most important factor that influences the decision to select one strategy over another is the students themselves as shown in several of the exercises.

Instructional strategies may be selected to help motivate learning, meet individual differences in learning styles, or account for a learner's lack of prerequisite knowledge. The learning assumptions stated in Chapter 2 can be used as guidelines in identifying and selecting instructional strategies on the basis of the needs of the learners.

Finally, the strategy selected by the teacher must be one that the teacher feels comfortable with and is enthusiastic about implementing. Identifying and using different approaches in teaching mathematics not only helps to make instruction more successful, but it provides challenge and excitement in what might otherwise become dull routine for the teacher.

6-3. An important criteria for selecting an instructional strategy is mathematical correctness. Examine the instructional strategy proposed by a prospective teacher who wished to devise an unusually clear way to lead students to see why a negative integer times a positive integer is a negative integer. Find the fallacy in this strategy:

We now must consider what happens when we multiply a negative integer times a positive integer. Let ^-a be a negative integer and b be a positive integer. We ask:

$$^-a \cdot b = ?$$

But

$$^-a = {}^-1 \cdot a$$

so

$$(^-1 \cdot a) \cdot b = ?$$

Applying the associative property we get

$$(^-1 \cdot a) \cdot b = {}^-1 \cdot (a \cdot b)$$

Hence,

$$^-a \cdot b = (a \cdot b)$$

6-4. There are many factors a teacher must consider in selecting a particular instructional strategy for any given situation. For each situation described below, indicate one or more of the approaches listed in Example 1 in the textbook for teaching linear equations in two variables. Which of these would you consider the better one and justify your choice(s).

(a) During the previous unit of work, Mr. Robbins' students have been asking questions such as: "What good is it to learn all this stuff?" "What good will knowing algebra ever be to me?" and, "What will we ever use algebra for?"

(b) The students in Mr. Robbins' class are convinced that there is no need to learn all these procedures for doing problems. The teacher wants them to do everything the long way, when they can get the right answer by just looking at the problem and writing the answer.

(c) Mr. Robbins' class is an advanced algebra class that has studied this topic before and can generally do the problems both algebraically and graphically.

(d) Mr. Robbins feels that it is important for this class to realize that the solution set to this type of problem will consist of ordered pairs, and that these ordered pairs must be solutions common to both equations.

(e) Mr. Robbins feels it is extremely important that the students do not get into a rut and use only one way of solving these problems. He wants them to examine each problem and choose the most efficient way of solving the problem.

EXERCISES

    7-1. It has sometimes been said that a good speech has three major categories. They are:

    (a) An introduction where the speaker tells the audience what he is going to tell them.

    (b) A body where the speaker tells the audience.

    (c) A conclusion where the speaker tells the audience what he told them.

1. Relate these three categories of a speech to the various types of developmental activities.
2. Discuss the purpose of each category and its relative contribution to the speech or lesson as a whole.

7-2. The major portion of classtime in some classrooms is spent in going over an assignment. This is basically a remediation process based upon the assumption that the students were unable to complete the exercises in the assignment.

Suppose that in a given classroom fifteen exercises were assigned as homework. These exercises all illustrated a single behavior, however, this behavior was approached in varied contexts. On the class day that this assignment was due, the teacher spent 35 of the 55 class minutes in going over these fifteen exercises.

1. What assumptions would you make about the development and assimilation activities prior to this assignment?
2. What type of teaching and what purpose did the teacher emphasize during the 35 minutes described above?
3. Is it possible that all of the students could do these problems and hence, this 35 minutes of class time was wasted? If so, how could this have been avoided?
4. Should class time be spent working an assigned problem if one student was not able to complete it? Two students? Half the class?
5. If the guidelines for homework given in the introduction were followed, would this situation frequently occur? Why?

7-3. Homework or assignments should be as carefully planned as the developmental lesson. The effects of a carefully developed lesson may be lost if the assignment consists of exercises which are not representative of the behaviors that were taught. Remember that the purpose of an assignment is to provide practice on relevant behaviors in varied contexts after assimilation has occurred. Discuss each of the following assignments with regard to its merits or deficiencies.

(a) Odd problems 1-59 (answers in back of book).

(b) Odd problems 1-59 (answers to even problems in back of book).

(c) Ten problems selected for the manner in which they illustrate the concepts taught that day in class. (Answers to several but not all of these provided in back of book.)

(d) Ten problems selected and the teacher tells the students why each problem was chosen and how completing each item should help them. (No answers provided.)

7-4. It was stated in the chapter that correct answers to several of the exercises in a homework assignment should be provided. The argument for providing answers is to provide a student with immediate confirmation of his response and hence he knows if he has practiced correct or incorrect behaviors. The major argument against providing answers to homework problems is that the students will use this information incorrectly—that is, they will copy the answers without working the problem.

1. Give arguments which could be used for and against providing all of the answers to homework problems.

2. State your opinion with regard to the availability of answers to problems in textbooks i.e., should the textbook have no answers, some answers, or all answers?

If students are too immature to use answers to assigned exercises correctly, the teacher may:

(a) Never provide answers,

(b) Provide answers on a limited basis with no instruction,

(c) Provide answers on a limited basis with instruction on the proper use of answers.

3. Discuss each of these courses of action.

7-5. An often expressed opinion is that it is preferable to teach only one technique to solve a certain type of problem. The proponents of this view argue that if more than one technique is taught, students will become confused and not know which procedure to follow.

1. Give arguments that might be used to refute this view.
2. Under what conditions is it preferable to teach more than one technique for solving a certain type of problem?
3. Give a specific illustration in secondary school mathematics where more than one procedure should be developed.

7-6. In a tenth-grade geometry class a teacher was developing the theory of similar triangles. In the course of this development it was stated that the measures of corresponding sides are proportional, that is, if a and x are measures of corresponding sides and b and y are measures of corresponding sides, then $a/x = b/y$. This concept was used in the assignment and many students in the class could obtain the correct proportion but then could not solve for an unknown value in the proportion.

One easy manner in which the geometry teacher could rationalize this problem is to remark that the algebra teacher did a poor job of teaching. It is always much easier to blame someone than try to correct a deficiency that was uncovered. This type of argument is also used in a general way when college teachers condemn secondary school teachers and secondary school teachers condemn elementary school teachers.

1. Is this argument valid? Discuss.
2. When a person uses this argument, what type of activities have generally been neglected or omitted?
3. How might the problem described above for the geometry class be overcome?
4. How might the student inadequacies have been detected before the development?

7-7. Suppose that the objectives for a lesson in algebra were as follows: Presuming a rectangular coordinate system, the student should be able to

(a) Graph functions of the type $y = ax^2 + bx + c$ where $a \neq 0$.

(b) Recognize that a graph is a parabola if and only if the function is $y = ax^2 + bx + c$ and $a \neq 0$.

(c) Recognize that if a parabola is concave up, then $a > 0$, and if concave down, $a < 0$.

1. Make a list of the prerequisite skills and concepts which must be possessed by the students if these objectives are to be attained.

2. Write a preview that might be used to introduce this lesson.

3. What developmental activities could be used to teach objective (a)?

7-8. On the class day following the lesson considered in Exercise 7-7, the teacher's opening remarks were:

(a) Yesterday we learned that the graph of a function of the type $y = ax^2 + bx + c$, where $a \neq 0$ is a parabola. We could illustrate a part of a parabola by the path that a ball travels as it is tossed into the air. (At this point the teacher actually tosses a small ball into the air and catches it.)

(b) In order to see if all of you remember how to graph a parabola, I would like for you to graph $y = {}^-3x^2 + 5x - 2$. (During the time the students are working, the teacher is walking around the room, observing their progress, and giving help where needed.)

(c) Following this, the teacher asks:
   (i) Is the graph concave up or concave down?
   (ii) How do you know from the function that the graph must be concave down?

(d) Today we wish to continue graphing quadratic functions of this type but we are going to look for shortcuts that will permit us to sketch a parabola, representing the graph of a given function, more rapidly. In order to do this we are going to look at properties possessed by all parabolas.

1. Name the type of activities illustrated in each of the four paragraphs above.
2. How might paragraph (d) be modified if paragraph (b) uncovered extensive difficulties?
3. What might be the objectives for the new lesson?

7-9. Return to Exercise 1-6 and read it carefully. The process described in the first paragraph of identifying clues in a new problem, using the clues to search our memory for similar problems and mathematical models, and modifying the models recalled to fit the new situation is an example of transfer. This means that we remember something we have already learned and try to apply it in a new and novel situation that we have not encountered before.

Imagine you are a student who has learned the mathematical model $h = rt - 16t^2 + k$ by studying the specific problem presented in Exercise 1-4. Now, suppose your teacher wanted to test your ability to transfer this mathematical model and chose one of the situations in Exercise 1-6 as a test item.

1. Which of the three situations would require the least amount of transfer from the way in which you originally learned the model?
2. Which of the three situations would require the most transfer mathematically in modifying the model as originally learned to what is necessary to fit the situation?
3. Which situation provides the fewest clues that the model you learned previously could be modified and used to fit this problem?

7-10. Referring to the last exercise, you, as a student may fail to pass the test your teacher set for you. Your failure to transfer your knowledge of the original problem to one of the new situations could stem from quite a few sources. Your teacher may observe that you have encountered one of the following difficulties:

(a) You cannot recall the formula $h = rt - 16t^2 + k$, but you recognize it when it is told to you, and you can modify it to fit the first two situations.

(b) You do not recognize the use of the model $h = rt - 16t^2 + k$ in the problem with the sandbag and balloon or in any other problem using objects except those involving a ball tossed in the air.

(c) You can recall the model, comprehend its meaning, and apply it in two of the problems, but you cannot figure out a way to express the initial upward velocity of a ball tossed at an angle of 30 degrees to the horizontal.

(d) You can recall a problem like this and remember that it used the formula $h = rt - 16t^2 + k$. You are unable to use or modify the formula to fit any of the problems, even the first situation.

(e) You recall the formula $h = rt - 16t^2 + k$ and apply it without modification in every situation involving time and the height of any object in the air. You apply it correctly when it fits, as in the first situation.

1. Each of the student behaviors described above indicates a specific difficulty. Name the difficulty in each case.
2. For each difficulty, what type of teaching activity was supposed to have helped the student, to avoid encountering that difficulty?

SUGGESTED ACTIVITIES

7-11. In Exercise 6-6 the term review was used in an intuitive manner. The hoped-for outcome of Exercise 6-6 is a synthesis of ideas as shown in Fig. 7-1. Determine the meaning of review as used in Exercise 6-7.

7-12. The twenty-first yearbook of the National Council of Teachers of Mathematics was devoted in its entirety to the learning of mathematics. As such, it provides material on drill, practice, and transfer of training. Compare the treatment of these topics by Sueltz (1953) and Rosskopf (1953) to that presented in this chapter.

7-13. One way of helping students to retain important facts and also add some light moments to classroom instruction is to use mnemonic devices. One such device is "My Dear Aunt Sally." By looking at the first letter of each word, one should think of the order of operations; multiplication, division, addition, subtraction. Another dealing with the multiplication of binomials is FOIL. Identify the meaning of each letter in this acronym.

ADDITIONAL SOURCES

Rosskopf, Myron F. "Transfer of Training," *The Learning of Mathematics Its Theory and Practice*. Washington, D.C.: National Council of Teachers of Mathematics, 1953, pp. 205–227.

Sueltz, Ben A. "Drill-Practice-Recurring Experience," *The Learning of Mathematics Its Theory and Practice*. Washington, D.C.: National Council of Teachers of Mathematics, 1953, pp. 192–204.

Chapter 8

Modes of Instruction

A central responsibility of a mathematics teacher is to structure classroom conditions and instructional materials so that his students have an opportunity to learn mathematical behavior. When a visitor enters a classroom and observes the students working problems, or sees groups of students playing mathematical games, or hears a student report, he is observing ways in which the student is interacting with his environment. Each of these classroom organizations is called a *mode of instruction*, which is more formally described below.

> A *mode of instruction* is a planned organization of the conditions in the environment intended to cause an interaction between the student and these conditions.

Notice that the mode of instruction is the organization of the stimuli external to the learner. These external conditions are arranged to impinge on the learner and cause an interaction between him and a selected part of the external environment. Student learning is expected to occur as a result of this interaction. (See assumption 1, Chapter 2.)

An arbitrary classification system is now introduced for modes of instruction so that the ensuing discussion and exercises can be more readily understood. The categories in the classification scheme are named by the type of student interaction produced by the modes in that category. The six categories and their descriptions are:

1. *Listening.* An exposition type of mode of instruction in which a group of students listens to or watches a presentation and may be permitted to ask questions.
2. *Responding.* A question-answer type of presentation where the burden of the interaction rests with the students responding orally to questions.
3. *Discussing.* In this type of mode, the burden of the interaction is between students talking together in an effort to achieve some common goal.
4. *Manipulating.* The interaction in this kind of mode of instruction is between the student and physical devices that must be manipulated to achieve purposeful learning.

5. *Reading.* Modes in this category have stimuli that are printed materials and the student behavior is that of reading.

6. *Writing.* Observation of these kind of modes of instruction would reveal the student's writing.

In Fig. 8-1 an example of a mode of instruction for each category in the classification scheme is illustrated. The student is

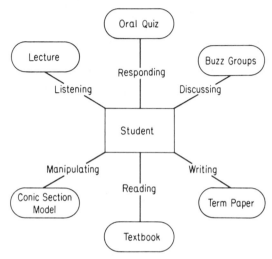

Fig. 8-1. Examples of external conditions that produce the type of student interaction corresponding to the classification of modes of instruction.

interacting with six different external conditions. The type of student interaction that each external condition produces is shown along the connecting line segments.

The categories described above are not necessarily mutually exclusive and there are modes of instruction such as programmed learning that span more than one category. Yet the classification system provides a frame of reference for examining classroom interactions in mathematics and indicates the variety of organizational patterns available to the competent teacher.

VARIETY OF MODES OF INSTRUCTION

Knowledge of many modes of instruction and their distinctive advantages and disadvantages can help the teacher organize the classroom environment and materials to insure maximum efficiency and effectiveness in learning. The teacher can increase the probability that his students will learn a given task when he selects and implements the mode of instruction most appropriate for optimal learning of the given task and when he uses a variety of modes of instruction in his classroom. A variety of modes of instruction elicits more student involvement, promotes a longer attention span, and provides more ways to meet different individual styles of learning.

Many modes of instruction can be employed in mathematics classrooms. Not all of them will be named in this chapter, but numerous activities will be mentioned in the hope that these will prompt the reader to use his imagination to think of many more that are suitable to his own personality.

The art of using any particular mode of presentation effectively can be acquired only with practice and experience. A teacher cannot improve his techniques unless he knows many modes of instruction and also is familiar with the precautions and planning requirements necessary for successful execution. The most important thing to remember about modes of instruction is that there should be a variety—not just one—used during most daily lessons.

8-1.

1. Four statements of a teacher to his class are listed below. In which of the statements is the teacher telling the class the mode of instruction that he wishes to use in class this day?

    (a) I am going to hand each of you a chart that you are to work on individually without my aid or the aid of your textbook. Complete the unfilled spaces in the chart and see if you can discover a pattern.

    (b) Today we are going to begin the study of the next chapter in your textbook on exponents.

    (c) Before we begin the new material on logarithms, we will spend part of the period reviewing exponents.

    (d) Instead of developing the concepts of exponents first and then doing logarithms, I am going to change the order found in your textbook. We will first study logarithms and then use these ideas to develop the properties of exponents.

2. For each "no" response in (1) what is the teacher telling the class? (i.e. is it a purpose, an instructional strategy or something else?)

8-2. A class has been studying similar triangles. The teacher decides to wrap up the chapter by having the students use their new knowledge in solving some problems outdoors.

(a) The teacher tells the class that she is going to break them into five groups and each group is going to have a different problem to solve. They will not know how to do the problem at first, but by working cooperatively they can figure it out. She tells them how to select a leader, how to write a step-by-step procedure for what they have to do, and how jobs are to be assigned within the group.

(b) Each group gets a problem such as "Find the distance across the street without crossing the street" or "Find the latitude of our school without looking it up." Each group begins to discuss the problem to decide how it can be solved and to determine the materials needed.

(c) Several groups have difficulty with their problems and ask for help. The teacher asks them questions about what they have done and other leading questions. She doesn't answer questions, but having anticipated just these difficulties, she skillfully gets the students thinking on the right track.

(d) The next day the students go outside and set up stakes and lay off triangles similar to triangles containing the unknown distances. Each one knows his job. Some set up equipment, some measure, and some record data.

(e) The students return to the classroom and each group writes a report of its problem, the procedures they followed, and the results they found.

(f) The third day each group reads its report to the rest of the class. They use charts and diagrams to present their procedures and results.

1. For each paragraph above, determine the mode of instruction that was used. In which of the six categories does it best fit?

2. Referring to the previous chapter on Purposes of Teaching Activities, how would you classify the purpose of this outdoor activity?

8-3. Several modes of instruction that could be classified as Listening are described below. For each mode described, give an example of a topic in mathematics that could be presented with that mode of instruction.

(a) *Lecture*. The class listens to ideas verbally communicated from a teacher who may supplement talking with visual aids or permit questions from the audience.

(b) *Demonstration*. The class watches a procedure, skill, technique, or experiment performed by the teacher that is usually accompanied by an explanation, but in which the learning occurs mainly from imitating the procedure rather than hearing the operations orally.

(c) *Audio Device*. The class listens to ideas verbally communicated from an audio device like a record or an audiotape that acts as the lecturer.

(d) *Visual Device*. The class watches or listens to devices such as television, videotape, films, closed film loops, filmstrips, and slides that replace the teacher as lecturer or demonstrator.

(e) *Reading*. The class listens to a writer communicating an idea or story through the medium of the teacher or a student reading.

(f) *Student Lecture-Demonstration*. The class listens or watches a student who acts as the teacher by lecturing or demonstrating.

(g) *Panel Presentation*. The class listens to two or more people jointly present and discuss a topic.

(h) *Debate*. The class listens to two teams take opposing positions on some issue and engage in a confrontation of views.

(i) *Dramatic Skit or Play*. The class listens and watches a play or skit designed to communicate or depict some issue, topic, or life situation.

8-4. As the name implies, modes of instruction in the Responding category use questions by the presenter to which the learner responds orally. Now questions may be used in other modes also, but again, the key here is what the student does. If the burden of the interaction lies with the student responding (not with the teacher asking rhetorical questions or the teacher answering his own questions) and the student responds orally (not in writing or manipulating), then it is a mode of instruction in the Responding category.

One of the hardest modes in this category to gain skill in using is the *heuristic* mode of instruction. The activity of the student is continually directed through carefully worded and well-directed questions that lead the student to the discovery and understanding of concepts or principles new to him. The word *heuristic* stems from the Greek word meaning "I discover" and implies the active search of a learner after knowledge. It requires patience, planning, and persistent effort on the part of the instructor, for progress is usually slow at first, but the students' ability to think for themselves increases rapidly after several exposures.

Some other Responding modes are:

(a) *Recitation.* The student recites from memory some piece of knowledge or even long passages, as in reciting a poem.

(b) *Oral Drill.* Essentially like an oral test to gain feedback on previously developed material or to promote recall.

(c) *Question-Answer Competitive Game.* Teams of students compete against each other in fielding questions for points in a game situation like a quiz program, an arithmetic bee, or a baseball game.

1. In which of the following activities could the heuristic mode of instruction be used profitably?

(a) Inventory

(b) Preview

(c) Development

(d) Assimilation

(e) Reteaching

(f) Review

(g) Drill

(h) Generalizing a task to a new setting or problem

2. Repeat Question 1 for the other three modes of instruction described in this exercise.

8-5. Statements that teachers make to their students and other teachers are often revealing about their modes of instruction. For example, a teacher may say, "The purpose of my teaching is to work myself out of a job—that is, get my students to the point where they can study mathematics without depending upon my explanations." Such a teacher would probably teach his students to do independent study. Independent study would cross several categories of modes of instruction, but would be confined mainly to reading and writing on the part of the student.

Analyze the teacher statements below to get suggestions for the type of mode of instruction that the teacher would favor.

(a) Learning proceeds from the concrete to the abstract. A student has to get experience and get actively involved with things he knows and can see and feel. Then he is able to understand verbal abstractions.

(b) I believe students learn more from one another than they do from listening to me. I set the task to be learned and then I let them work together to arrive at a solution, helping whenever I am needed.

(c) A teacher's job is to show them how to do mathematics and get the material that they will need later covered.

(d) A person who asks one good question is a better teacher than one who has all the answers.

(e) Students learn in spite of the teacher.

8-6. Statements that students make to teachers can reveal a need for improvement or refinement in teaching methods. A student may say: "I understand it when I see you do it in class, but when I get home, I can't do it myself." This statement suggests that some class time needs to be devoted to the students writing examples under the guidance of the teacher. Only when the teacher is certain that the students can write exercises successfully under his guidance should he expect the student to be able to do them without guidance.

1. What phase of developmental activities discussed in the previous chapter seems to be lacking when students make this comment?

2. The remedial mode of instruction recommended above is writing examples by the students under the guidance of the teacher.

For each student statement below, indicate a remedial mode of instruction.

(a) I understand it when you do it, but I can't get anything out of reading the textbook.

(b) Some kids seem to get ideas for doing these proofs and the rest of us don't know how to begin. How do they do it?

(c) When you explain the material in class, those smart kids understand it and you go ahead assuming that everyone understands. We don't want to ask questions and look stupid. Yet when some person does ask a question, I hear other students say the same problem was bothering them.

8-7. A teacher decided to have her students do some constructions in geometry. When the class began she asked the students to take out paper, a ruler, and a compass. Some students said they did not have their compass or ruler with them that day. She told the class to study the examples in the book and start to work on the construction problems in the exercises, while she went to another teacher to get some equipment. When she returned, she found the students making circles, marking the desk tops, and stabbing each other with their compasses. When she got control of the class, she told some of the students they would have to share some of the equipment.

As the students started to work, hands were raised all over the room; students began to ask questions about how to do the exercises. Some of the other students were bisecting line segments by measuring with the ruler. Finally in desperation the teacher called every student's attention to the board and told them to watch her and on their paper do everything she did as she demonstrated each of the constructions. She silently vowed to herself to never have another laboratory lesson. ("They may work in theory, but they don't work in practice!")

The situation described above is typical of poorly planned and poorly executed laboratory lessons.

1. Identify at least two difficulties in the first paragraph that developed in the lesson that could have been avoided.
2. Identify at least two errors that the teacher made in the second paragraph.
3. List several precautions that the teacher should have taken so that the lesson would have been a smooth one and would have avoided the difficulties that arose.
4. What mode of instruction did the teacher finally use at the end of the lesson?

8-8. A teacher wishes to introduce her students to the concepts of congruence and similarity of geometric figures and some properties of these figures. An envelope was prepared for each student that contained cutouts of pairs of different geometric figures, some of which were congruent, some similar, and some neither congruent nor similar. Each student found in the envelope on his desk a ruler, a protractor, a detailed instruction sheet, and a prepared laboratory sheet for recording data. The student's instruction sheet included such items as:

(a) Sort into a group, pairs of figures that have exactly the same size and shape.

(b) Write on the lab sheet in the space provided how you could show another person that two figures have the same size and shape.

(c) Sort into a group, pairs of figures in which one of the figures looks like a photographic enlargement of the other.

(d) Write on your lab sheet in the space provided whether the figures found in (c) can be described as having the same size and shape, only the same shape, only the same size, or none of these.

(e) Write on your lab sheet how you would give directions to another student who wishes to make a $1^1/_2$ times enlargement of quadrilateral A.

1. What are some advantages of the manipulative mode of instruction described in the example above that would not be present if a different mode were used for this lesson?

2. Compare this exercise to the previous one and list some problems that the teacher anticipated and avoided.

3. Upon which purpose of a teaching activity (Chapter 7) is this lesson concentrating?

8-9. The laboratory lesson is an excellent example of a mode of instruction that can permit students to discover new relationships, rather than simply being told. To do this, however, requires detailed planning and a guided approach.

To illustrate how to guide pupils to discover, design a laboratory sheet to be used with the lesson described in the previous exercise. You may wish to specify the type and number of geometric figures that you would want in each student's envelope. This will help you in designing the lab sheet.

In making the lab sheet, you must meet each of the following requirements.

(a) Design the sheet so that space is provided for the students to answer the questions shown in (a)-(e) of the last exercise.

(b) Design the sheet so that the questions on congruent figures are separated from questions on similar figures.

(c) Make sure that students have to collect and record data about relationships between sides and angles of pairs of figures. (Should this be done only for congruent and similar pairs or for other pairs also? Why?)

(d) Ask questions that direct the students to search for relationships between corresponding parts of congruent figures and similar figures.

(e) Ask questions that in some way gets most of the students to discover and be able to state several conjectures about similar figures and congruent figures.

8-10. If we are sufficiently clever as teachers we could presumably use every type of mode of instruction with each topic we teach. Suppose we wish to teach the probability of getting a head on a fair coin. We could consider each classification of instructional modes as follows:

Listening. The teacher might simply tell the class the probability of getting a head on a fair coin.

Responding. The teacher might ask leading questions like: How many possible ways can a coin land? How many of these would yield a head?

Discussing. The teacher could organize the students into groups and ask them to try to arrive at some conclusion with justification for the question: What are the chances of getting a head on a fair coin?

Manipulating. Give each child a coin and let him try to answer the question by flipping the coin.

Reading. Let the students read to find the answer to the question.

Writing. The teacher could ask each student to do some thinking and write his answer with justification for the question: What are the chances of getting a head on a fair coin?

1. Repeat the same procedure described above for the following topics:
   (a) Finding the solution graphically for two simultaneous linear equations in two variables.
   (b) Learning that the diagonals of a rectangle bisect each other and are congruent.
2. State which mode of instruction you think would be better for 1(a) if the teaching activity is:
   (a) Assimilation
   (b) Development
   (c) Review or recall
3. State which mode of instruction you think would be better for 1(b) if the teaching activity is:
   (a) Assimilation
   (b) Development by a discovery approach
   (c) Transfer of learning to a novel situation within mathematics
   (d) Drill

SUGGESTED ACTIVITIES

8-11. A chart is provided below for use in observing modes of instruction in the classroom. The chart contains six headings corresponding to the six classifications of modes of instruction given in this chapter. You select a constant time interval such as every 2 or 3 minutes. At the end of each time interval you place a check in the row that corresponds to the activity the students are engaged in at the time. After one or more class periods you can observe patterns and get an indication of the extent and variety of student involvement.

Type of Mode	Time Intervals	Total
Listening		
Responding		
Discussing		
Manipulating		
Reading		
Writing		

1. Use the chart to record data in a mathematics class. Using the data in your chart answer the following:
   (a) What kind of interaction are the students usually using in this class?
   (b) How often does the type of mode of instruction change in this class?
   (c) After observing for several periods, do you notice any patterns in the positioning and amount of time spent in one mode?
2. Use the chart to observe in physical education classes, history classes, science classes, English classes, and industrial arts classes. Do the frequencies and spacing of modes of instruction vary from one kind of class to another?

8-12. Read the dialogue between Socrates and the slave boy in Fadiman (1958), pp. 49-57. This story is the source of the now famous method of instruction called the Socratic method. In which classification would this mode of instruction be found?

8-13. The Committee on Educational Media of the Mathematical Association of American has produced several films that show great mathematicians teaching. One man whose teaching has been captured on film is George Polya. The title of Polya's film is "Let Us Teach Guessing." It can be obtained from Modern Learning Aids, Atlanta, Georgia. You should find it an enjoyable task to preview this film. Decide the type of mode of instruction used in this demonstration lesson.

8-14. Avail yourself of the opportunity to competitively play such games as Monopoly, chess, checkers, Wiff 'n' Proof, Equations, Configurations, Rook, Chinese checkers, and cribbage. Can you think of a way to use each of these games for instructional purposes in mathematics? In which category in the classification system for modes of instruction would these games be found?

8-15. You may have heard of the "genetic" method of teaching mathematics advocated by many mathematicians. This method of teaching is briefly described in the Introduction of Polya (1963), p. ix. This book is devoted to illustrations of this method of teaching. Sometimes the genetic method of instruction is confused with the heuristic mode of instruction. Read this description of the genetic method of teaching and tell how it differs from the heuristic mode of instruction. Is the genetic method a mode of instruction?

8-16. There are certainly more modes of instruction that can be used in mathematics besides those encountered in this chapter. Two other sources that give additional suggestions are Davis (1951), pp. 27-38 and Dubisch (1963), pp. 23-25.

ADDITIONAL SOURCES

Davis, David R. *The Teaching of Mathematics*. Cambridge, Mass.: Addison-Wesley Publishing Company, Inc., 1951.

Dubisch, Roy. *The Teaching of Mathematics*. New York: John Wiley & Sons, Inc., 1963.

Fadiman, Clifton. *Fantasia Mathematica*. New York: Simon and Schuster, Inc., 1958.

Polya, George. *Mathematical Methods in Science*. Studies in Mathematics, Vol. XI. School Mathematics Study Group, 1963.

Chapter 9

Instructional Materials

One of the main assumptions listed in Chapter 2 is that new behavior is acquired as a result of the learner's interaction with his environment. The learner's senses are the pathways that carry the impressions and sensations that the pupil receives from the external environment to his mind. The teacher is a part of the learner's external world and, therefore, the teacher's only means of "reaching" the learner is through the roadways of his senses. Teaching that focuses primarily on one sense, that of hearing, is much less effective in influencing the acquisition of new knowledge than a multisensory approach. A variety of stimuli that appeals to all the senses is needed in the teaching environment to allow as many avenues as possible to the learner's mind.

Instructional materials and audio-visual equipment are the tools that enable a multisensory approach to mathematics teaching. Many teachers of mathematics undertake teaching with a limited knowledge or neglect of the many tools that are available for their use. As an analogy, suppose a cabinetmaker were hired to construct an elegant and exquisite piece of furniture using the finest and most expensive wood. If the cabinetmaker arrived to do the job with only one tool, a hatchet, what would you think of his chances? Teachers undertake an infinitely more important project, shaping the behavior of children, and expect to do so with a tool chest that usually contains one basic textbook, a chalkboard, and a piece of chalk. The purpose of this chapter is to increase your awareness of a wide variety of teaching tools.

A wide variety of materials is available to a teacher who wishes to utilize all of the possible tools that can give each child an opportunity to learn mathematics. An arbitrary division of these materials is made as follows: models and manipulative materials; audio-visual presentation equipment; and printed materials. A short description of some of the materials available in each category will be given. However, the best way to become familiar with the available resources is to personally search, collect, and organize materials. You will find that many of the exercises are designed for you to investigate some model, try equipment, or compare printed material.

MODELS AND MANIPULATIVE MATERIALS

Mathematics is learned not only through seeing and hearing, but also through the sense of touch and tactile movement. Models are designed to take full advantage of this avenue to mathematical understanding and to assist the learner in bridging the gap from the concrete involvement necessary for a foundation of understanding to the abstract concepts that comprise mathematics. The use of concrete objects, models, and manipulative devices is increasing in mathematical instruction, particularly in conjunction with the growth of laboratory lessons.

A perusal of any one of the many commercial catalogs will reveal a multitude of models, simulators, and demonstration aids for every branch of secondary school mathematics. Other devices that make mathematics meaningful and fun can be found, such as geoboards, colored rods, and academic games. Caution should be exercised with any device, since it is only as effective as the person using it. Little benefit is derived from objects that the students are not permitted to handle or experiment with. Conversely, students gain little from mere manipulation without some skillful guidance or gentle direction from the teacher. The guidance should be in the form of open-ended questions that require the pupil to produce the desired learning outcome with the aid of the concrete object.

Perhaps the best manipulative devices are the ones designed and constructed by the teacher or students. The activity of conceiving and producing homemade objects assures that the teacher has given unusual thought to the benefits and best use of the aid. When a teacher invests much time and involvement in some project, he usually makes sure that the execution is successful.

There is a danger with the use of models and demonstration devices that a teacher must guard against. Students should constantly be reminded that physical models *do not prove* any theorems or relationships in mathematics. The medians of a triangle are not proved concurrent by experimentation with a model. Showing that a right circular cone only holds one-third as much sand as a right circular cylinder with the same base and height is no proof that the volume of a cone is one-third its base times its height. The final test of the validity of a mathematical statement rests not upon experimentation but with its logical derivation within the deductive system. Models can be used to demonstrate physically a mathematical relationship that has been stated to help determine its meaning. They can also help students discover relationships and engage in inductive thinking to produce conjectures and generalizations.

AUDIO-VISUAL AND SUPPORT EQUIPMENT

Numerous machines have been designed to fulfill special functions in supporting a teacher. Some are simple and readily available while others are sophisticated, expensive, and require special competencies to use. Each item of equipment has certain advantages and disadvantages. Any particular machine should be used only in those situations where its unique features can be best utilized. Some of the devices commonly used are overhead projector, opaque projector, filmstrip projector, slide projector, motion picture projector, closed film loops, record player, audiotape, videotape, teaching machine, calculator, copying machine, spirit duplicator, and overhead transparency production equipment.

The advent of computers has added a new dimension to instructional equipment. Schools are beginning to install terminals that are connected to large computer installations and are operated on a time-sharing basis. Students learn to solve interesting and often complex problems by analyzing the problem, writing a computer program, and then running the program on the computer. In this way the computer is used as a tool to solve problems that ordinarily would be impossible, and as an agent that greatly motivates students to work on mathematics The computer is being utilized in a second way as a very complicated teaching machine in what is called "computer-assisted instruction." The machine contains various programs that provide branching instructional routines and visual displays. The learner interacts with the machine much like he would with a questioning teacher through the use of a typewriter keyboard and a light pencil on a television screen. Proponents of this type of arrangement argue that the computer can relieve the teacher of such chores as drill activities and remedial work and free him for more individual and creative teaching.

Audio-visual aids are useful tools, but they will not substitute for inspired teaching or cover over poor teaching. Like tools in a tool chest, they should be used only in those situations where their special features and the teacher's expertise can be brought together to produce good results.

SUPPLEMENTARY PRINTED MATERIALS

In most classes the students will have a basic textbook. However, one basic textbook cannot be expected to fulfill adequately the needs of every student in the class. If any class of 35 students were considered with respect to their dietary needs, it would certainly be found that the exact same foods in the same amounts would not suffice for all. Likewise, the same mathematical meal from a basic textbook for all students is inadequate. Rather, the teacher must select many materials to place before the students, as in a cafeteria. From this smorgasbord of mathematical nourishment, the particular learning activities required by each individual student can be prescribed and administered.

Supplementary materials should include enrichment materials for the more able students, remedial and drill activities for those who need to build necessary skills, books and pamphlets to create interest in mathematics, games and puzzles for mathematical recreation, applications and uses of mathematics to increase motivation, and bulletin-board displays to enliven the learning environment.

Remedial materials to supplement the teaching of any topic can be obtained in various ways. Programmed instruction offers a way of providing remedial instruction in a topic or can be used to drill basic skills. A classroom set of old textbooks, a book of drill problems, a set of workbooks, or a collection of dittoed sheets providing practice on different skills also are practical means of supplementing the textbook for the purpose of remedial instruction. A classroom kit of materials on basic computation is commercially available in which a student needing help is instructed to withdraw from the kit the material on the specific skill that he lacks. He takes a diagnostic test which directs him to a short instructional narrative that explains that part of the skill he does not understand. It provides practice with answers so that he can attain the skill and return to the main topic of the class. These are some of the methods that can be used to help students who require more instruction or remedial work.

Enrichment activities for mathematics are also becoming more abundant. More books are being published for student readers that deal more deeply with usual topics or introduce related topics new to the student. Programmed instruction is an alternative for a student who is interested in learning more about some area or wishes to study a new topic. Recreational books are available that contain fantasy stories about mathematics; students find these interesting and thought-provoking. Puzzle books in mathematics can be displayed on a materials table for the student to peruse as a reward for finishing regular work. Other printed materials for a materials table would be volumes that have mathematical pictures and colorful illustrations that the students can leaf through like a picture magazine.

Amassing a wealth of supplementary materials is a gradual and continual process. Excellent charts and pamphlets can be obtained from companies interested in the promotion of the study of mathematics that are particularly helpful for applications and bulletin board material. Other teachers are an excellent source of ideas and resources, and they may lend you such things as pictures and biographical sketches of famous mathematicians. It takes a long time to assemble and organize books, problems, pictures, programmed instruction, and drill activities for topics. A beginning teacher will not have acquired many resources. With a conscientious effort to search for, organize, and systematically file supplementary material, an excellent collection of resources can be gradually assembled.

EXERCISES

9-1. A model often used to represent the relation $x^2 + 2xy + y^2 = (x + y)^2$ is pictured below:

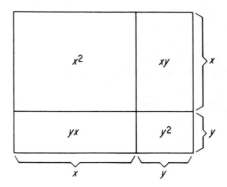

1. How could a physical model be constructed to show that the relationship $x^2 + 2xy + y^2 = (x + y)^2$ holds for various values of x and y? (That is how can the idea of x and y as variables be emphasized physically?)
2. State how a model could be designed and constructed to show the relationship $(x - y)^2 = x^2 - 2xy + y^2$.
3. Show how a model could be designed and constructed to show the relationship $x^2 - y^2 = (x + y)(x - y)$.
4. Show how a model could be designed and constructed to show the relationship $(x + y)^3 = x^3 + 3x^2y + 3xy^2 + y^3$.

9-2. Many of the concepts that are taught in algebra can be illustrated by pictures or representations from the physical world, as shown by the previous exercise.

An illustration that might be used to show the graph of the function $y = ax^2 + bx + c$, $a \neq 0$ would be to bring a ball into the classroom and observe its path as it is tossed from one pupil to another. It is felt that illustrations of this type motivate the learning of the task and increase the probability of its retention.

1. Devise a physical example to illustrate direct and inverse variation.
2. Devise an illustration of a physical example for the principles of addition of equals to either equals or unequals.

9-3. A commercially available aid that is very useful in geometry is a board with holes in it as shown in the illustration below.

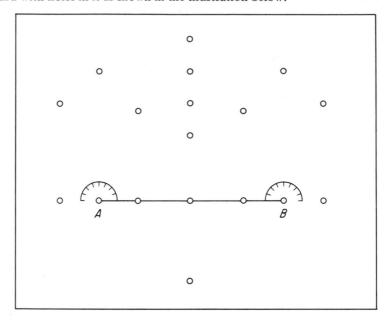

Line segment $\overline{AB}$ has printed protractors at its end points. Pegs are fixed at A and B and pegs can be placed in the remaining holes shown. Elastic bands are stretched over the pegs to form geometric figures.

This model can be used to illustrate the meanings of many of the relationships in geometry after they have been stated.

1. State how you could position the pegs and elastic bands on this model to show
   (a) the different kinds of triangles
   (b) the relationships among angles of a triangle and its exterior angles
   (c) the dependence of the area of a triangle on measures of its base and altitude
   (d) another theorem or definition in geometry

Experimentation with this model can be used to get students to generate conjectures.

2. Devise a way you could use this model with students so that they will experiment with the equipment and discover each one of the geometric statements that are listed at the end of the introduction to Chapter 18.

9-4. Assume that you are a member of a mathematics department in a newly opened senior high school and your department has been allocated $150 per teacher for the purchase of equipment. This equipment must be other than audio-visual aids or supplementary books and printed material. Using the list provided below as well as equipment catalogs, make a list of items and the quantity of each that you would purchase for your room with the $150. (The prices or the amount of money you are allocated may not be realistic.)

Item	Approximate Price
Place-value board or demonstration abacus	$ 6.00
Dissectable wood cone model	22.00
Colored rods demonstration kit	60.00
Cube and pyramid volume model	3.00
Dandelin's cone model	12.50
Wooden chalkboard drawing instruments	11.50
Set of geometric solids fillable with water	35.00
Reversible chalkboard panel with rectangular and polar coordinate graphs	49.00
Gravity protractor	7.50
Hexstat to show normal distribution	2.00
Liter block	9.00
Logarithm and trig table wall chart	9.50
Pantograph	6.00
Multibased arithmetic blocks	90.00
Trisectable prism	7.00
Demonstration slide rule	20.00
Student's beginner slide rules (per dozen)	12.00
Adjustable quadrilateral with plastic protractor at vertices	11.00
Trig function demonstrator	22.00
Model of Cavalieri's principle	25.00
Slate globe	43.50
Manual desk calculator	140.00
Demonstration Model for πr^2 as area of circle	12.00
Wiff'n' Proof, the game of logic	6.00
Configurations, geometry game	4.00
Map projection model	22.50

9-5. Overhead projectors can be used as a very effective instructional aid. One use of this device is to carefully prepare drawings or illustrations before class. In this way it is not necessary to spend valuable classroom time constructing a complex figure. A second value is that the transparency can be used many times rather than just one time as a picture on the chalkboard. One valuable tool that a teacher should have at his disposal is the art and know how for making transparencies for use with an overhead projector.

To illustrate the intersection of two sets, a teacher may make a transparency with one overlay as follows:

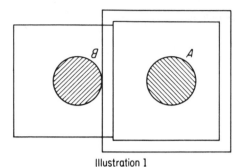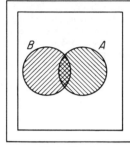

Illustration 1   Illustration 2

Put a transparency with the set A on it in a frame and tape to it a transparency with a set B on it. This latter transparency is called an *overlay*. Illustration 1 shows the overlay taped to the frame and in an open position. Illustration 2 shows the picture when the overlay is placed over the transparency containing set A.

1. Design a transparency with one or more overlays to show that one altitude of a right triangle separates the original triangle into two similar right triangles.
2. Design transparencies with one or more overlays to illustrate graphically a function that is onto, a function that is one-to-one, and the relationship between a function and its inverse.

9-6. One very useful teaching tool that has recently been developed is a closed-film loop or single-concept film. A short film on a single idea is placed into a cartridge and the two ends are spliced together. The cartridge is inserted into a special projector and can be shown over and over or stopped at any time. It requires no rewinding or threading.

Like any teaching aid, there are some ideas that it can present well and some others that can be better presented by a different technique. Some descriptions of the concepts taught by several commercially available film loops are listed below. For each one, decide if the concept is most practically, efficiently, and effectively taught by a film loop or would be better or more practically taught by the student manipulating a model.

1. This film loop illustrates with animation how an ellipse can be constructed as the locus of a point on a stretched string, whose fixed endpoints form the foci and, hence, shows that the sum of the distances from each foci to any point on the ellipse is the same.

2. In this loop, two ball bearings are simultaneously released from the same height; one has no initial horizontal velocity and the other one does. Slow-motion photography shows that both strike the ground together. (Recall Exercise 1-7.) How is this concept important in finding the mathematical model for Exercise 1-7?

3. The area of a rectangle is shown to consist of the number of small unit squares which exactly cover the rectangle. The area formula is shown to be a fast way of counting the number of unit squares.

4. This loop develops the trigonometric functions using the unit circle. The idea of arc length on the circle measured in terms of radians is animated. The relationship between real numbers or measures of arcs and the trigonometric functions of these real numbers is illustrated as well as an animation showing the winding function. (Compare with the display you prepared in Exercise 6-10.)

9-7. Students many times have difficulty learning mathematics because of the one track approach of the teacher lecturing and always working abstractly. For each situation described, think of a model or visual aid that would help the student understand the presentation.

1. "Suppose we had twenty-seven objects and I wished to group them into groups of four. Every time we have four bundles of four, we regroup them into one group of four. So, we would have one group of four bundles and two groups of four each and three single objects. Is that clear?"

2. "Let us look now at the rectangle *ABCD* drawn on the board. If I flipped it around the vertical axis and then rotated it 180 degrees, would that be the same result as if I rotated it 180 degrees and then flipped it around the vertical axis?"

3. "Imagine a plane cutting through this sphere so that it passes through the center of the sphere. Why is the circle made by this cut larger in circumference than any other circle made by a cutting plane not through the center?"

9-8. Bulletin boards can be used as teaching aids and to stimulate interest in the classroom. One use that can be made of bulletin boards is to present interesting historical anecdotes about mathematics or mathematicians. There is, for example, the story of Karl Friedrich Gauss who in his first class in arithmetic was given a long arithmetic progression to add by the laborious method of writing the numbers and adding. Gauss had never seen or been told the formula for a sum of an arithmetic progression but discovered this formula at the age of ten, completed the difficult problem in a very short time, and was the only student in the class to get the correct answer.

Several excellent sources for historical anecdotes or biographical sketches relating to mathematics are:

E. T. Bell, *Men of Mathematics.*

Tobias Dantzig, *Number, The Language of Science.*

Howard Eves, *An Introduction to the History of Mathematics.*

Use one or more of these sources to find a story which could be used to motivate a mathematics lesson with respect to

(a) A historical origin of amicable numbers

(b) An anecdote associated with the $\sqrt{2}$ as an irrational number

(c) Fermat's last theorem

(d) The life and death of Evariste Galois

9-9. Another way in which bulletin boards are useful is as a problem center. Most mathematics students are challenged by working puzzles and if this becomes a competition among students in various classes, a great deal of lively enthusiasm is generated. These problems should be challenging and differentiated for varying backgrounds. They can be changed after several students have demonstrated their ability to solve the problem.

1. See if you can solve them.
    (a) Divide an obtuse triangle into several other triangles so that each new triangle is acute. Example:

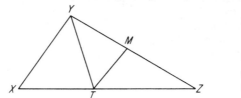

The condition is not satisfied since △ *MTZ* is obtuse.

    (b) Substitute digits for each letter to make the problem a true addition problem. Each letter is to be replaced by the same digit each time it occurs and no digit can be used for more than one letter.

$$
\begin{array}{r}
\text{FORTY} \\
\text{TEN} \\
\text{TEN} \\
\hline
\text{SIXTY}
\end{array}
$$

    (c) A traveler on a train notices that 4.5 times the number of telegraph poles that the train passes each minute yields the speed of the train in miles per hour. Find the distance between the poles.
2. Find several sources (at least three) which can provide problems which could be used on a bulletin board.

9-10. In most schools there are three main collections of supplementary books in mathematics:

One collection is in the main library and includes books of general interest to students for reading, study, or entertainment.

A second collection is the classroom library. Here would be found books showing uses of mathematics, references needed in class and books intended to be "eye-catchers" and "interest-grabbers." Books should be included that the students would find interesting to glance at for five minutes during a lull in the period.

Finally, the third collection is the professional library which would contain works of interest to teachers of mathematics.

Examine the following books and determine the library in which they would best serve.

Irving Adler, *The Giant Golden Book of Mathematics.*

David Bergamini, *Mathematics.*

Morris Kline, *Mathematics in Western Culture.*

L. Lieber and G. Hugh, *Human Values and Science, Art, and Mathematics.*

James Newman, *The World of Mathematics.*

Eric T. Bell, *Men of Mathematics.*

Lancelot Hogben, *Wonderful World of Mathematics.*

National Council of Teachers of Mathematics. *Mathematical Challenges.*

L. G. Brandes, *Yes, Math Can Be Fun.*

Billy L. Turney, *Geometry Teaching Aids You Can Make.*

H. Martyn Cundy and A. P. Rollett, *Mathematical Models.*

9-11. Many teachers do not use the mathematics books in the library for their classes because they do not know what is available. Knowing sources to go to when the need arises is half the battle.

Choose a source from the list below that would aid the teacher in each situation described.

1. The teacher is looking for a story about mathematics to read to the class the day before a vacation.
2. The teacher is looking for an easy reading book to recommend to a student for enrichment in mathematics.
3. The teacher wants a source for a student who has asked about geometry in more than three dimensions.
4. The teacher would like a source that would give applications of modular arithmetic.

    National Council of Teachers of Mathematics. *Secret Codes.*

    Clifton Fadiman, *Fantasia Mathematica.*

    E. A. Abbott, *Flatland.*

    Eric T. Bell, *The Last Problem.*

    L. Lieber, *Mits, Wits, and Logic.*

9-12. Source materials can be a valuable aid to the teacher. One common source that has information on many of the problems faced by secondary school mathematics teachers is the journal, *The Mathematics Teacher*. There are also various other source books, such as yearbooks of the NCTM, with which the teacher should be familiar.

1. For each of the following situations, find one specific section of a yearbook of the NCTM which would provide useful information for the teacher.

    (a) An enrichment lesson for a seventh grade mathematics lesson.

    (b) The purpose and function of drill in the learning process.

    (c) The role of mathematics in the secondary school.

    (d) A PTA speech justifying "modern math."

    (e) A definition of evaluation.

    (f) The development of the concept of function in the mathematics education of students.

    (g) Historical material that can be used in the classroom.

2. Find at least one other source, not in an NCTM yearbook or *The Mathematics Teacher*, which would provide information for each of the above situations.

SUGGESTED ACTIVITIES

9-13. One of the best listings of instructional materials available in mathematics can be found in the Appendixes of Johnson (1967). The listing contains suggestions for exhibits, displays, and student projects. Many books and teaching aids are listed as well as the names and addresses of publishers from whom the materials can be obtained. Examine this listing for ideas and suggestions.

9-14. Obtain an equipment catalog for mathematics and observe the wealth of teaching aids that are available in mathematics. If no catalog is available to you, use the book named in the activity above to obtain the addresses of companies and write letters requesting their catalogs.

9-15. This activity provides a list of questions that you can use to make a check of equipment and materials available in your school. This is especially important for a beginning teacher or a teacher that moves to a new school.

1. Which of the following pieces of equipment are available in your school?
   - (a) Overhead projector
   - (b) Opaque projector
   - (c) Closed-film-loop machine
   - (d) Motion picture projector
   - (e) Slide projector
   - (f) Filmstrip projector
   - (g) Record player
   - (h) Audiotape machine
   - (i) Videotape machine
   - (j) Spirit duplicator
   - (k) Copying machine
   - (l) Projection screens
   - (m) Computer terminal

2.
   - (a) How is equipment scheduled?
   - (b) Where and how is equipment stored?
   - (c) Who sets up and operates the equipment?
   - (d) How are transparencies for the overhead made?
   - (e) How are films and filmstrips ordered?
   - (f) What kind of copies can be made on the copying machine and who makes them?
   - (g) Where is the spirit duplicator?

3.
   - (a) Where are the mathematics materials kept?
   - (b) What models are available?
   - (c) How do you order new materials?
   - (d) Is there a collection of filmstrips in the school?

(e) Where are the programmed materials kept and what is available?

(f) What mathematics books are found in the main library and when were they last checked out?

(g) Where is the professional library and what is available?

(h) Where are old sets of textbooks kept and can they be used as a classroom set of supplementary books?

9-16. Commercially produced materials are becoming increasingly available. Investigate the advantages and disadvantages for instructional purposes of such materials as:

(a) Cusinaire rods

(b) Geoboards

(c) Tinker Toys

(d) Logic or attribute blocks

(e) Mirror cards

(f) Artin braid boards

(g) Madison Project shoebox kits

9-17. There is a surprising number of films available for mathematics. A listing of films in mathematics with accompanying reviews can be found on pp. 578–605 of the December 1963 issue of *The Mathematics Teacher.* A subject index is shown as well as the names and addresses of film distributors. Look at some of the film reviews in this source; they are very interesting and educational to read. More recent films can be added to this listing by looking in the index for subsequent volumes of *The Mathematics Teacher* found in the December issues.

9-18. An excellent booklet on making and using multisensory teaching aids in mathematics is Krulik (1963). Ideas can be found in this source that range from using the chalkboard more effectively to how to plan and implement field trips. You would profit a great deal from perusing this source, particularly the section that gives suggestions for preparing your own aids.

9-19. Mathematics teachers are sometimes asked by the school librarian to make an inventory of the mathematics books in the library and make recommendations for books that need to be purchased. A useful guide in this kind of an undertaking are the three booklets, Schaaf (1963), Schaaf (1967), and Schaaf (1970). Read the list of fifty essential mathematics books found on pp. 44–45 of the 1963 edition or the starred entries in the later editions and see how closely you would agree with the selections made by Schaaf.

ADDITIONAL SOURCES

Abbott, E. A. *Flatland*. New York: Dover Publications, Inc., 1932.

Adler, Irving. *The Giant Golden Book of Mathematics*. Wayne, N.J.: Golden Press, Inc., 1960.

Bell, Eric T. *Men of Mathematics*. New York: Simon and Schuster, Inc., 1937.

———. *The Last Problem*. New York: Simon and Schuster, Inc., 1961.

Bergamini, David. *Mathematics*. New York: Time, Inc., 1963.

Brandes, Louis. *Yes, Math Can Be Fun*. Portland, Maine: J. Weston Walch, Box 1075, 1959.

Charosh, Mannis, compiler. *Mathematical Challenges*. Washington, D. C.: National Council of Teachers of Mathematics, 1965.

Cundy, H. M., and A. P. Rollett. *Mathematics Models*. New York: Oxford University Press, Inc., 1965.

Dantzig, Tobias. *Number, The Language of Science*. Garden City, N. Y.: Doubleday and Company, Inc., 1954.

Eves, Howard. *An Introduction to the History of Mathematics*. New York: Rinehart and Company, Inc., 1953.

Fadiman, Clifton. *Fantasia Mathematica*. New York: Simon and Schuster, Inc., 1958.

Hogben, Lancelot. *Wonderful World of Mathematics*. New York: Random House, Inc., 1955.

Johnson, Donovan, and Gerald Rising. *Guidelines for Teaching Mathematics*. Belmont, Calif.: Wadsworth Publishing Company, Inc., 1967.

Kline, Morris. *Mathematics in Western Culture*. New York: Oxford University Press, Inc., 1953.

Krulik, Stephen, and Irwin Kaufman. *Multi-Sensory Techniques in Mathematics Teaching*. Teacher's Practical Press, Inc., Prentice-Hall Education Series, 1963.

Lieber, Lillian. *Mits, Wits, and Logic*. New York: Institute Press, 1954.

———, and Hugh G. Lieber. *Human Values and Science, Art and Mathematics*. New York: W. W. Norton and Co., Inc., 1961.

Newman, James. *The World of Mathematics*. New York: Simon and Schuster, Inc., 1956.

Peck, Lynn C. *Secret Codes, Remainder Arithmetic and Matrices*. Washington, D. C.: National Council of Teachers of Mathematics, 1961.

Schaaf, William. *The High School Library*. Washington, D. C.: National Council of Teachers of Mathematics, 2d ed., 1963; 3d ed., 1967; 4th ed., 1970.

Turney, Billy. *Geometry Teaching Aids You Can Make*. Portland, Me.: J. Weston Walch, Box 1075, 1958.

Chapter 10

Long-Range Planning

One of the prerequisites for successful teaching and maximum learning is careful and detailed planning of the goals for mathematics learning, the specific objectives to be achieved, instructional strategies, purposes of activities, modes of instruction, and the instructional materials. Each of these has been considered in a previous chapter. Planning is viewed as the molding together of these various aspects of the teaching and learning processes. In a sense, planning is analogous to a blueprint which specifies both the end result and the means for achieving this result.

There are several levels or stages of planning which we designate as planning for the year, unit planning, and daily lesson planning. The first two of these types of planning will be discussed in this chapter and consideration of daily lesson planning is deferred to the next chapter.

PLANNING FOR THE YEAR

As planning becomes further and further removed from the students and classroom it becomes more and more general. Planning for the year is probably the most general type of planning, and for this reason, it is sometimes regarded as the least essential type of planning that teachers do. There are however several types of activities in which a teacher should engage prior to beginning the school year. As a teacher gains experience these activities may become internalized and more or less automatic. For the beginning teacher, on the other hand, some time should be set aside for planning the year's work.

Activities that should occur in planning for the year include:

1. Establish the major goals and objectives for the course.
2. Survey all content to be taught.
3. Organize the subject matter in terms of units.
4. Assemble the units in a suitable sequence.
5. Determine approximate time allotments for units, review, and testing.
6. Construct a pretest for the course.

Probably every teacher should give some thought to the first five of the above activities. A good pretest measuring specific behavioral objectives can more easily be constructed after having taught the course one or more times.

Establish goals and objectives. The first question to be asked of any course is, "Why should this particular content be taught?" or "What purpose does the teaching of this content serve in the mathematical education of the student?" We get some help in answering these questions by a careful study of Chapter 1, dealing with the nature of mathematics. For each course, such as a first course in algebra, the teacher should identify content goals, process goals, and affective goals as were described in Chapter 3. Planning specific objectives for the course may or may not be done at this time.

Survey the content to be taught. One manner of surveying content is to specify the "last content" to be taught and then to work backward, that is, to identify prerequisite skills and concepts for achieving this "last content." One disadvantage to this procedure is that it offers a single-track program to achieve a final objective in the course. This procedure may not consider some very interesting and profitable side trips into a variety of concepts that do not contribute directly to the attainment of the specified "last content."

Another procedure is to critically survey the content in the textbook and then to select those portions of the textbook which contribute most to the attainment of the specified goals. This determines what you as a teacher feel to be a minimal course and then other topics or portions of the textbook may be identified and included in the course, if there is time. In any case, some set of priorities should be determined for inclusion of particular content in the course of instruction.

Organize and sequence the subject matter. Perhaps a first-year teacher would wish to use the organization and sequence of mathematical topics that is presented in the textbook. After having taught a course, however, it seems that the material from a textbook may be reorganized and resequenced to better suit the needs of the teacher and the students in the classroom.

In assembling the units of instruction, a more careful analysis of the content in the textbook should be made. At this time an indication of specific topics to be covered and to be omitted would be noted. This aspect of planning will be treated in more detail in the next section on unit planning.

Sequencing is somewhat more complex because this must take into account prerequisite skills necessary for attainment of any particular concept. At times, units may be sequenced in any order if they are on a somewhat parallel level and the development of one unit does not require an understanding of the other unit. This is not usually the case in mathematics, and so, careful attention must be given to the sequencing of units.

Time allotments for units, review, and testing. Any time allotments that can be made in this stage of planning must by necessity be approximate, since the teacher does not know the abilities or attributes of the students in the class. Very rough estimates of time allotments can be made to determine the extent of materials that may be taught in the class. It may be useful to specify a minimal time for completion of each unit and a maximal time for completion of each unit. This would permit an estimate of the maximum amount of material that could be covered in the year as well as a minimum amount of content that could be taught. Within these estimates, it is essential that sufficient time be set aside for review and testing.

UNIT PLANNING

The basic ingredients that went into long-range planning are also essential to unit planning. Unit planning, however, is a step closer to the students and the classroom, and as a result the planning done here is somewhat more specific. This is a comprehensive plan which provides many activities, special materials, different procedures, and finally sources of help for teaching the particular unit. Contained within a unit plan should be a statement of the goals and objectives for that unit, a pretest, a list of special materials, rough sketches of lesson plans which will be considered in detail in the next chapter, a list of films and filmstrips applicable to the particular content, a bibliography, and plans for a specific testing program.

Goals and objectives. After a careful analysis of the material to be covered has been made, the teacher should formulate unit objectives and goals in line with the yearly goals that had been stated in planning for the year. The objectives should be stated in behavioral terms wherever possible and we should be aware of the hierarchy of objectives in the cognitive domain that was presented in Chapter 5. After the objectives have been listed, it may be a good practice to attempt to identify the classification in the hierarchy that applies to each objective. This will assure us that the specific behaviors we would like the students to exhibit are not restricted to the levels stated as knowledge, comprehension, and application.

At this time it may also be beneficial to attempt to sequence the objectives in an order in which they should be attained. This sequencing will provide a rough estimate of the sequence of content or topics that will be presented to the students. This should provide one strand of an instructional strategy and may or may not follow the sequence of topics presented in the textbook. It should also be noted that a teacher should be selective about the material from the text that contributes to a given unit of instruction and the attainment of the objectives for that unit.

Pretest. The purpose of a pretest given prior to beginning a unit is to determine if the students have the necessary prerequisite skills for beginning the unit and also to assess the extent to which students have attained some of the specific objectives for the unit itself. Thus a pretest should contain two types of items. The first of these should be items testing prerequisite skills or concepts. To identify these items the teacher should ask, "What must the student be able to do in order to successfully attain the objectives for this unit?" Once these behaviors have been identified, diagnostic test items can be written to determine if the students have attained these prerequisite skills. Secondly, it would be assumed that the students have very little knowledge of a new unit. They may, however, be familiar with some of the knowledge objectives or even comprehension objectives stated for this unit. Thus the second type of item would be to help the teacher determine the extent to which the students have attained the objectives specified for the unit prior to beginning instruction. This procedure may also identify certain misconceptions that the students have about new terms to be used. This is helpful in that the teacher can correct these misconceptions before they have caused further damage.

If used in these ways, the pretest can be a valuable adjunct to the teaching of a unit. It should never be used as a means for grading; rather, it should be used as an aid to planning. Another purpose is to determine if any remedial instruction is necessary before beginning the unit.

Materials and special activities. Each unit of instruction has a variety of materials and special activities that can be used effectively to teach the specified skills and concepts. For example, to teach a unit in probability, it is essential to have such materials as coins, dice, and cards. It would also be useful to have random samplers which may consist of a bingo number selector or may be a manufactured device specifically for this purpose. Another example might be some of the specially prepared transparencies illustrating complex diagrams in geometry. Materials of this type that can be used to facilitate instruction should be listed in the unit plan along with the availability of these materials. By *availability* we mean the amount of time and money necessary to arrange for the use of the materials in your classroom.

The planning of special activities should also be a part of unit planning. For example, if indirect measurement is being considered in a junior high school mathematics program, special activities should be planned to utilize the skills and techniques from this unit. Plans should be made for estimating the height of buildings, width of roads, and the like. Other more routine classroom activities should also be considered both for the development of the skills and concepts as well as for application of the techniques that have been learned.

Titles of specific films or filmstrips that could be used in conjunction with the development of the unit should be listed. There may also be general interest films which would perhaps motivate the need for the study of the concepts in the particular unit. If films or filmstrips are available, planning for their use is essential. Since films must be ordered well in advance, it is necessary to carefully plan where they will best fit into the instructional sequence. Finally, we should mention that films should always be previewed by the teacher prior to their use in class. This permits the teacher to motivate the use of the film, tell the students what to look for, and then to discuss the film with the class following its showing. Hence, indications of the content of the film should be included in the unit plan, if possible.

A bibliography of source materials should also be included in the unit plan. Within the bibliography there may be a separation of materials for student use and materials for teacher use.

The materials and activities gathered for a particular unit should be comprehensive in nature and should provide sufficient activities, both for remediation as well as for enrichment. In many cases the listed activities would not be used in the classroom but rather would be materials that could be used either for the slow learner or for the fast learner in an individual setting. Finally, we might mention that gathering these materials and activities is a continuous job that is never complete. The list is always expanded by teaching the unit another time and consciously seeking to identify new materials, activities, or procedures that could be used.

Testing program. We have already mentioned the need for having a pretest in the unit plan. Also included should be test items which can be used to assess both achievement and transfer of the objectives for this unit. These may be included in the form of a unit test or they may just be listed as test items from which to construct a unit test. After having taught the unit one or more times, however, there should be copies of any test that have been used within the unit.

There should also be specific time allotments made for a testing program. This testing program would include allocation of times for diagnostic tests as well as for performance tests.

CONCLUSION

If the various aspects of unit planning are carefully considered it should make the daily lesson plans much easier to construct. To be sure, not all of the above phases of unit planning can be accomplished prior to teaching the unit for the first time. If, however, careful records are kept as a unit is being taught, the unit plans can take shape and be of valuable assistance the second time it is taught. Many of the activities that should go into unit planning as well as materials that can be used for some specific units will be considered in more detail in the Exercises. An outline that can be used when constructing a unit plan and that nicely summarizes this activity follows.

OUTLINE OF A UNIT PLAN

1. *Overview.* A brief introduction to the unit followed by a calendar of days with a general description of the activities for each day.

2. *Goals.* The contribution(s) of this unit to the learner. (Chapter 3.)
3. *Objectives.* Observable student behavior (terminal behavior) for both content and attitude (Chapter 4.)
4. *Materials and/or equipment.* (Chapter 9.)
   (a) Films, filmstrips, film loops, or audiotape
   (b) Transparencies for the overhead projector
   (c) Models and manipulative materials
   (d) Enrichment materials
   (e) Remedial materials
   (f) Programmed instruction
   (g) Library books
   (h) Games
   (i) Free and inexpensive materials from businesses and other sources
5. *Daily lesson plans with homework assignments.* As these are prepared they would be included in the unit plan. (Chapter 11)
6. *Applications.* Examples of the usefulness of the ideas in the unit.
7. *Tests.* (Chapter 5).
   (a) Pretest
   (b) Unit test
   (c) Standardized tests or items from a standardized test.
8. *Bulletin Boards.* Drawings of possible bulletin board displays that would be appropriate for the unit (Chapter 9).

10-1. Suppose that in planning for the year you have developed a pretest which reflects a sampling of specific objectives which you have established for Algebra I. After administering and scoring this test on the first day of class, the following distribution of scores was obtained for the 100 item test.

Score	Number of Students
90–100	2
60–70	3
30–40	8
0–10	17

In planning for the year the teacher should make some provision for students who have already attained many of the objectives of that course. For example, the two students scoring 90–100 may sit in the back of the room and work independently on enrichment materials such as an extended study of probability or vector arithmetic.

1. What provisions might the teacher make for the three students who scored 60–70?
2. What provisions might the teacher make for the eight students who scored 30–40?
3. What might be the consequences if the results of the pretest are ignored and the whole class is required to listen to the same lecture, do the same activities, complete the same assignments, and take the same tests?

10-2. One way of planning for the year is to specify the last content to be taught. For example, the yearly plan for a first course in algebra may be to finish the course by developing the quadratic formula. For geometry it may be to finish the course with a section on secants and tangents to a circle. There are many disadvantages to plans of this type. One disadvantage is that no intermediate goals or content are specified. This could mean that in order to achieve the yearly plan, many necessary concepts and behaviors were not learned. Ignoring the logical sequencing of skills and behaviors in a course can have detrimental effects on the long range mathematics training of students.

1. Another fact that is ignored in this type of long range planning is the ability of the students in the class. Discuss the consequences of plans such as those above for very bright students and for very slow students.

2. Discuss the disadvantage of ignoring the logical sequences of behaviors to be developed.

10-3. Many times the goals established for a particular textbook are stated in the teachers manual. These are yearly goals and must be quite general. For example, several yearly goals from a textbook for an introductory course in algebra might be:

(a) To help students to understand the structure of the real number system.

(b) To provide students with algebraic techniques that can be used to solve real or contrived problems.

(c) To help students to use inductive reasoning to formulate hypotheses which utilize algebraic skills or procedures.

(d) To provide opportunities for students to use deductive reasoning in the verification of hypotheses.

(e) To help students appreciate the wide applicability of the content of algebra.

1. Each of the yearly goals above are stated as teacher goals rather than as student goals. Translate each of these goals into statements which reflect the contribution that attainment of this goal has for the learner.

2. Write several more yearly goals for a beginning course in algebra.

3. For each goal written in parts 1 and 2 of this exercise, classify the goal as content, process, or affective. (For a description of types of goals, see Chapter 3.)

4. Write one content goal, one process goal, and one affective goal for a first course in plane geometry. Compare your goals with those of several classmates and in this way generate a set of yearly goals for the study of geometry.

10-4. One responsibility of the teacher is to sequence the instructional content in a fashion that will hopefully permit maximum learning. This implies that prerequisite skills are attained prior to teaching a concept that utilizes these skills, i.e., we would not teach addition of integers until addition and subtraction of whole numbers have been attained.

The following list of topics comes from a unit on congruence of triangles. Order the topics as you would teach them and justify your sequencing. Note that this is not an inclusive list.

(a) Hypotenuse-leg congruence theorem.

(b) Recognizing corresponding parts of congruent triangles.

(c) Congruence of triangles is an equivalence relation.

(d) The base angles of an isosceles triangle are congruent.

(e) The side-angle-side congruence theorem.

(f) Use of angle addition or subtraction as an aid in proving triangles congruent.

(g) The angle-side-angle congruence theorem.

(h) Proving overlapping triangles are congruent.

(i) Use of auxiliary lines which are properly determined.

(j) Proving that angles are congruent when they are corresponding parts of congruent triangles.

10-5. Directions for a pretest should emphasize that this test is not for the purpose of grading students but rather is to determine what the students already know about the unit as well as prerequisite skills for the unit.

1. Write a clear set of directions that can be used as a pretest.

Suppose that the content to be taught was "congruent triangles" which was considered in the last exercise. A pretest for this unit might test vocabulary items such as congruent, included angles, or corresponding sides; conditions for congruence of triangles such as SSS or SAS; and consequences of triangle congruence theorems such as isosceles triangle theorems or theorems about parallelograms. Several items that might be on this test appear below:

   (a) In $\triangle ABC$ and $\triangle DEF$, $\angle A$ corresponds to $\angle E$ and $\angle B$ corresponds to $\angle D$. What side of $\triangle DEF$ corresponds to $\overline{AC}$ of $\triangle ABC$? _____

   (b) In $\triangle ABC$, $\angle C$ is included between what two sides? _____

   (c) If $\triangle NMP$ is isosceles and $\overline{MN} \cong \overline{MP}$, which angles are congruent? _____

   (d) If triangle 1 is constructed from three unequal segments and triangle 2 is constructed from three segments each equal to one and only one segment from triangle 1, then what can we conclude about the two triangles? _____

2. Answer each question above.

3. State an objective from the unit that is being tested by each item.

4. Write three more test items that could be used on a pretest for this unit.

10-6. The introduction to a unit should inform the students of the goals for the unit and how it relates to past and future mathematical content. This introduction should be brief and should place the content of the unit in its proper perspective. The next paragraph is an example of an introduction to a unit on measurement for seventh-grade students.

Measurement is a very important aspect of our everyday life. From the ancient world to present times man has needed to determine the distance between two cities, the weight of things, the time of day, or the size of a particular object. These are all measurement type problems which can be thought of as assigning a number to represent a property of a set. In this unit we will study only linear measure or finding numbers to represent the length of various line segments. It is hoped that a study of this unit will increase your awareness of the importance of measurement, will help you to understand some of the fundamental problems encountered in measuring infinite sets, and will increase your ability to measure accurately.

1. From the preceding paragraph, identify several of the goals of this unit.
2. Does the above paragraph imply any content that should have been studied before beginning this unit? If so, what?
3. Does the above paragraph imply any content to be studied following the completion of this unit? If so, what?
4. Write a paragraph that could be used as an introduction to a unit on congruent triangles.

10-7. A student activity that can be used to illustrate the SSS theorem is as follows:

> Provide each student with several (at least three) slapsticks (popsicle sticks) with holes in each end and with the same number of brass paper fasteners. Instruct the students to make a triangle with three slapsticks and compare it with a triangle made by another student. If the slapsticks for the two triangles are pairwise congruent, then the students should recognize the triangles as congruent.

Other points to emphasize in a discussion following this activity is that since we have the SSS congruence theorem (or axiom), we call a triangle a rigid figure. Questions that may then be asked of the class are:

(a) Do you think a quadrilateral is a rigid figure?

(b) How could we find out?

(c) Will you show me with your slapsticks?

Sometimes it is not possible to have a student activity but it is possible to have a model or illustration prepared. In any case, activities and models should be used as much as possible in your teaching so that the learner remains actively engaged in the learning process.

1. Answer the questions above. You may need to obtain slapsticks and paper fasteners and experiment with them.

2. Devise a model which illustrates why there will never be a SSA congruence theorem.

3. Devise a student activity that can be used to demonstrate the AAS theorem.

10-8. A listing of films, filmstrips, and transparencies that can be used is an essential part of a unit plan. There are many sources for identification of available films. One review of films and list of film suppliers for use in secondary school mathematics was published as a report of some reviewing committees (1963). Since December 1969 *The Mathematics Teacher* has periodically included a section entitled, "Reviews of Films." Using these two sources above it is possible to obtain a good idea of films that are available. In addition to these sources many schools maintain their own film and filmstrip library, commercial suppliers of films maintain up to date catalogs of films, and audio visual facilities at colleges and universities are often depositories for films. The new teacher should become familiar with each of the above mentioned sources.

1. Make a list of mathematics films which could be used in teaching the unit on congruent triangles.
2. Exercises 10-4-10-8 give some indication of the scope of a unit plan on congruent triangles. To be sure, large omissions have been made in identification of materials and in much of the detail. Select one of the categories 4b-4i in the outline of a unit plan and prepare a list of materials that could be used in this unit. Share your list with a classmate.

10-9. In Appendixes A and B there are lists of selected goals and objectives for a unit in statistics. Within each of the goals there is a cluster of the more specific objectives which contribute to the attainment of that goal. For example, goal 2 specifies skill in computing summary statistics from ungrouped data. In order to achieve this goal the students must be able to state descriptions of the summary statistics (a portion of objective 1); be able to portray data graphically (objective 2); and be able to calculate the summary statistics from the ungrouped numbers (objective 3). From this description we see that goal 3 is attained when the student attains the behaviors specified in objectives 1–3. Each of the objectives listed in Appendix B must contribute to at least one of the goals of Appendix A and every goal subsumes a nonempty set of objectives.

1. Determine the objectives which contribute to each of the goals 1, 3, and 8.
2. Each of these goals are of a different type, i.e., content, process, or affective. Can you make any distinction between the types of objectives which contribute to these different type goals? If so, what?
3. To what goals does the student behavior specified in objective 15 contribute?

This exercise is an extension of Exercise 3-8.

10-10. Applications of the content in a unit serve to make the material more meaningful to the student as well as provide a method for achieving affective goals. In the statistics unit partially described in Appendixes A and B, a number of applications were inferred. Objective 17 clearly states that statistical information is presented in a variety of everyday sources; objective 15 states that there are courses of action based upon statistical data; and objective 18 implies that statistics helps people do things in their occupations. Specifically, when we hear the weatherman make the prediction, "There is an 80 percent chance of measurable precipitation this afternoon," we will take an umbrella or raincoat with us. Another application of the content of this unit occurs when a newscaster states that with 2 percent of the precincts reporting, the election has gone to Mr. X.

It is the teacher's responsibility to gather applications for the content of each unit that is taught and then to formulate objectives which specify student behavior relating to the applications. Suppose that a unit on modular arithmetic was being developed for a seventh-grade class.

1. What applications does this unit have to other mathematical topics?
2. What applications does this unit have to situations or events in the physical world? [One type of application is given in Peck (1961).]
3. Write several student objectives for this unit which reflect these applications.

10-11. One activity of teachers in planning for the year is to survey a textbook and assign priorities to the content of the course. By carefully examining the content, a suitable sequence of topics can be established as a minimal course. Depending upon the time available, additional topics can be included on the basis of previously established priorities. Select a secondary school mathematics textbook, survey its content, and assign priorities for inclusion of topics in a year long course.

10-12. Prior to using a film in a classroom it should be previewed. In this preview, the teacher should actually formulate a review of the film which includes length, cost, grade levels for which applicable, strengths and weaknesses. This review should then be kept in the unit plan for handy reference. Review some mathematics films.

10-13. One concern of every mathematics teacher in long-range planning should be to teach students how to study mathematics. One pamphlet written to help students learn to study mathematics is Swain (1970). Every teacher should read the useful information in this source and then implement its suggestions in planning and teaching.

10-14. An interesting description of a source unit on normal variability is included in the Progressive Education Report (1940), pp. 385–402. As stated there on p. 385, "...*source unit*...means a preliminary exploration of a problem showing its possibilities for study." This source unit includes an overview of the work along with activities to illustrate the content. It is a worthwhile experience to read this unit.

ADDITIONAL SOURCES

Peck, Lyman C. *Secret Codes, Remainder Arithmetic, and Matrices.* National Council of Teachers of Mathematics, 1961.

"Reviews of Films," A Report of Some Reviewing Committees. *Mathematics Teacher*, December 1963, pp. 578–605.

Report of the Committee on the Function of Mathematics in General Education. *Mathematics in General Education.* New York: Appleton-Century-Crofts, Inc., 1940.

Swain, Henry. *How to Study Mathematics: A Handbook for High School Students.* Washington, D.C.: National Council of Teachers of Mathematics, 2d ed., 1970.

Chapter 11

Daily Lesson Planning

The primary duty of the mathematics teacher is teaching the daily lesson. All other instructional activities which the teacher performs are merely supportive of this function. The main emphasis in this chapter is *planning* for the daily lesson, whereas the next chapter will deal with the act of *teaching* the lesson. Unit planning, discussed in the previous chapter, is an effective aid in preparing and teaching successful daily lessons, but it does not replace the need for careful, diligent, daily planning.

BENEFITS OF GOOD PLANNING

While planning the daily lesson the teacher decides and learns what he is going to do when he manages the learning activity of his class. Much of this planning may be quite informal, unscheduled, and not written down. It may occur while driving the car, taking a shower, eating, or walking down the hallway. Thinking about a previous lesson or an upcoming one can occur at any time, and some of the best ideas may be forthcoming when they are least expected. Yet one thing seems to be universally true: diligent planning may not always result in successful learning by the students, but lack of adequate thought focused on teaching will always become quickly evident.

Although successful planning or thinking about what should be done in the classroom may be informal, it is not unsystematic. There are several aspects or components of every lesson that must be consciously considered if continued success in teaching is to result. Several of these components that have already been studied separately are: goals and objectives, instructional strategies, purposes of activities, and modes of instruction. A daily lesson consists of these components meshed and molded into a plan of action.

Some experienced teachers, many of whom are successful, do not bother to write out their plan for the daily lesson. They sometimes make notes to themselves or write down examples that they may wish to have available to use during the course of the lesson.

This is not recommended for inexperienced teachers. One benefit of writing out a lesson plan complete with examples, questions to be asked, and assignment is that the teacher internalizes or memorizes the content and procedure so well that he does not need to rely on his written notes or his "quick wits." Instead, he can be so confident and assured of what he is doing that he can focus his primary attention on more important things such as "reading" the comprehension and attention of the class for feedback, maintaining discipline, and spotting students who need individual attention. A teacher groping for what he should do next or an appropriate example cannot at the same time attend to other important aspects of the teaching act discussed in the next chapter. Thus a written lesson plan assures the teacher that he has given the thought and preparation necessary to know his main procedure and alternatives before he gets into the classroom, rather than "fly by the seat of his pants."

PLANNING AREAS

The format of the written lesson plan is a matter of personal taste and preference. However, some format should probably be followed at the outset to make sure that important considerations in planning are not overlooked. Two different lesson plan formats are shown in Appendixes C and D. The main areas that require attention and thought in planning, whether the plan is actually written out in detail or not, are the following:

Objectives
Materials
Preview
Activities
Assignments
Summary

A discussion of the function of each of these planning areas in the entire lesson will now be discussed, but not necessarily in the order in which they might be planned or occur in a lesson.

Objectives. Any lesson is just part of the total instructional program. Likewise, the hoped for outcomes of any one lesson contribute to only a small percentage of the goals to be attained. But, together with the many other objectives, they unite to complete the spectrum of goals for the unit or course. The function of stating objectives is to provide guidance in the selection of the learning activities. There should be a close correspondence between the objectives of the lesson and the type and nature of activities chosen. Each activity selected for use should contribute to the attainment of the specified objectives for the lesson. The activities may help to attain other objectives as well but this is peripheral to the major purpose.

If the objectives are stated behaviorally in terms of student performance, there is the added advantage of clarity about what is expected of the learner. This in turn facilitates measuring the attainment of the objectives by the learner. The objectives may be written before, after, or during the writing of the rest of the plan.

Preview. A preview or introduction should be given to inform the students of what they are expected to do and learn during the lesson. It should be short and to the point, telling the pupils in a couple of sentences how the day's lesson is related to what has already been learned and what is yet to be encountered. The purpose is to give the student direction, a sense of perspective, a chance to review, and an opportunity to "place himself" in the mathematics class.

Summary. Like the preview, the summary is intended to help the student gain perspective about the content in the lesson—to permit him to see the forest as well as the trees. It should sum up the day's work, indicate why it is important to learn this bit of knowledge, and, if possible, relate it to the learner's world of experience.

Materials. Sometimes special materials are required that are not usually available without prior planning. Possible materials include models, board instruments, colored chalk, projection equipment, an extra set of books, handout sheets, or laboratory equipment. While you may decide not to include such a category in your personal lesson plan format, obviously you will have to plan ahead to have materials available when needed.

Activities. The learning activities are the heart of the lesson and hence require the most thoughtful planning. Most periods of instruction in mathematics should consist of several distinct activities incorporating different modes of instruction. Not all the activities in a lesson would necessarily deal with the same topic, but rather they would have different purposes. For example, one hour of instruction may consist of the following activities:

1. A *short* oral drill on a previously learned skill that is needed in the new development.
2. A developmental lesson on a new concept using a laboratory method.
3. An assimilation activity on the content in the previous day's developmental activity with some of the students working at the chalkboard and the rest of the class working at their seats.
4. A short written quiz with a couple of problems on fundamental skills that 90 percent of the class should be able to do correctly and rapidly.

In planning each activity, the sample problems, key questions, directions and procedures should be written. Reading the description of each activity should make obvious the purpose (developmental, maintenance, or transfer), the mode of instruction, and the instructional strategy.

Assignments. This is an area in which current practices in mathematics teaching are receiving increasing criticism and justifiably so. Massive homework assignments are unthinkingly piled on youngsters in the belief that this practice increases mastery and understanding. Often just the opposite is the result. Together with other subjects, it is not unusual for students to have at least five hours of homework for one night. In an effort to finish, the student does his work poorly or copies the work of others just to get done with it. It is no wonder that pupils become frustrated and develop hostile attitudes toward mathematics and school work in general.

A few well-chosen homework problems can be helpful to a student in increasing his mathematical competence. Three general suggestions for making homework assignments helpful and rewarding for students are:

1. Keep the assignments short and tell the students the benefits of doing these few problems.
2. Do not assign homework problems on newly developed techniques that the students have not yet tried under your supervision.
3. Do not assign all of the problems on the same topic but, instead, include some variety.

Students will be more willing to do short assignments, and hence will probably do more homework in the long run for short assignments than for hopelessly long ones. In addition, they are more willing to work when they know the problems have been carefully selected to help them. Homework assignments based upon ideas that were just introduced in the class can result in disaster in several ways. The student may spend endless hours vainly working on procedures that he has not had sufficient time to assimilate. He should first try new procedures under the direction of the teacher before he is expected to practice them in the absence of help or guidance. Also, as a result of insufficient experience he may learn incorrect practices either on his own or from some inexpert person trying to help him. Finally, by including problems on more than one topic, the homework can aid the retention of previously learned concepts and maintain needed skills.

Many mathematics teachers plan a spiral type of homework assignment. The problems are chosen very carefully from previous topics that already have been studied. The student is not allowed to forget the mathematics once it has been studied. Instead he has to continually go back to use and review what he has previously learned. The homework becomes a planned program of maintenance. Another clever technique is to include one word problem in the homework assignment. The study of word problems should not be confined to one chapter in the textbook. Word problems are much less frightening and more easily done when they are met continually and as a matter of course in mathematics.

SAMPLE LESSON PLANS

Several sample lesson plans are included in the appendices. They will be referred to in some of the exercises in this chapter and they should be read carefully. They certainly contain much more written detail than would normally be necessary or practical in daily planning. They are written to be read by another person, and hence do not leave many items overlooked. However, they do indicate the extent of thinking necessary to teach a really good lesson.

EXERCISES

11-1. Students react negatively to a teacher who does not think enough of them to attempt to plan for their class. Lack of planning is quickly noticed and resented by students.

Identify the actions of the teacher in the situations below that betray a lack of thought and planning by the teacher.

(a) " . . . If triangles have two angles congruent and a side not included by the angles congruent, that will not make the triangles congruent. For example, in $\triangle ABC$ and $\triangle A'B'C'$, $m(BC) = m(B'C') = 6$ inches, $m(\angle A) = m(\angle A') = 65°$, and $m(\angle B) = m(\angle B') = 25°$."

(b) " . . . For homework tonight, do some problems on page er . . . page er . . . well, page 215. Why don't you do numbers 2 . . . and number 4 . . . and number 9—number 9 looks like a good one—yes, and any other ones that have answers in the back of the book."

(c) " . . . Just as with integers, we will be able to find the least common multiple of two algebraic expressions. Let's start with an example of finding the least common multiple of two expressions. Let me see. Let's try $(8x^2 + 24x + 18)^2$ and $16x^4 - 81$."

11-2. Poor planning outside of the classroom results in wasted time and motion which is often indicated by the distribution of time to the various activities during the class period.

Two philosophies of distribution of class time are:

I. 25 percent. The students do one or two notebook exercises, check them, copy homework assignment, and place previous night's homework on side or rear chalkboards of the classroom, while the teacher observes and checks attendance.

50 percent. Developmental lesson on new topic with student trying some problems.

25 percent. Discussion of solution to previous night's homework exercises.

II. 50 percent. Discussion of solutions to previous night's homework exercises.

20 percent. Explanation on how to do the new set of homework exercises.

30 percent. Supervised study in which students begin homework exercises and the teacher gives help and guidance where needed.

1. Read each statement below and place a check mark in column A, if the statement is more true of I; B, if the statement is more true of II; C, if the statement seems to be true of both; D, if the statement is not true for either I or II.

	A	B	C	D
(a) Provides review on previously learned topics....				
(b) Students receive guidance before working problems on their own....				
(c) Makes efficient use of class time....				
(d) Provides a variety of activities using many modes of instruction				
(e) Provides a systematic maintenance program....				
(f) Requires more remedial teaching....				

2. What do you think an ideal allocation of classroom time might be? Justify your answer.

11-3. Many critics of mathematics teachers say they can tell exactly what will happen when they observe a mathematics classroom. It usually goes something like this:

> Teacher: "All right, the bell has rung. Sit down and get out your homework. Are there any questions on the odd-numbered problems you had for homework dealing with the new topic we developed yesterday?"

At this point, hands and questions are raised all over the room and the teacher launches into a long explanation of each problem, reteaching all of yesterday's lesson in the process. The class becomes bored and unmanageable as the teacher "loses himself" at the board.

Finally, with 10 minutes left in the class period the teacher begins a hasty development of the new material breathlessly finishing at the bell. The homework assignment, consisting of the odd problems following the newly introduced material, is shouted at the students as they ready themselves for dismissal. The next day a majority of the class period is again spent working all the homework problems that the students were unable to do.

Obviously something needs to be done in this situation to get more time for a careful development of new material. Without a careful development, with the new material clearly understood, the students cannot do their homework without encountering a great deal of difficulty.

Discuss some remedies that are needed in the situation described above with regard to

1. Nature of the homework assignment.
2. Routine tasks.
   (a) Start and finish of class.
   (b) Mechanics of assigning and checking homework.
3. Provision for other types of teaching besides developmental.
4. Modes of instruction.
5. Distribution of time in the classroom.

11-4. Often concepts or procedures which are needed in the development of a new topic and which can cause difficulty can be identified and worked on separately before they are needed for the new material. Examples of short warm-up activities that pave the way for the developmental activity can be found in the sample lesson plans in the Appendixes.

Suppose the new developmental activity is to discover with guidance, the proof of the Pythagorean theorem. In the figure below, the areas of the large square, the triangles, and the small square are used to prove that $c^2 = a^2 + b^2$ in the right triangles.

1. As you work out the proof, identify one or more difficulties that the students might encounter in trying to discover this proof of the Pythagorean theorem.

2. Devise a *short* warm-up activity for the students to do at the beginning of the class period that will allow them to get over any anticipated difficulties so that they can more easily discover this proof.

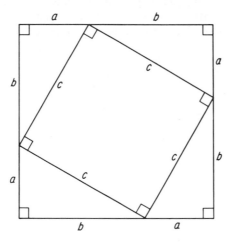

11-5. We have seen in Chapter 7 that activities must be designed for drill as well as development, transfer, and assimilation. Drill is most effective when the students are motivated. One way is to provide drill in an interesting or novel setting. One of the best ways for doing this is to use competitive games as a mode of instruction.

Suppose you were teaching the sample lessons on addition of integers. You decide that after the two lessons given in Appendix D, the students need to drill in adding integers so that they can do them quickly in their heads.

1. Modify the following competitive game so that it could be used to drill addition of integers. A race track is made of spaces labeled with the numerals 1 to 25. Each child draws a card with a numeral on it which indicates the number of steps to move his horse. The first to cross the finish line is the winner.

2. Devise another competitive game that could be played by several children in a group. Make it a game in which they can manipulate objects but where they must do additions in their heads with positive and negative integers. Also, make the game so that several students are given the opportunity to win during the duration of play in the class.

11-6. Looking at the lesson plan for addition of integers on Day 1, you should note that there is a close correspondence between the objectives of the lesson and the activities composing the lesson.

The activities found in the lesson plan on statistics were chosen to give the students the opportunity to attain several of the objectives listed in Appendix B for a unit on statistics.

1. Find the objectives in the list in Appendix B that correspond to the developmental part of the lesson on statistics.

2. Find the objectives in the list in Appendix B that correspond to the exercise on mean, median, and mode.

11-7. The developmental activity in the second lesson on the integers under addition concentrated on explaining why the integers are added the way they are. Inevitably, there will be some students who can carry out the procedures after only the bare minimum of explanation given in the development. Most of the students will need assimilation time to decide on which procedure to use with which integers and how to carry it out.

Devise two types of assimilation activities for investigating the addition of integers. The first one for the students who need to do more work on their own. The second one for those students who already know the techniques well but who might be curious about such questions as:

(a) Why must the positive integers be the ones to act like the whole numbers?

(b) What would happen if we started by saying that $^+2 + {}^+3 = {}^-5$ rather than $^+5$?

11-8. One of the objectives of the second lesson on addition of integers is that the students be able to construct shortcut rules for adding integers. Shortcuts are to be encouraged when the students understand why and under what conditions the shortcuts are applied.

Write a class exercise that is designed to get the students to

(a) Discover and verbalize the shortcuts for adding a positive and a negative integer.

(b) Write the rules symbolically using variables.

(c) Explain the reason why the shortcut rules work, based on the procedure learned in the development.

11-9. The instructional strategy for adding integers shown in the sample lesson plan is a good one for introducing students to the why of adding integers. But, like many other places in mathematics, the student needs to learn to compute quickly and skillfully rather than go through all the steps of a long procedure every time he needs an answer.

Opinions differ about the teaching of shortcuts. Some of them are:

(a) All the students should learn is the shortcut rules. The explanations of why they work just confuse them. All they need and want to know is a rule they can follow.

(b) Get them to memorize the shortcut rules first so that they are at least able to apply them. Give them the explanations of why they work later when they are interested and know what is supposed to be explained.

(c) The students should be taught the shortcut rules only when they understand the fuller process and can state why and under what conditions the shortcut rules work.

(d) The students should not be taught to use shortcut rules but rather they should discover these rules by themselves. For example, after a student adds columns of 2's, 3's, 5's, etc., long enough he'll discover that multiplication is a shortcut way to add and he'll know when and how to multiply.

(e) Students should not be taught or permitted to use shortcut rules. They simply learn them by rote and always use them unthinkingly and incorrectly.

Perhaps the best policy is to use a variety of tactics when teaching shortcuts, depending upon the level of the students and the particular subject matter.

Discuss the approach you would adopt in the following situations.

1. Use of the Euclidean algorithm to find the greatest common factor of two numbers with seventh-graders.
2. Checking base-ten computations by casting out nines with sixth-graders.
3. Cancelling common factors in multiplying and dividing polynomials in ninth-grade algebra.
4. Use of synthetic division in second-year algebra.

11-10. As indicated in the sample lesson on statistics in Appendix C, the next lesson could concern bias and precision in sample estimates. In particular, it could be devised to meet objectives 5 and 8 listed in the objectives for the statistics unit.

Devise a developmental activity after the manner of the one in the sample lesson that would correspond to objectives 5 and 8. In some way, get the student to generate some of the causes of sampling bias and relate them to situations involving polls, surveys, and results of experiments used in advertising.

11-11. Getting feedback is often a very informal process. Usually it is not asking direct questions since they tend to put the student "on the spot" and a lesson may seem more like an inquisition with the teacher acting as a prosecuting attorney. Feedback should be gathered as a natural part of the lesson. There are many ways of obtaining feedback such as

    (a) Observing students putting homework on the chalkboard.

    (b) Overhearing one student explaining a problem to another.

    (c) Letting the students talk you through a procedure after they have seen it demonstrated.

1. List as many different techniques as you can find that were employed in the sample lessons to gain feedback during the lessons.
2. List several more ways besides those listed above and those used in the sample lessons that could provide information on the students' understanding and need for remedial help.

11-12. The lesson-plan format used for the statistics lesson has a column headed *feedback*. This indicates that the teacher plans to constantly gather information from the learners to see how well the lesson is going and note places where reteaching may be necessary.

Notice that the feedback column does not include the questions intended to guide the development of new concepts. Rather, it contains techniques of checking up on concepts that have already been encountered.

The advantage of the lesson-plan format with the feedback column is that the teacher is reminded to plan to occasionally "tap into" the students' thinking to get information and to evaluate.

Identify the places in the two lesson plans on integers that provide the teacher with feedback and would be placed in the feedback column in the other lesson-plan format.

11-13. In Appendix E you will find a list of suggestions indicating good planning practices to use in preparing for the daily lesson. Few lessons will meet all the standards suggested by this list.

Read over the items to see how many of these suggestions you can determine were followed in constructing the sample lesson plans. For each item, indicate a "yes" if it was adhered to in one of the plans; a "no" if it was not adhered to; and " undecided" for all others.

11-14. Construction of thoughtful, worthwhile homework assignments has been stressed in this chapter. Well-planned assignments whose purpose and function is clear to both the students and the teacher can make a mathematics course both interesting and profitable.

The homework assignment can serve many purposes. For example:

(a) Practice on recently developed concepts and skills.

(b) Recall and maintenance of topics previously studied and assimilated by the students.

(c) Application of mathematics to everyday life by assigning students to carry out projects and activities at home such as making measurements, keeping shopping logs, or gathering and organizing data.

(d) Gathering of information and materials concerning mathematics that could be brought to class and used in later class activities.

Construct a short homework assignment that could be helpful to students finishing the sample statistics lesson for each purpose of homework listed above. That is, make up four different homework assignments that differ in their purpose but will be recognized by the students as being useful, interesting, and worthwhile. You may assume that the students will soon be constructing and interpreting the several different types of graphs.

SUGGESTED ACTIVITIES

11-15. Interest in a topic can be heightened by reading the students a story from the vast literature of mathematics. One such story, written by Robert Coates, is found in Newman (1956). Read this short story and decide which of the goals for the unit on statistics could be stressed by using this story in class.

11-16. The unit on statistics stresses not only content but appropriate use and detection of misuse of statistical procedures. One of the most helpful sources for attaining objectives 12 and 13 is Darrell Huff, *How To Lie With Statistics*. Look at this book to get ideas of the way in which statistics are sometimes misused to manipulate and confuse people.

11-17. Find a line graph in a newspaper or magazine and radically change the spacing of the units on one of the axes. How does this distort the message to be communicated? Would a critic or an advocate of the idea to be communicated be benefited by your alteration?

11-18. A good source for activities that could be used to teach operations in the system of integers is articles from *The Arithmetic Teacher*. Articles for elementary school teachers often present devices that can be modified for use with older children. Find three devices that are described in this journal and which could be used with ninth-grade algebra students.

ADDITIONAL SOURCES

Coates, Robert M. "The Law," in James R. Newman, *The World of Mathematics*, Vol. 4. New York: Simon and Schuster, Inc., 1956, pp. 2268-2271.

Huff, Darrell. *How To Lie With Statistics*. New York: W. W. Norton and Company, 1954.

Chapter **12**

Teaching the Lesson

After all of the plans have been made, all of the writing done, the most enjoyable task of the teacher is in implementing these plans in the classroom. In a sense, this is analogous to a stage play where the script has been written and rehearsed and is now ready for the opening-night performance. In the case of the teaching process, lesson plans correspond to the script, and rehearsals are generally mental rather than physical. Then comes the day of the lesson when the teacher walks confidently into the classroom to begin the teaching process. The different activities that comprise this classroom performance will flow smoothly only if there has been adequate planning and rehearsal.

It is not possible to explicitly describe the best behavior of a teacher in the classroom. A technique used by one teacher may be completely adaptable to his personality while this same technique may be a very poor practice for another teacher. For this reason each teacher must develop his own style of presenting the lesson in the classroom. The purpose of this chapter is to discuss various behaviors that each teacher in his own way could accomplish while teaching the lesson.

TEACHER BEHAVIOR

In Chapter 11, Daily Lesson Planning, it was stated that the purpose of writing a lesson plan was actually to memorize the instructional strategies to be used in the classroom. This by no means implies that the specific words that a teacher will say in the classroom are to be memorized. In order for a short presentation to be effective, it cannot give the appearance of being memorized. The teacher should appear to be talking to the students. There should be varying tones of voice and pauses. These pauses, although not long, will serve to provide time for a student to reflect on a previously mentioned concept.

One of the most challenging and rewarding aspects of teaching the lesson is in asking questions of the students. By using carefully phrased questions it is possible to have active student participation, guide the thinking of the students in the learning process without appearing to lecture, and to assess the strengths and weaknesses of the members of the class.

Prior to teaching a lesson using questions, there are several types of student response for which the teacher should plan. To be sure, a student may answer the question correctly and the lesson can proceed as planned. A response, however, may be incorrect and the teacher should attempt to identify means of correcting these responses efficiently and without punishment of the individual. Finally, the most difficult type of response with which the teacher must cope is a correct response different from the anticipated one. In many instances this occurs when the question is poorly phrased or when students have insufficient knowledge of the concepts under consideration. Several of the exercises will deal explicitly with student responses to teacher questions.

The atmosphere of a classroom should be relaxed and there should be many opportunities for students to raise questions or to add supplemental information to the talk. For this reason the teacher should plan situations in which students may interject relevant questions or comments. When a student is talking, the teacher should be a good listener—should be attentive to these student questions or comments and should not interrupt the student. After the student has finished, it is the teacher's responsibility to respond to this question or comment. This implies that the teacher may need to alter the plans for that particular lesson.

Student questions may pose the most difficult task for the teacher because these may require the teaching of concepts for which there has been no planning. This is one of the critical times when it is essential for a teacher to think on his feet. During the time that the question is being asked and shortly thereafter, the teacher must identify what the student is really asking, identify the concepts that need clarification, formulate an answer to the question, and finally, decide on an instructional strategy for answering these questions.

The interpretation of a student question is sometimes one of the most difficult aspects of answering student questions. When a student is asking the question he may not be entirely sure of the concepts that are not understood. It is often true that the students do not have sufficient knowledge to ask an intelligent question but they realize that they are lacking some skills or concepts. For this reason they may say, "I don't understand any of this," or they may ask a question that appears irrelevant. When this occurs, it is the teacher's responsibility to make an effort to identify the specific concepts that need clarification.

Another type of student comment in the classroom relates to the questioning of a procedure or statement that you have made or that was made in the textbook. For example, you may have omitted a step in a development and the student cannot see how you went from one statement to the next. One way of responding to this type of a comment is to answer it with questions. The questions should be carefully constructed so that the student is led to answer or develop the concept which he was questioning. Another way of proceeding is to have another student from the class answer the question.

Finally, we should mention that there are times when questions are asked and the teacher does not feel competent to answer immediately. Under these conditions, the teacher should feel perfectly free to answer, "I don't know, but I will find out for you." It is much better to admit not knowing than it is to attempt to give a response which will confuse the students. There are also times when a question is beyond the scope of that course. Under these circumstances, the teacher should state this and then talk privately with the individual who asked the question. This private conversation may give reasons why this concept is beyond the scope of the course, an indication of how the concept may be developed, and provide outside sources which could be used.

Perhaps one of the greatest condemnations of the teaching profession as a whole is that we stifle student comments and questions. In many classes it is hard work to get students to be confident enough to express their feelings. This is a result of previous exposure to teachers who were not good listeners and who did not have sufficient confidence in their ability to respond to these comments in a satisfactory way. It takes an extremely confident person and a relaxed atmosphere in the classroom for meaningful student participation in the teaching-learning process.

While teaching the class, it is essential that the teacher know what the students are doing. Careful observation of facial expressions and of activities in which the students are engaging will provide the teacher with feedback information relating to the effectiveness of his teaching. This in some way serves to evaluate the teaching-learning process at any particular point in time. One way of reading the class is to select five or six students scattered throughout the classroom to watch during a lesson. These students should represent differing ability and motivational levels. A careful examination of the facial expressions and activities of these students will give an indication of how well the members of the class are paying attention, a notion of how well these students are comprehending the material under consideration and, hence, an evaluation of the instruction. To be sure, students will generally wear a facial expression that they believe the teacher likes to see. A frowning face may indicate a lack of comprehension; a blank stare or a student gazing out of the window indicates inattention; while a look of surprised pleasure may indicate the breakthrough of a concept or procedure. If there are signs of inattention, the teacher should change the mode of instruction. For example, if the mode of instruction is a lecture, it should gradually be changed to a question and answer or discussion type mode of instruction. If, on the other hand, it does not seem reasonable to alter the mode of instruction, there should be some changes made within the mode of instruction, such as the changing of voice inflection and tone of voice.

This reading of the classroom should also detect any discipline problems that exist. If preventive discipline such as interesting lessons and respect for the individual fail, as they sometimes do, it is essential that a discipline situation be identified and remedied as soon as possible. This can occur only if the teacher is constantly aware of the behavior of the students and the small signs which indicate behavior that is not conducive to learning.

When teaching the lesson, the teacher is telling, asking, listening, answering, writing, manipulating, or reading. The students should also be engaged in these types of activities and when these activities conform to the specified objectives of the lesson the student should be rewarded. Thus instead of a continual flow of comments from the teacher such as "Be quiet Tim," "Let's pay attention, Susan," "We don't have time for that now, Mark," there may be comments such as "That is an interesting notion," or "That shows some very good thinking." It is certainly more conducive to learning to tell students when they have done something correctly rather than merely to correct their mistakes. Some positive recognition should always be provided for a penetrating comment or an unusual solution to a given problem.

Perhaps one of the more rewarding experiences that can be provided for a student is to exploit a learning opportunity that was suggested by the student. If, for example, a student questions a particular derivation that is relevant to the concepts under consideration, it may be worthwhile to change the lesson plan for that day and to consider the suggestions made by the student. The plans that were made for this day can be used at a later time, but the opportunity presented by this student and the interest of the class in this particular concept may never again be quite as great as it is at the given time. It may be that on one of those days when the students felt that they "got the teacher off the track" that the most profitable learning occurred. Several specific examples of this are included in the exercises at the end of this chapter.

Also included in the exercises at the end of this chapter will be situations dealing with changes in routine, the positioning of the teacher in the classroom, as well as other situations that pertain to teacher behaviors while teaching the lesson. These notions will not be discussed in further detail here.

STUDENT BEHAVIORS

The purpose of all of the activities that go on in the classroom is to enhance student learning. In teaching the lesson we should always be aware of the student behaviors we are trying to induce as well as the student activities that lead toward the final behaviors. It is essential that we as teachers realize that learning mathematics is not a passive activity such as osmosis; rather, the learner must be actively involved in the teaching-learning process. We should also remember that we as adults would not sit quietly and listen attentively to people talk to us for five or more hours a day. We as teachers must consciously attempt to vary the activities in which we wish students to engage.

It is not reasonable to have students remain quiet for the entire class period. This would be the case if the modes of instruction were lecture, working problems, and independent study. If listening, reading, and writing are the only interactions in which a student may engage while we are teaching a lesson, he will never learn to express orally his views on mathematics. We should encourage board work, perhaps plan for small-group discussion sessions, encourage verbal participation in each class, encourage experiments with physical objects whenever applicable, and in general, provide for more physical activity of students in the mathematics classroom. If teaching the lesson provides for many varied student behaviors of the type mentioned here, we must expect some noise in the classroom. If the procedures and concepts, however, are of extreme interest to the students, the existence of moderate amounts of noise will probably not deter to any great extent the learning that occurs. It should also be pointed out that students need to be instructed in using time profitably in small-group discussion or laboratory type experiences. It is the mathematics teacher's responsibility to teach more than mathematics; that is, to teach efficient use of time and to teach general problem solving activities.

Another very useful activity for the more capable students in the classroom is to assist some students who are having problems. It has often been said that you do not learn a concept completely until you have taught it to someone else. If students are used in this way, a teacher can cope with individual differences to a greater extent. This technique may work very well while students are doing board work. For example, if one student has completed a problem correctly while another is having difficulty with this problem, the teacher may ask these students to work together while he is helping someone else. This technique would permit explanation of correct procedures to more than one student at a given time. Several additional examples of student behaviors that are desirable while teaching the lesson will be provided in the exercises.

12-1. A hypothesis pertaining to the type of question asked in most mathematics classrooms is, "Ninety percent of all questions that are asked by the teacher are either poor questions or rhetorical questions." Several examples of poor questions are as follows:

P1   Can you tell me if these two angles are congruent?

P2   Do you see that?

P3   Are there any questions?

P4   Can you do problem x?

P5   Is that clear?

Each of these questions can honestly be answered by the students as yes or no. This answer requires no thought on the part of the student and tells the teacher very little.

We could gain a great deal by rephrasing these questions in a meaningful way either as questions or requests. Under these circumstances the question or request should require some thought by the student and provide the teacher with some knowledge about the effects of the previous instruction. For example, in P1 we probably do not care if you can tell the angles are congruent but rather, "how can you tell if the angles are congruent?" and then "are they congruent?" A meaningful replacement of P1 might be

P'1   What are some ways by which we could tell if these two angles are congruent?

If a proper response to this was obtained then

P''1   Which, if any, of these ways apply to this specific situation?

P'''1   Are these two angles congruent?

For each of the remaining questions above, rephrase the question as either a question or as a request to demand a certain amount of thought by the student and to provide the teacher with a measure of the previous instruction.

12-2. As in the last exercise there are meaningless questions which need a short response (not yes or no) and require no thought by the student at the time the question is asked. Some examples are:

P6   In an advanced class, what is the sum of 7 + 6?

P7   What is the answer to problem x?

P8   Who can work problem x?

P9   What should we do now?

Again, there are a variety of better means which could be used to generate student participation and thought. For example, P6 might be handled by a short speech in the beginning of the year to the effect that "This year we will be doing a lot of computational work and from time to time it is only natural that I will make some mistakes. Sometimes these mistakes will be intentional—so that I can see how many of you are following the work we are doing in class. Part of your job will be to detect my intentional and unintentional mistakes." When a student detects one of your mistakes, provide praise and thanks for this and continue with the lesson.

Give a procedure or alternative question which would be more meaningful and provide the teacher with better information for each of P7 through P9.

12-3. One sure way for a class to degenerate to bedlam is to conduct a question-answer review lesson in the following fashion. The teacher stands in the front of the classroom and asks open questions such as, a parallelogram is a quadrilateral with____; a rhombus is a parallelogram with____; etc. After each question, the students are permitted to shout out their notion of the answer without being called upon to do so. For some questions three or more different answers are stated at the same time. The teacher then selects the correct response and says, "That's right," and reiterates the correct response.

A situation like this might arise in the beginning of the school year when the teacher is not sure of the names of many of the students in the class or it may be used to stimulate enthusiasm. In either case, it is a poor procedure.

1. List several reasons why this is a poor procedure to follow in questioning students.
2. What effect might the teacher's statement, "That's right" have for a student who made an incorrect response?
3. What is an argument against the practice of the teacher always repeating and embellishing for the class, a correct response by the student?
4. List at least five correct ways to complete the statement, "a parallelogram is a quadrilateral with ____."

12-4. When a teacher asks a question he must be prepared for a variety of responses, several of which might not have been anticipated. For example, suppose that an introductory class in logic was considering conditional sentences of the form $P \longrightarrow Q$. The teacher may ask the question, "What are the names for P and Q?" The anticipated response was that P is called the *antecedant* and Q is called the *consequent*. The obtained response was that P and Q are variables.

There are a variety of procedures that the teacher might follow when this occurs. Several of them are:

(a) To say "that's not what I'm looking for."

(b) To say "yes, but are there any names for P and Q? If so, what are they?"

(c) To provide an analogy by referring to $a + b = c$ where a, b, c are variables but we also call a and b addends and c the sum. Then returning to $P \longrightarrow Q$ and trying to determine other names for P and Q.

The first of these procedures tells the student that he hasn't guessed what is in the teacher's mind and will inhibit students when they are asked questions. If this is done often the students will be leery about answering questions unless they know the answer that the teacher wants. This technique may be useful when the answer provided by the student is irrelevant but should not be used if the answer is relevant and correct, but not the expected answer.

1. Discuss the effects of 2 and 3 above.

2. What are several other procedures that could be used?

12-5. There are a variety of procedures that may be used for asking questions in class. For example, the teacher may say: "Otto, what is a parallelogram?" Asking a question this way immediately alerts Otto that he is on the spot and will be expected to respond to a question. The effect of this is that Otto will pay careful attention to the question and, hence, will have a better chance of answering it. The rest of the class also hears that Otto is asked to perform and feel that they can relax. This results in many members of the class tuning out the question and perhaps missing a necessary part of the instructional process.

A second way of asking the question is: "What is a parallelogram? (pause) Otto."

1. If questions are asked in this manner, what will be the effect on the class?
2. Can the teacher expect to get as many correct responses when questions are asked this second way rather than the first way? Discuss.
3. Into what traps might a teacher fall if questions are asked this second way?

12-6. While teaching the lesson, it is essential that the teacher use precise language. If a lack of precision is permitted, some students may formulate a concept that is not always true. One fundamental problem that often arises in the classroom is a failure to specify the domain for which a statement is valid. Thus the statement, "Anything over itself is one" is false because a domain of definition has not been specified. First of all, this statement only applies to numbers and then it is false for the number 0. Rephrasing the statement as, "Any nonzero number over itself is one," results in a precise valid statement in the specified domain. For each of the following, specify the domain of definition for which the statement is true and formulate a way to make this statement to a student.

(a) You cannot factor $x^2 + y^2$.

(b) You cannot trisect an angle.

(c) Every linear equation has a solution.

(d) $\sqrt{a}\,\sqrt{b} = \sqrt{ab}$

(e) The sine of an angle is the side opposite over the hypotenuse.

(f) The product of two numbers is greater than or equal to either of the factors.

12-7. We also make many other categorical statements which are false. Each of us at one time or another has heard, π equals 22/7, which is absolutely false since π is an irrational number and 22/7 is a rational number. To correct this erroneous statement we should say, "A rational approximation for π is 22/7 "or" π is approximately equal to 22/7." For each of the statements below, point out the problem that exists and rephrase the idea in a manner that is clear and true.

(a) You can't add 2/3 and 4/5.

(b) x^n, where n is a positive integer, is x times itself n times.

(c) In the subtraction, 75 – 69, you can't subtract the 9 from the 5.

(d) Two lines are parallel if they do not intersect.

12-8. Another problem in precise use of language is using synonymously two words which have slightly different meanings. To be sure, it is helpful to explain concepts in different ways and to use different words in these explanations. In every instance, however, caution should be used to insure that no false concepts are being learned.

An example of this might arise when talking about the construction of various lengths. By construction, we would mean the production of a segment of given length using only a compass and straight edge. In the course of the lesson, the teacher made remarks such as:

We can represent a segment with length $2\frac{3}{5}$.

We can construct a segment with length $2\frac{3}{5}$.

We can construct a segment with length r^2, given r.

We can represent a segment with length r^2, given r.

We cannot represent a segment with length π.

We cannot construct a segment with length π.

1. Which of these statements are true and which false?
2. Can construct and represent be used interchangeably? Explain.
3. What false concepts might be learned by the students?

12-9. In the classroom there are two types of conversational interaction both of which are highly desirable. They are teacher-student and student-student. We all know that teacher-student conversations are essential to learning but the question of who should be talking when, is open to debate. For each of the situations below, discuss who has the major responsibility for talking. Might this responsibility shift from time to time during the lesson?

   (a) Introducing the concepts of line, ray, and segment in a beginning lesson on nonmetric geometry.
   (b) Explaining an erroneous problem that was put on the board.
   (c) Constructing a proof of the congruence theorem, AAS if ASA is already known.
   (d) Constructing a proof that the set of prime numbers is infinite.
   (e) Solving a linear equation similar to one that had been on a previous assignment.

12-10. There are also many questions related to student-to-student exchange of ideas and conversation. If this is directly relevant to the subject under consideration, in this case mathematics, and is not detrimental to the best interests of the remaining students, this interchange of ideas can be a valuable tool in learning. Many times a student will more readily understand an explanation from a peer than if the explanation is given by the teacher. There are also benefits that are derived by verbalizing ideas because it causes us to more carefully organize and structure the ideas to be presented.

1. How much student-student interchange in the mathematics classroom is desirable if:
   (a) It is known that it relates to mathematics
   (b) It relates to a different school subject
   (c) It relates to current affairs
   (d) It relates to student social life
2. If the noise level due to these conversations become such that other students cannot work efficiently, what is the responsibility of the teacher?

12-11. In most secondary school mathematics classes there is very little positive reinforcement. For example, we are much more likely to hear, "Johnny, turn around and be quiet" than we are to hear, "Your behavior was excellent today, Johnny." Another instance of this is the emphasis that is placed on mistakes rather than on good questions or clever solutions.

1. State several means whereby we could, at least verbally, introduce positive reinforcement in the mathematics classroom.
2. Discuss the implications that positive reinforcement may have for motivation to learn mathematics.
3. Would it be possible to give more tangible rewards, such as five minutes of free time before the bell for certain behaviors?
4. What other rewards might be used?

12-12. In most classes students enjoy going to the board to work problems. This can create an atmosphere of mild competition and also provide the teacher with an immediate check on the effect of the previous instruction. All of this is good, however, there is one problem that sometimes occurs—that is, the remainder of the class is ignored by the teacher. If the remainder of the class can sit back and talk while their classmates work at the board, most of the good effects of this type of instruction has been lost.

When part of the class is doing boardwork,

1. What procedures can be used so that the remainder of the class at their seats are constructively occupied?
2. Could some healthy competition be encouraged by having the class evaluate the student work done at the board? What are some disadvantages of this procedure?
3. Should the teacher explain the student work or should the student explain his own work? Why or why not?

12-13. Analyzing student mistakes is often quite helpful. If the incorrect concept(s) that the student performed is (are) known, the teacher has a base from which to work. In a recent algebra class a student put the statement, $(x + y) \cdot x \cdot y = x^2 + y^2$ on the board. A number of problems are obvious from analyzing this work:

(a) The student does not make a clear distinction between indicated additions and multiplications.

(b) The student has the misconception that only like terms can be multiplied.

(c) The student does not understand the distributive property of multiplication over addition.

For each of the following false statements identify, if possible, the incorrect concept(s) that is (are) being applied.

1. 2/7 is renamed as 8/42.
2. $(a + b)^2 = a^2 + b^2$.
3. $\dfrac{7 + x}{x + 9} = 8/10$.
4. $\sin (a + b) = \sin a + \sin b$.

12-14. In ninth-grade algebra a student is sent to the board to solve the inequality, $\frac{2}{3}p - 1 > {}^-3$. The work of the student is as follows:

$$\frac{2}{3}p - 1 > {}^-3$$
$$(\tfrac{3}{2})\tfrac{2}{3}p - 1 > {}^-3\,(\tfrac{3}{2})$$
$$p - 1 > {}^-4\tfrac{1}{2}$$
$$p - 1\,(1) > {}^-4\tfrac{1}{2}(1)$$
$$p > {}^-4\tfrac{1}{2}$$

1. The student has obviously learned some incorrect concepts. What are they?
2. How can the student be retaught to correct the incorrect concepts?
3. If you as a teacher spend class time working with this student, what is the remainder of the class going to do during this time?
4. After you have retaught the student, how could you make sure the correct concepts were learned?

12-15. One of the more challenging aspects of planning a lesson is in attempting to anticipate the problems and difficulties that students will have. One goal of the developmental lesson should be to help the students avoid misconceptions. If the developmental lesson is lacking for particular students, many incorrect student behaviors can be observed.

Suppose that in an introductory algebra class the topic under consideration was rules of exponents. Three very common student errors in this lesson are:

(a) $2x^2 + 3x^2 = 5x^4$
(b) $2^2 \cdot 2^3 = 4^5$
(c) $(2b)^3 = 2b^3$

A teacher should anticipate that problems of this nature may occur and attempt first of all to forestall these errors and if that fails then the teacher should have planned methods for remedial work. What procedures could be used to correct each of the three erroneous statements given above?

12-16. In tenth-grade geometry, a class exercise was to prove the theorem, "The diagonals of a parallelogram bisect each other." During the course of the analysis (i.e., talking about what must be proved and how to go about it) a student asked, "Don't we have to show that the diagonals intersect inside the parallelogram?" There are a variety of alternatives open to the teacher at this point. For example, the teacher might comment that it can be seen from the picture that the diagonals will intersect inside the parallelogram. Alternatively the teacher might commend the question but inform the student that its answer is beyond the scope of the course. A third procedure might be to assume an affirmative answer to this question in order to complete the proof of the theorem under consideration and then return to this problem for further discussion. These are only three possible procedures which might be used in the classroom.

1. Which procedure do you think stands the best chance of success?
2. What problems might arise if the teacher used the first procedure? the second procedure? the third procedure?
3. What is another procedure that you might use to handle this instructional problem?

12-17. In a geometry class, the following exercise was being considered:

"Prove: In a trapezoid, neither diagonal is bisected by the other."

The argument used to prove this exercise is given below:

  Given:

Trapezoid $ABCD$ with $\overline{AB} \parallel \overline{DC}$

Diagonals $\overline{AC}$ and $\overline{BD}$ intersect at O

  Prove: $DO \neq OB$ and $AO \neq OC$.

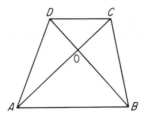

When proving two segments are unequal it is often convenient to use the indirect method of proof. We will use that type of argument here, so assume that $DO = OB$ and $AO = OC$. Hence, we have a quadrilateral in which the diagonals bisect each other. We have previously proved that under these conditions the quadrilateral is a parallelogram. This contradicts the hypothesis; hence our assumption is false and $DO \neq OB$ and $AO \neq OC$.

1. What is wrong with this argument?
2. How would you correct a student if he had given this argument?
3. Write a correct proof for this exercise.
4. How might an alternative definition of trapezoid invalidate this theorem?

12-18. An excellent technique for convincing a student that he has made an error is to exhibit a counterexample or to lead the student to the discovery of a counterexample. Some possible student-made statements which can be shown erroneous by a counterexample appear below. Find at least one case where each of the statements fails to hold. Also, devise a procedure that could be used to convince a student that the statement is false.

1. Two triangles are congruent if in triangle one, two sides and the angle opposite one of the sides are congruent to the corresponding sides and angle in triangle two.
2. If $a > b$, then $ac > bc$.
3. If $a > b$, and $c > d$ then $a - c > b - d$.
4. If the angles of one triangle are congruent to the angles of a second triangle the triangles are congruent.
5. $\sin \frac{1}{2} \alpha = \frac{1}{2} \sin \alpha$.

12-19. In any mathematics class illustrations and examples should be selected with care. If illustrative materials are not carefully thought through prior to their use, they may fail to exhibit a clear picture of the concept under consideration, they may cause students to learn an incorrect behavior, and hence, they may create more confusion than clarification.

An example of this could arise in geometry when trying to illustrate that SSA is not a sufficient condition for triangle congruence. To illustrate this concept, the two figures below were used.

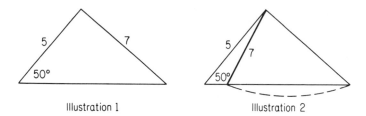

Illustration 1   Illustration 2

One of the more perceptive students in the class might say that it is not possible to obtain Illustration 2 from Illustration 1.

1. Why is the student response correct?
2. What effect may this student response have on the other members of the class.
3. What type of figures should have been used?

12-20. Writing on the chalkboard is one of the important activities of mathematics teachers. Several rules that should be followed when doing boardwork are:

(a) Write legibly and large enough to be seen by all students in the room.

(b) Erase all unnecessary marks on the board before each class.

(c) Each new concept should be started on a clean section of the board.

(d) Concepts should be orally explained while you are writing on the board.

(e) Be aware of the class when you are writing on the board.

1. List additional rules that should be followed for good boardwork. (The above procedures and rules should also be followed if the mode of presentations utilizes an overhead projector.)

Usually a teacher can watch only a part of the class when he is writing on the chalkboard. To watch different students some teachers have learned to write with either hand. Another procedure that might be used is to place a mirror above and to one side of the chalkboard. This enables the teacher to watch most of the class at any given time.

2. Do you feel that this is a good procedure to follow? Discuss.

12-21. Even before teaching a lesson there are a number of ways for a teacher to get some feedback about how he will sound or look when teaching. Some of these are to record a portion of the lesson using either an audiotape or videotape recorder. These can then be played back for you to see and hear yourself teach. If either or both of these facilities are available to you, try this and critically analyze yourself.

12-22. Another technique which provides feedback about your teaching is to teach some mathematical content to other students preparing to be teachers. They in turn can criticize your teaching techniques and offer constructive suggestions for you to try. Try teaching a mathematics lesson to some group of prospective teachers.

12-23. An article which provides much guidance for teaching the lesson, as well as an overall approach to instruction was written by Davis (1964). The abstract to this article states, "The reader is presented with a clinical approach to the development of a theory of instruction which seems consistent with modern views on learning." Read this article.

12-24. A regular section in *The Arithmetic Teacher* is entitled, "In the Classroom." Activities, strategies, or games are often provided that may be applicable to junior high school mathematics. Find several classroom activities in recent issues of this journal that could be used in a junior high classroom.

12-25. For a somewhat different view of teaching, read Skinner (1954). In this article, Skinner described classroom teaching as he saw it and then described his views of what teaching should be. This report, although not the first about programmed instruction, gave impetus to a great deal of activity relating to programmed instruction and teaching machines.

ADDITIONAL SOURCES

Davis, Robert B. "The Madison Project's Approach to a Theory of Instruction," *Journal of Research in Science Teaching*, Vol. 2 (1964), pp. 146–162.

Skinner, B. F. "The Science of Learning and the Art of Teaching," *Harvard Educational Review* (Spring 1954), pp. 86–97.

Chapter 13

Maintaining a Learning Atmosphere

Structuring the conditions for learning involves not only subject matter and teaching methods but also includes the management of the classroom environment. That part of teaching that requires managing the atmosphere or climate for learning will be called *classroom management*. Classroom management can be conceived of in three parts: *physical appearance* of the classroom, *routine tasks*, and establishing and maintaining *discipline*.

PHYSICAL ENVIRONMENT

One goal of mathematics instruction is to interest and motivate students to appreciate mathematics and make them want to approach mathematics learning opportunities. When students can envision mathematics learning as an activity that is associated with and occurs in comfortable facilities and pleasant surroundings, positive student attitudes toward mathematics are formed, and student achievement is indirectly enhanced.

The appearance of the physical setting in which mathematical learning occurs is one area that any conscientious teacher can markedly improve and make a positive contribution to student achievement in the process. Bulletin boards, displays, models, and classroom libraries can make a drab room look more cheerful and pleasant, and most importantly, a person entering the room can observe immediately that the study of mathematics is the central activity in that room. Changing the room arrangement occasionally and providing a special materials table for reading and independent study are other innovations that can transform a classroom from a dull, impersonal institutional cell to be avoided into a place that is pleasant, interesting, and has some character.

ROUTINE TASKS

Much of a teacher's time will be devoted to such pursuits as taking attendance, checking homework, discussing test results,

231

keeping student records, and filling out reports. All of these routine tasks and many more are irksome and can become over-burdening if the teacher is not wise enough to devise time-saving ways of handling them.

Each teacher will have to find his own best way to handle routine tasks in his situation. (Opportunities will be provided in the exercises, as well as some suggestions.) It may take several years of constant striving and experimentation to become really organized to the point where routine tasks are efficiently handled in an unobtrusive manner. Like collecting instructional strategies, finding better methods of handling routine tasks can be achieved by continually trying to think of better practices, reading professional literature, attending professional meetings, and seeking suggestions from fellow teachers, your department head, or the mathematics supervisor. Handling routine tasks efficiently and unobtrusively will result in reducing the opportunity for students to get into mischief, the conservation of student and teacher time for instructional purposes, and easing the unpleasantries that can overshadow the joys of teaching.

DISCIPLINE

When individuals gather in a group for some purpose, it becomes necessary to establish rules of conduct and standards of acceptable behavior so that the purpose of the group can be achieved and so that the rights of each individual are protected. When the group is a class or a school, the rules of conduct are established to maintain an atmosphere considered conducive to learning and to insure the right of each student to develop his own abilities free of encroachments. The rules and standards of behavior act as boundaries separating classroom behavior considered acceptable and classroom behavior considered unacceptable. The act of disciplining students is making sure that they obey the established rules and conform to desired patterns of behavior.

Problems arise when students are unwilling to obey the rules (often with good reason) and engage in activities that are outside the boundaries of behavior deemed desirable by authority or custom. When a student does cross the usually vague boundary from acceptable behavior to behavior deemed unacceptable, a breach of discipline occurs, and the teacher is expected to get the student to return to acceptable behavior and compel him not to stray again.

The ability of individual teachers to insure that students adhere to the behavior considered appropriate for the classroom varies greatly. The methods they use are as different as their personalities, and a technique used effectively by one person may be disastrous when used by another. Yet each teacher will use his personal mixture of the following ways to attempt to get students to comply to his will.

1. Cultivate a relationship of mutual respect and admiration

that the students will not want to jeopardize by knowingly overstepping the boundaries.

2. Elimination or modification of conditions that may heighten the temptation to misbehave or make misbehavior rewarding or reinforcing.

3. Intimidation or threats that make the students fearful or unwilling to risk the possible consequences of violating the rules of conduct.

4. Punishment of breaches of discipline when they do occur to discourage students from a repetition of the behavior because of the unpleasantness of the associated punishment.

The extent to which the teacher can perfect the first two practices described above and limit the use of the second two is the degree to which he is truly a disciplinarian.

The teacher's role in discipline is twofold. One function, preventive discipline, is to do whatever possible to keep the student from initially engaging in breaches of discipline. The other is one of controlling or acting upon misbehavior after it occurs. These two aspects of discipline will now be considered separately.

PREVENTIVE DISCIPLINE

The cornerstones of good preventive discipline are efficient routines, pleasant physical environment, excellent teaching, and good rapport between the students and teacher. Following practices found to be effective in these areas, many breaches of discipline can be prevented. There will always be, however, a few students who will inevitably engage in misbehavior. Physical surroundings and routine tasks were discussed for a different purpose, but their part in preventive discipline is explored in the exercises.

Much of the minor misbehavior that occurs in classrooms is nurtured by too little imagination in teaching techniques and too little active involvement by the students. Sitting quietly in an uncomfortable seat hour after hour and day after day listening to some person talking can become very boring for anyone, even if highly interested or motivated. Classrooms in which there is little chance to do much but listen or work problems can be unbelievably dull, particularly for students who see little worth in studying mathematics or who have difficulty learning mathematics. It is no wonder that pupils, who have short attention spans and an unlimited amount of restless energy, seek relief from the boredom associated with learning in any way they can and in ways that will release some of their pent-up energy and frustration.

There is no substitute for an enthusiastic, well-prepared teacher who gets and keeps all the students actively involved in learning mathematics. Practices such as using several modes of instruction, making the purpose of instruction clear and construct-

ing short, distinct activities that vary in amount of student participation will greatly increase the attractiveness of learning mathematics. Students who are interested and engaged in the activities
of the lesson will be less inclined to want to disrupt the classroom.

Teaching methods relate to preventive discipline in another
way. Planning and experience can be used to identify and avoid
situations that often tempt students to misbehave. When students
are required to deviate from normal procedures such as in laboratory lessons or working in small groups, careful planning is necessary to insure a good learning atmosphere. The start and finish of
class, discussing test results and homework, students working at
the chalkboard, or when the teacher is writing and talking at the
chalkboard are recurring activities that are potentially troublesome. A wise teacher practices awareness in the classroom by fac-
ing the class as much as possible, circulating about the room observing everything, and modifying procedures and activities that
are going badly. Also, it is advisable to work out a plan of action
with a school administrator when it appears that serious problems
may be developing with a student.

Use of good teaching techniques is simply part of the whole
process of establishing good rapport. By good rapport we mean a
cooperative, harmonious relationship between the students and
the teacher. This is a relationship of mutual respect and consideration, but where the teacher always acts and feels like the adult in
the classroom. Concern and interest are shown for each student as
a worthy individual, and the opportunity is taken to listen, talk,
and encourage students individually and make them feel important. Teachers who achieve this fortunate relationship do so not
by acting as the student's pal but by achieving a certain aloofness
or formality. They are friendly, but never familiar. They are interested, cooperative, approachable, decisive, businesslike, efficient,
and aware. By their actions and their thinking, they make their
presence felt in the classroom at all times; and there is never any
doubt in anyone's mind, including their own, who is in charge in
that classroom.

CONTROLLING MISBEHAVIOR

In spite of all efforts and good intentions, some students will
misbehave. The misbehavior is usually minor and requires little
response on the part of the teacher. When a classroom agreement
is broken, the teacher needs to take only that action required to
redirect behavior into appropriate channels and restore a good
learning atmosphere. Whatever action that the teacher takes
should be in the direction of restoring a good environment for
learning.

The variety and seriousness of the breaches of discipline that
will be faced are great, and hence the response of the teacher will
need to be fitted to the particular offense. The misbehavior may
result from boredom, mischief, rebellion, deep-seated emotional or

biological problems. No one teacher action will suit all breaches of discipline, but rather judgments will have to be made. Often it is better not to react in haste but take time to find out as many circumstances as possible surrounding any disturbance of more than a trivial nature. The violation can be noted but not acted upon until later instead of in the heat of the moment. There is no danger of the other students thinking that the offense went unpunished, since the word inevitably spreads to the other students.

Of course, there are many "dont's" in handling breaches of discipline.

1. Don't use sarcasm against a student or try to embarrass him so that he must try to save face.
2. Don't escalate trouble by engaging in verbal battles with students.
3. Don't act the "friendly young teacher" or allow students a familiarity such as calling you by your first name.
4. Don't make impossible threats.
5. Don't favor certain students or pets.
6. Don't reward misbehavior with favored treatment or special privileges.
7. Don't punish students by assigning school work, either related or unrelated.
8. Don't use physical torture such as running, sitting on the hands, or holding a chair overhead.

Some of these techniques may work from time to time in controlling misbehavior. However, engaging in all of the above practices and others that could be added to the list are obviously the opposite of the purpose of classroom management: the maintenance of a classroom atmosphere conducive to learning. (Not to mention that all of these don'ts are probably more immature teacher behavior than the misbehavior of the student.)

CONTROL TECHNIQUES

It may seem that teachers have few ways of enforcing their will in the classroom. In fact, there are really few physical ways of compelling compliance, and in some states where corporal punishment is illegal the use of physical force by a teacher can result in a lawsuit. The major force that a teacher can employ is the force of his own personality and the reservoir of good will built up with the class.

There are actions that a teacher can take that in most cases will suffice to control breaches of discipline. Some of these are listed below as a guide.

1. Stop talking and wait for the disruption to stop.
2. Walk nearer to the individual causing the disturbance.
3. Direct a stern stare at the individual that clearly concentrates and conveys your disapproval.

4. Ask the student to stop what he is doing since he is disturbing other members of the class, and direct his attention to what he should be doing. Perhaps do it privately at his desk so that he is not forced to save face.
5. Put the class to work, then talk to the pupil privately in the hall or in some private place convenient to the classroom.
6. Ask the student to see you privately, either after class or at another time. Let him know the breach of discipline, and clearly register your disapproval.
7. Isolate the student, perhaps by sending him to the back of another teacher's room after a prior agreement with that teacher.
8. Note to the parents.
9. Note to the counselor.
10. Note to the disciplinary officer.
11. Conference with the parent or school officials and student.
12. Take the student to the disciplinary officer of the school.

Three considerations should be kept in mind with respect to student misbehavior.

1. A large majority of students are friendly, cooperative, respectful, patient, and forebearing a majority of the time.
2. All teachers will have occasions when they will encounter difficulties with discipline.
3. The main concern in classroom management is constantly promoting and maintaining a good atmosphere for learning.

13-1. Suppose you walked into a classroom in which the floors were dirty and paper and apple cores could be seem lying in the desks. The teacher's desk looked unkempt, and the student's desks seemed to have no systematic arrangement but rather were askew, with some crowded together and a few pushed against the back wall. The chalkboards and chalkrails were dirty, and the overhead projector needed cleaning. Although it was a rainy day, the blinds were fully open, and the lights were off. The bulletin boards held newspaper clippings of school events and school notices, and the bookshelves were bare except for dust.

1. If you were a student in the class, how would you feel about the room? The teacher who taught in that room? The subject matter taught in the room? How might you expect to act in this room?
2. If you were the teacher in this room, what could you do to improve the physical appearance?
3. List specific things from the surroundings described above that could contribute to discipline problems in this classroom.
4. Name as many ways of improving the physical environment as you can which are also examples of practicing preventive discipline.

13-2. Good housekeeping should be developed to the point of being second nature. Some chores can be done by students, while others should be done only by the teacher, depending upon the class. Of course, some things should not be done by either, but left for the custodial staff.

Decide whether the teacher and students, teacher alone, or neither should have the responsibility for each of the following housekeeping chores, and indicate the provisions or rules you would establish for carrying out those duties that fall under the teacher's direction.

(a) Adjusting blinds, heating, lighting, and windows.

(b) Cleaning of erasers, chalkboards, and chalkrails.

(c) Cleaning and straightening of book shelves, displays, materials and models.

(d) Keeping the floor and desks neat and free of paper and trash.

(e) Cleaning the floor, walls, and windows.

(f) Cleaning and storing of the overhead projector and other equipment.

(g) Alignment of seating arrangement at end of each class.

(h) Changing the arrangement of the room and seating.

13-3. School policy probably will establish the school attendance procedures and require that class attendance be kept.

1. Why is it important for schools to keep accurate school attendance records?
   (a) Enforce compulsory school attendance.
   (b) Inform parents of child's attendance.
   (c) Distribution of tax money for education.
   (d) Keep statistics on national school population.
   (e) Meet school's legal obligation to care for and protect pupils.
   (f) Plan needs of school for facilities, teachers, and classes.
2. Why is it important for a teacher to keep accurate class attendance records?
   (a) Help the school account for students during the school day.
   (b) Teacher is legally responsible for his students, even when they are skipping his class.
   (c) To be able to account for students in case of a fire or air raid.
   (d) Show evidence to parents for poor quality of student's work when related to absenteeism.
   (e) Use of class attendance in evaluation of the student's grade.

13-4. Consider the following methods of obtaining the attendance.

(a) Call each student's name on the class roll.

(b) Construct a seating chart, and mark the absentees by noting the vacant seats while the students are working on some assignment.

(c) Remember who was absent and mark it down at the end of the hour or the end of the day.

(d) Construct a card for each pupil, flip through them as you observe the class, and mark the students' absences on the card.

(e) Appoint a student in the class to take the roll each day by one of the above methods.

(f) Mark the absentees at the end of the day from the list of students absent from school that circulates each day.

1. What are the advantages and disadvantages of each method for getting school attendance? Class attendance?

2. Which method would you use at the beginning of the year to get class attendance? Why?

3. Which is most saving of teacher time? Student time?

4. Which method would you use as a regular routine after you had learned the students' names?

13-5. Checking homework is a routine task that can be overwhelming if no provisions are made for efficiency and variety. One procedure frequently used by teachers is to collect the homework. They may grade each paper, simply spot-check a few papers, merely glance over all papers to get an impression, or require the students to do all their homework in a notebook and collect the notebook periodically. Some advantages of the teacher collecting the work is the obvious pressure on the students to do their homework, no class time required, and the teacher has a way of getting feedback to indicate how well the students are doing. Some disadvantages are the inordinate amount of teacher time for such checking and the length of time before the students know if they are working the problems correctly.

1. Discuss each procedure for handling homework listed below with regard to its advantages and disadvantages for the students and the teacher.
   (a) Don't assign homework or do not check it if it is assigned.
   (b) Check homework by quickly going around the room and looking at the homework papers laid on the corner of the desks while the students are working on some other assignment.
   (c) Have answers prepared on the chalkboard or the overhead and let the students check their papers as soon as they enter the room.
   (d) Call out answers or call on students to give answers to problems and allow them to check their papers or their neighbor's paper.
   (e) Give students a quick quiz that requires the knowledge found in the homework but that is easy and quick to check.
   (f) Call on different students to put different problems on the chalkboard when they enter the room.
   (g) Assign groups of students to prepare specific homework problems on a sheet of acetate and have it ready to place on the overhead projector when the class begins.
   (h) Ask the students if they had any questions on the homework and explain only the ones that a majority found troublesome.
2. List at least two more procedures that can be used to handle the homework assignment.

13-6. Initiation of classroom routines is most important for the start and finish of the class period. The wise teacher who wishes to prevent serious discipline problems will always have an understanding or unwritten rule with the class that the sound of the bell means to be in their seats and ready for business. Consider the following ways of beginning a class:

    (a) Call the roll and sign excuses while the class sits and waits or sharpens pencils and gets out paper.

    (b) Have students copy the homework assignment.

    (c) Have students place previous night's homework problems on the board.

    (d) Ask: "Are there any questions on last night's homework?"

    (e) Make the students say in unison, "Good morning, Mr. Jones."

    (f) Have one review problem for all to work on at their seats.

    (g) Have a *short* quiz that is marked and recorded for each student immediately.

    (h) Have a student call out the answers to the homework problems.

    (i) Stand and wait for the students to stop talking so that you can begin the developmental lesson.

1. Which of these gets the class quiet and down to the business of mathematics immediately?

2. Which of these would be best for a class that easily gets out of control and likes to cut up with each other?

3. What other ways of starting the class can you think of that will set the right tone for the period and prevent misbehavior?

13-7. The close of class should be a routine procedure, but it need not be so strict as the opening. The students need some time to relax and gather up their belongings, particularly if they have worked diligently during the rest of the class period.

A situation that often occurs in mathematics classes is where with only seven minutes remaining in the period the teacher finishes the development and directs the students to begin working on their homework until the bell rings, then plops down at his desk. Many of the students, realizing that there is little time remaining, pack up their books, get their belongings together, start a conversation with their neighbors, roam about the room, or stare out of the window. A few seconds before the sound of the bell they edge toward the door, position themselves like track stars, and at the bell dash from the room en masse, leaving paper and trash, scattered everywhere.

Reviewing the situation described above, devise an end-of-class routine in which the learning atmosphere remains in the teacher's control when there are fifteen minutes remaining in the period, five minutes remaining, and two minutes remaining. In each case, provide time which the students know will be available to them to gather their belongings and leave on time.

13-8. While classroom regulations are established by the teacher as the responsible adult, the reasons behind their establishment should be clear to the students.

What procedures or rules would you want and how would you justify them to your students for the following recurring problems?

(a) Seating assignments in the classroom.

(b) Clearing students' desks of notebooks and books when working on class work.

(c) Use of the pencil sharpener.

(d) Use of the wastebasket.

(e) Talking in class.

(f) Leaving the room by a student.

(g) Leaving the room by the teacher.

(h) Use of equipment and materials.

13-9. The kinds of rules and regulations established in a class are not always so important as the personality and temperament of the teacher making and enforcing them.

For example, some teachers do not seem to mind if a student sharpens a pencil any time during the class period, and many of them have no problems with discipline. Others insist that all pencils be sharpened prior to class and none sharpened during the class period. Still others allow students to use the pencil sharpener except when someone is talking to the entire class and then only one person at a time. One imaginative teacher simply kept a cigar box of pencils about $1\frac{1}{2}$ inches long which could be borrowed by those pupils who needed a sharpened pencil during class. Although it was considered a fine joke, students learned to provide themselves with sharpened pencils prior to the beginning of class.

1. Think of several ways the following problems might be handled by teachers with different personalities:
   (a) Walking around the room by students.
   (b) Use of the wastebasket.
   (c) A student who wishes to leave the room.
2. Can you think of a subtle way of handling the problems listed above such as that recounted for sharpening pencils?

13-10. While the rules are established by the teacher, consideration must be given to the feelings of the students.

One routine commonly practiced is to seat the class alphabetically. This is certainly an efficient way to take attendance, hand back papers, and learn the names of students. Yet, one of the authors remembers a college class in which the teacher made the class sit alphabetically after everyone had chosen his seat with his friends. The question was then asked, "Do you like the way you are sitting? Do you feel more or less secure in this class and in the surroundings you find yourself?" All agreed that they felt less inclined toward the class and further vowed that it would cure them of seating their own students alphabetically.

1. How would you handle seating assignments in your classroom? Under what conditions would you change the seating arrangements?

2. In what way do the following procedures show lack of consideration for student feelings?

    (a) Placing a student in charge of discipline when the teacher leaves the room.

    (b) Seating the girls on one side of the room and the boys on the other side.

    (c) Recording test scores or grades by asking students to say them aloud as the teacher records them.

    (d) Making a student stand to ask or answer a question or speak in the class.

13-11. Tardiness to class is sometimes a problem. Most schools have some policy with respect to handling it, but the teacher also may have to set some guidelines of his own.

Consider the following alternatives for handling a student who comes to class tardy.

(a) Students coming in late get a dirty look from the teacher but are allowed to go to their seats.

(b) Student can only be admitted with a written note from another teacher or the office after the sound of the bell.

(c) Student coming in late goes directly to his seat and waits for the teacher to get around to seeing him privately to determine the cause of his tardiness.

(d) Student coming in late is stopped and asked by the teacher for the cause of his tardiness and perhaps reaps a public reprimand.

(e) Student who is late is not permitted in the room after the bell and must take his chances on not getting caught out in the hall without a hall pass.

1. Which of these procedures is least in keeping with promoting and maintaining a good learning atmosphere? Why?

2. Which of these procedures is most in keeping with the practice of preventive discipline? Why?

13-12. In most classes students enjoy going to the board to work problems. This can create an atmosphere of mild competition and also provide the teacher with an immediate check on the effect of the previous instruction. All of this is good; however, there is one problem that sometimes occurs—the remainder of the class is ignored by the teacher. If the remainder of the class can sit back and talk while their classmates work at the board, most of the good effects of this type instruction has been lost. When part of the class is doing boardwork,

1. What procedures can be used so that the remainder of the class at their seats are constructively occupied?
2. Could some healthy competition be encouraged by having the class evaluate the student work done at the board? Why or why not?
3. Should the teacher explain the student work or should the student explain his own work? Why or why not?

13-13. The location of a teacher is also an important phase of classroom management. It is obvious that if the students are working at their desks, the teacher should be checking students' success and providing help to individuals. This would imply that the teacher would be roving up and down the aisles of the classroom.

1. Where should the teacher be while a test is being given? What should the teacher be doing during this time? Justify your answer.
2. Is it necessary for the teacher to be in the front of the classroom during the developmental lesson? Discuss.
3. Where should the teacher be during a laboratory lesson? What should the teacher be doing during this lesson? Discuss.

13-14. Good rapport is a desirable condition in a classroom, but the distinction between activities that produce it and those that don't are not always clear. Distinguish between those teacher characteristics or behaviors that you think will generally enhance rapport and those that usually will erode it.

(a) Start each class with a joke or funny story.

(b) Make known to the students the methods of grading, evaluating, and how they are progressing.

(c) Establish classroom rules that are impartially and consistently enforced.

(d) Look and act very stern, giving directions and presenting instructions very curtly and crisply and glowering at anyone who does not immediately comply.

(e) Allow the students the freedom of making their own class regulations and let them enforce these regulations.

(f) Show evidence of planning and a good grasp of the subject matter.

(g) Get to know students by soliciting information about their social activities and join them at the movies or in a restaurant.

(h) Try to give each student some encouragement or special notice of something he does well as often as possible.

(i) Take advantage of humorous situations as short stopping points before returning to the business at hand.

(j) Add some humor to the class by calling a student by a nickname or some name like "Hotshot," "Son," or "Boy."

13-15. A special type of discipline problem which occurs frequently is cheating. Let's take a hypothetical situation which portrays a situation where cheating may occur. All of us are familiar with students who write off to one side leaving their work exposed to other students. Suppose Boy A does this and Boy B has wandering eyes and an unrestricted view. Further suppose that Boy A and Boy B are the best students in the class so that Boy B could use any information he obtains judiciously. This situation portrays possible cheating. However, it is practically impossible to be certain that cheating has occurred.

There are several courses of action open to the teacher. Some of them are as follows:

(a) Ignore the situation since both boys will get an A anyhow.

(b) Tell Boy B to keep his eyes on his own paper.

(c) Accuse Boy B of cheating in front of the whole class.

(d) Accuse Boy B of cheating after the test, and in private.

(e) Tell Boy A to keep his work covered.

(f) Several days after the test, move Boy A to a seat where his peculiar writing style does not leave his work exposed to other students.

1. Discuss each of the above situations with respect to
   (a) The possible effects on the two boys involved
   (b) The possible effects on the rest of the class
   (c) The probability of success that the action may have

2. Can you think of any other procedures that could be followed?

13-16. Another form of cheating of which the teacher must be aware occurs when the homework papers for two students have identical work and errors. It is obvious that an infraction of honesty has occurred. Several procedures that can be followed are:

(a) Discuss the purpose of homework with the class and the need for completing their own work. Mention that two identical papers were received which indicated that at least two people were not being honest. (Mention no names.)

(b) Same as (a) but mention the names of the guilty students.

(c) Call the two students in after class and explain that neither of them would receive credit for this work since their papers were identical implying that one of them copied with the other's consent.

(d) Ignore it.

1. Discuss each of these procedures with respect to
   (a) The possible effects of the two students involved
   (b) The possible effects on the rest of the class
   (c) The probability of success that the action might have

2. What would be another procedure that could be followed?

13-17. In the last exercise suppose that you followed procedure (c) and the students came back with the argument;

We do study together and it seems that we learn more when we cooperate on our assignments. This is why our papers are alike but neither of us copied from the other. Rather, we did the work jointly.

1. Is this a valid argument? Discuss.
2. Do you want to encourage cooperation of this sort? Discuss.
3. How might you suggest that the students cooperate in the future so that their papers are not carbon copies?
4. Would you reverse your decision about credit for the assignment? Discuss.

13-18. Another common discipline problem is sleeping in class. The causes for this are varied and to handle this type of problem effectively, the teacher should make every effort to determine the cause. For example, one case may be due to biological necessity. This may occur if the student works the equivalent of a full shift after school. This problem should probably be discussed with the parents to determine the necessity of working and the detrimental effects it may have on the child's health. Needless to say, it is having a bad effect on his school work and should be resolved if at all possible. If working is essential it may be possible to rearrange the student's schedule to provide for more sleep out of school. Other causes may be

(a) Boredom because the material is not challenging

(b) Boredom because the material is too difficult

(c) Lack of motivation to learn

Discuss each of these with respect to several corrective measures that might be used to remedy the situation and the probability of success that each measure might have.

13-19. As you are writing on the chalkboard and have your back turned to the class, an eraser hits the board close to you, and showers chalk dust over an area near you. Procedures that you as a teacher might follow are:

(a) Ignore it.

(b) Comment that whoever threw it had poor aim.

(c) Ask a general question of the class; "Who threw it?"

(d) Inspect each student for traces of chalk dust and speak to each student who shows indication of chalk.

(e) Tell the class that you are using an honor system and would like to speak to the individual who threw the eraser after class.

(f) Give the entire class an extemporaneous lecture on respect of individual rights.

The first of these is a poor procedure to follow in any class for in a sense it condones the act of defiance. Some action is obviously necessary and each of the other five alternatives provides an action. Some of these are more appropriate than others.

1. Comment briefly on each of the remaining five alternatives. Your comments should reflect the effect of this action on the class and the possible success of this action.

2. Try to think of two other procedures which would have a high probability of success.

3. If you identified the culprit, what would you do or say to this student if

(a) He was a chronic troublemaker?

(b) He was a mischievous but conscientious student?

13-20. Often classroom problems deteriorate into difficult classroom confrontations as a result of the teacher escalating the situation. The incident described below is broken into parts where the teacher did one or more things to aggravate a mild situation into a major crisis. After each part, list one thing the teacher did wrong and how he could have avoided escalating the situation.

(a) The teacher is making a presentation at the chalkboard. One or two students answer questions, but only a few students are attending to the work at the board.

(b) Three students in the back of the room begin to talk and the noise level of the classroom begins to rise. The teacher stops and says: "Everyone get quiet, right this minute."

(c) The teacher begins again and again the noise begins to rise. More students are whispering and the teacher picks out an individual and orders him to get quiet.

(d) The other students are quiet only momentarily. Soon the noise increases and the teacher calls on a student who is talking to answer a question.

(e) The student says in a smart manner: "I don't know," and the rest of the class giggles. The teacher shouts at the student that he better pay attention or he will not be able to pass the next test.

13-21. Part of good discipline is thinking on your feet and making the right decisions. One wrong decision will not ruin you as a teacher, but a lot of them will be damaging to the maintenance of a learning atmosphere. Consider the following examples:

(a) Susan, an excellent student, quietly uses the pencil sharpener during a teacher demonstration. The teacher does nothing. Sam, who often disrupts the class gets up to sharpen his pencil. The teacher orders him to take his seat.

In the example above, the teacher was obviously permitting a double standard, particularly if there was a rule that you do not sharpen your pencil while the teacher is talking. She might have given Susan a nod of the head to indicate she should wait or permitted Sam to sharpen his pencil. In the examples that follow, point out places where the teacher made a wrong decision:

(b) The teacher walks into the room to start the class and several boys are running and knock over a desk. They set up the desk and sit down giggling. She decides to ignore it this time, but next time she will make them go to detention hall.

(c) The teacher turns around and sees two students laughing and cutting up. The teacher shouts, "Jim and Joe, either you straighten up or I'm going to slap you till your teeth rattle." Joe replies, "You touch me and my old man will take care of you." "Oh yeah! You get out of this class and don't come back till you apologize to me."

13-22. As you know from psychology, punishment does not eliminate defiant behavior, but only represses it. Punitive actions may also repress other desirable behaviors such as class participation. Punishment is most effective when the student is given the opportunity to engage in a proper alternative that can be reinforced. Punishment with restitution is a better procedure than mere punishment, since it requires the defier to engage in desirable behavior that can be reinforced.

For example, a student who writes on a desk should be directed to clean the desk (i.e., directed to a desirable behavior) rather than write, "I will not write on desks" one thousand times. For the examples below, indicate ways the student can make restitution or be directed to practice desirable behavior that can be reinforced:

(a) Throwing paper in the room.
(b) Cheating on a test.
(c) Stealing money.
(d) Calling out answers in class.

13-23. Suppose you have tried to establish discipline in your classroom but you have failed. The students do not obey you and *you* have tried everything *you* can think of, but it has not worked. You have several alternatives:

(a) Just live with your mistakes and try to do better next year.
(b) Decide that things are going to change and you are going to march right in there on Monday and let them know who is boss.
(c) Hide a tape recorder in your room to try to analyze what is happening in your room.
(d) Read a book on disciplining a class.
(e) Ask another teacher whom you respect and trust to sit in the back of the room and observe and give suggestions.
(f) Ask the principal or assistant principal to sit in your class to help you manage them.
(g) Tell the principal your problem, and work out with him a procedure you can use in class as well as arrangements to use his backing in enforcing the new procedure.

If you select alternative (a) you will be maintaining a poor atmosphere for learning and, as a result, will be shirking your responsibilities as a teacher. Furthermore, you will be gaining little insight into the cause(s) which generates the lack of discipline.

1. Discuss the alternatives (b–g) with regard to the chances that these procedures have for bettering discipline and the effects they may have on you as a teacher.
2. Which of the above techniques do you think would be most useful for getting the class under control?

SUGGESTED ACTIVITIES

13-24. Two pamphlets which contain some excellent suggestions relating to discipline and classroom control are Schain (1961) and Schain and Polner (1964). These sources include several case studies with analyses and suggested remedial actions that could be followed. Reading these pamphlets should provide a variety of techniques for each prospective teacher to try in order to improve classroom discipline.

13-25. Issues of *Today's Education* (formerly *NEA Journal*) contain case studies on discipline. The incident is reported, followed by an analysis by "experts." Read some of these case studies and then
  (a) Relate the incident in a sentence.
  (b) Relate the teacher reaction in a sentence.
  (c) List the main suggestions of the experts.
  (d) List what you would have done.

13-26. The American Educational Research Association and the Department of Classroom Teachers of the NEA have published a research pamphlet series designed to show how research findings can help with classroom situations. One pamphlet in this series, Gnagey (1965), interprets research findings and indicates possible implementation of the findings for teachers. Reading this source will provide the prospective teacher with techniques that have been shown to be effective in the classroom.

13-27. There is more to maintaining a learning atmosphere in the classroom than maintaining order. One source which effectively describes additional ways to maintain a learning atmosphere is Hankin (1961). Read Hankin's short pamphlet and then relate the ideas found here to those presented here in Chapters 11 through 13.

ADDITIONAL SOURCES

Gnagey, William J. *Controlling Classroom Behavior*. Washington, D.C.: National Education Association, 1965.

Hankin, Aaron. *Meaningful Mathematics Teaching*. Valley Stream, N.Y.: Teachers Practical Press, Inc., 1961.

Schain, Robert L. *Discipline: How to Establish and Maintain It*. Valley Stream, N. Y.: Teachers Practical Press, Inc., 1961.

——, and Murray Polner. *Using Effective Discipline for Better Class Control*. Valley Stream, N.Y.: Teachers Practical Press, Inc., 1964.

Chapter **14**

Evaluation

We have already seem in Chapter 5 that test construction should reflect the goals and objectives of the instructional process. In particular, each item should measure some specific nonempty set of objectives. Following the administration of a test, it is necessary for the teacher to make an assessment of the extent to which each individual student has attained the specified objectives. This assessment must then be translated into a letter grade or a percent score which is meant to reflect the performance of the student. This process is one phase of student evaluation which is more generally the process of determining the degree to which the behavior of students conforms to the objectives of instruction. In this general characterization of evaluation we need not restrict ourselves to paper and pencil tests for evaluation of students. Rather, evaluation should be based upon the behavior of the student for any school relevant goals or objectives. The emphasis which different goals or objectives receive in the evaluation process, however, is a question open to debate.

Factors other than teacher-made tests which may be considered in the evaluation process include student behavior in or out of the classroom, evidence of completion of assigned tasks, the effect that the evaluation may have on the student, and results of standardized achievement, intelligence, ability and attitude measures. From observation of the student, inferences can be made about the effort expended in constructive classroom participation, the quality of classroom participation, the attitude of the student and overall citizenship qualities. These traits can in part be substantiated through the results of standardized tests and completion of assigned tasks. Finally, the evaluation will have some type of an effect on the student—that is, a grade may cause one student to work harder while the same grade may deter another student. Each of these factors should contribute to the overall evalution of the student. A schematic diagram of the relationships implied by the evaluation process is given in Fig. 14-1.

The Report to Students and Parents is a culmination of the evaluation process. It should reflect an attempt to evaluate more than an average of test scores. Note the variety of behaviors or

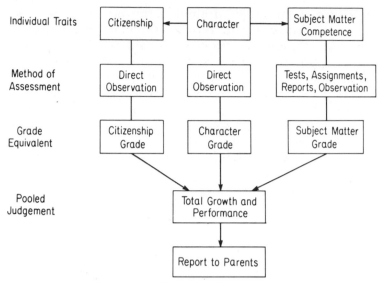

Fig. 14-1. The evaluation process.

attributes which contribute to the overall evaluation or Total Growth and Performance of the student. It should be realized that the categories are by no means exclusive. They do, however, serve to give a framework for evaluating separately different types of goals and objectives of education.

GRADES

Evaluation is a continual process in that we should always be observing the behavior of students in the classroom and attempting to assess the progress they are making in the attainment of the goals and objectives of instruction. At periodic intervals, however, it is necessary to inform the students and parents of the evaluation that we as teachers have made for each student. This report to students and parents usually is in the form of a letter grade (A, B, C, D, F) although some school systems report numerical grades based on a percentage system.

There are essentially three rationales available to a teacher in reporting a student's progress.

1. The number of objectives the student has achieved is compared to the total required objectives of the unit or course (that is, The student's performance is compared to some predetermined standard based on the objectives).
2. The student's performance is compared to the performance of some group of students, usually the class he is in.
3. The student's *actual* performance is compared to what he can *ideally* achieve.

The differences in the three methods relate to the standard to which the student's performance is being compared. It should be noted that two or more of these rationales may be mixed to obtain a modified system for reporting student progress.

The task of assigning grades is probably one of the most difficult tasks confronting teachers. One of the difficulties stems from the multitude of subjective decisions that the teacher must make in the evaluative process. There is no objective way of assessing to what degree a student is working up to his capacity, nor of determining the amount of positive attitude a student has toward mathematics. In fact, there is little if any concrete evidence for most traits or behaviors held to be influential in the evaluation of pupils. The one notable exception is the results of paper and pencil work such as test grades and homework. Even here, there are many subjective decisions to be made—the problems to be included, how the test is graded, or how grades are assigned to test scores.

A second difficulty is a consequence of the limited categories, (letter grades) that are available. This means that two students, both earning a grade of C, can exhibit behavior which is very different. For this reason, it may be preferable, although more time-consuming, to give written evaluations which indicate strengths and weaknesses of students. This type of evaluation may be more meaningful to parents and students than would a letter grade.

If a single grade is reported as an evaluation of a student, the factor that probably contributes most to this grade is some type of average of test grades or scores. Influential in the assignment of letter grades is the manner in which the tests are scored. There are several factors which introduce sources of variability when grading tests and about which the teacher must make subjective decisions. Several of these factors are:

1. The number of points or the weight to be assigned to individual test items.
2. The response(s) which constitute a correct answer.
3. Partial credit.
4. Extra credit.
5. Method of assigning letter grades to test scores.

Decisions relating to these and other factors should be carefully considered prior to grading the test and policies which will permit fairness in grading for all students should be formulated.

The manner in which test scores are averaged also contributes to the variability in a letter grade that is composed of performance on several tests. Several methods of averaging test scores are

1. Find the arithmetic mean of the percent scores.
2. Sum the numerical raw scores and then convert to a percent score.
3. Convert scores on each test to standardized scores (i.e., each test has the same mean and variance) and average these scores.

4. Assign letter grades to each test and average these letter grades.

Each of these methods of averaging has advantages and disadvantages and could result in widely different letter grades for the same set of scores. (See Exercise 14-4.)

From the preceding paragraphs it is obvious that the procedure of grading on the basis of test results has many pitfalls. The grade a student receives in a course is often an unreliable indicator of his achievement. This grade, however, is used to inform the student, parents, school, colleges, and employers of the progress of the student in that course. The grade is also often used as a predictor of future position. For these reasons every effort should be made so that grades more accurately reflect the student's performance on the specified objectives of the course regardless of factors such as the teacher and methods of assigning grades.

EXERCISES

14-1. A unit on systems of linear equations has just been completed and a unit test is being constructed. The assignment of points to test items is one source of variability in evaluation, just as is the items to be included on the test. The following test items were among those constructed for this test.

(a) What are inconsistent equations?

(b) The ordered pair (___, 3) is a solution of $3x - 6 = 2y$

(c) The solution of the system of equations $x - 2y = 5$ and $^-2x - 3y = 6$ is _____.

(d) Graph the solution of the system of inequalities "$x < y$ and $x + 2 > 3y$."

(e) The difference of two whole numbers is 30. The greater number is two more than three times the smaller. Find the two numbers.

1. Classify each question as knowledge, comprehension, application, or analysis. (For test item classification system, see Chapter 5.)

2. Should a knowledge question have the same number of points as a comprehension or analysis question?

3. Assign point values to each of the five questions so that the sum of the point values is 40. State the reasons for your assignment of point values.

4. Compare your assignment of point values with that of a classmate.

14-2. Letter grades may be assigned to test scores using a fixed or variable scale. A common fixed scale for a 100-point test is:

A: 92–100
B: 84–91
C: 76–83
D: 70–75
F: below 70

A common variable scale is based on the test scores themselves and necessitates the computation of the mean, $\overline{X} = \dfrac{\Sigma x_i}{n}$ and the standard deviation

$$s = \sqrt{\dfrac{\Sigma x_i{}^2 - \dfrac{(\Sigma x_i)^2}{n}}{n-1}}$$

where x_i $(i = 1, 2, \ldots, n)$ are the test scores and n is the number of test scores. Grades are then assigned as follows:

A: if $x_i > \overline{X} + 1\frac{1}{2} \cdot s$
B: if $\overline{X} + \frac{1}{2}s < x_i \leqslant \overline{X} + 1\frac{1}{2} \cdot s$
C: if $\overline{X} - \frac{1}{2}s < x_i \leqslant \overline{X} + \frac{1}{2}s$
D: if $\overline{X} - 1\frac{1}{2}s < x_i \leqslant \overline{X} - \frac{1}{2}s$
F: if $x_i \leqslant \overline{X} - 1\frac{1}{2}s$

Two sets of 20 scores appear below:

Set 1   96,91,89,88,87,82,80,76,75,73,72,70,69,67,64,62,59,57,55,41
Set 2   99,95,94,93,91,89,87,86,83,81,80,79,75,74,73,71,70,67,65,57

1. Assign grades for each of these two sets of scores using both of the types of scales defined above.
2. Do different scores receive different grades on the two types of scales?

14-3. There are arguments for and against each type of grading scale defined in Exercise 14-2. A fixed scale can be specified in advance of the test administration. Also, it explicitly states the criterion for achieving a certain grade. This may be an adequate scale if only knowledge and comprehension questions were being asked; however, if the questions on the test were application or analysis type questions, a fixed scale may be too demanding. In fact, if this type of scale is strictly adhered to, it would influence unduly the type of items to be placed on the tests.

1. Discuss other arguments for or against a fixed-scale marking system.
2. Discuss arguments that might be used for or against a variable-scale marking system. You should consider such factors as:
   (a) What does a grade of A mean in relation to the number of specific objectives achieved?
   (b) When is the grading scale defined?
   (c) Is this system fair if ability grouping is used for this class?
   (d) Will this system permit grades from A to F for tests of any type (i.e., comprehension, analysis, etc., type questions)?
3. Match each of these grading scales to one of the three rationales given in the introduction to this chapter.

14-4. Another popular method for assigning letter grades to test scores is to examine the distribution of scores. For this method it is convenient to order the scores from highest to lowest. Two useful statistics, the *range* and the *median* can then be obtained quite readily. The range is merely the difference between the largest and smallest observed scores and, if the scores are evenly distributed between the highest and lowest, serves as a rough discrimination index for the test. The median is the middle score and is a score which under normal circumstances should receive a grade of C. At this point, natural breaks in the distribution can be identified to be used as cutting points for grades.

Perhaps an example will clarify this procedure. The Set 1 scores from Exercise 14-2 are

96, 91, 89, 88, 87, 82, 80, 76, 75, 73, 72, 70, 69, 67, 64, 62, 59, 57, 55, 41

The range is 55 and the median 72.5. The arrows indicate one set of breaks in the distribution which could be used for assigning grades. These grades should then be compared with a fixed standard grading scale and if there is wide disagreement, grades may be modified to reflect a combination of the breaks and fixed scale method.

1. Use the method described above to assign grades to the scores in Set 2 of Exercise 14-2.
2. Which of the three methods (two from Exercise 14-2 and one from Exercise 14-4) appears to be more equitable?

14-5. Listed below is a set of thirty-four hypothetical test scores obtained on students in a homogeneously grouped, average-ability, ninth-grade Algebra I class. The test is assumed to be a unit test containing items (say 45 points) that all the students were expected to achieve as well as some items that required a little thinking beyond mere recall or ability to solve certain problems in a set pattern. The total number of points possible is 85.

Assign the letter grades of A, B, C, D, or F to the scores indicating the letter grade corresponding to each score. You may use any method of assigning grades you wish. Be prepared to describe your method of assigning grades and to justify it.

SCORES

80	66	55	47
74	65	55	47
73	64	53	47
72	63	51	46
71	62	51	45
70	62	50	45
69	60	50	45
68	59	49	45
67		48	

14-6. Suppose that a test item on a ninth-grade algebra test was:

Solve $\dfrac{x}{2} - \dfrac{x-5}{4} = 5$

The answers given by four students appear below:

Student A: $\dfrac{x}{2} - \dfrac{x-5}{4} = 5$

$2x - x - 5 = 20$

$x = 25$

Student B: $\dfrac{x}{2} - \dfrac{x-5}{4} = 5$

$2x - x + 5 = 5$

$x = 0$

Student C: $\dfrac{x}{2} - \dfrac{x-5}{4} = 5$

$x = 15$

Student D: $x = 25$

1. If this were a 5-point question, assign point values to each student response. Compare your point assignment with other students.
2. Suppose 2 points were awarded to Student A for his response. Since Student D has obtained the same value for x should Student D also be awarded 2 points? Discuss.
3. Is it possible that Student C made some error in his work yet obtained the correct answer? Are there circumstances under which this response might receive less than full credit?

14-7. In geometry a student gives the following proof for the theorem, "Sides opposite congruent angles in a triangle are congruent."

In $\triangle ABC$, let $\angle B \cong \angle C$. Draw AD such that $AD \perp BC$ and $BD = DC$. Therefore, $\triangle ABC \cong \triangle ADC$ by ASA.

1. What is wrong with this proof?
2. If you were scoring this proof on the basis of 10 points, how many points would you give?
3. Do you think other people will give different amounts of credit?

14-8. In second-year algebra a student is given the radical equation $2x - 2 = \sqrt{2x^2 + 4}$ to solve. His work appears below:

$$2x - 2 = \sqrt{2x^2 + 4}$$
$$4x^2 - 8x + 4 = 2x^2 + 4$$
$$2x^2 - 8x = 0$$
$$x = 4 \text{ and } x = 0$$

1. If this is a test item worth 10 points, how much, if any, credit should the student receive?
2. Have several other people score this item on the basis of 10 points.
3. Is there any variation in scoring. If so, how much?
4. If 90 percent and above is an A; 80–89 percent a B and so on, could the student's grade on this item range from A to F?
5. How can some of this subjectivity in scoring be avoided?
6. Presuming an error in the above work, how would you go about correcting it for the student?

14-9. Averaging grades across two or more tests is also a serious cause of variation in the assignment of grades. Suppose that there are three 100-point tests during a six-week grading period and that student X has scores of 75, 75, and 78, while student Y has 52, 76, and 93. The means scores for the three tests are 72, 80, and 78. If we average raw scores, we find student X has an average of 76 which is a C on the fixed scale while student Y has an average of 73$\frac{2}{3}$ which is a D. On the other hand, we could average letter grades for student X (D, D, C) which would result in an average grade of D, while for student Y (F, C, A) we obtain an average grade of C. The two procedures yield exactly reversed grades for the two students.

1. What grades do you think the two students should receive? State your reasons.
2. Which averaging procedure explained above is fairer?
3. Should each test be given equal weight in the averaging process? Why?

14-10. Four tests were given throughout one six-week period. The point values on the tests were 20, 40, 50, and 100. A student obtained scores of 10, 30, 45, and 85 respectively on the four tests.

1. Find the percent scores for these four tests and then find the average of the four percents. Using the fixed letter-grade scale given in Exercise 14-2, assign a letter grade to this average.
2. Find the sum of the students raw scores and then transform this sum to a percent score. Assign a letter grade to this percent using the fixed scale.
3. Use the percent scores obtained in part (a) and assign a letter grade for each test. Average these letter grades.
4. Which grade do you feel should be assigned to this student for a six-week evaluation on the basis of his test scores?
5. Is it mathematically sound to average percent scores as requested in 1?

14-11. Averaging several grades together to arrive at one grade can present many problems and result in inequities. For example, averaging raw numerical scores does not account for the difference in difficulty level of tests or other factors that should be weighted differently.

One method of arriving at a weighted grade is to assign a letter grade to each activity which contributes to the final grade. Each letter grade is converted to a numerical score by some scheme such as A-4, B-3, C-2, D-1, F-0. The activities are also assigned a relative weight factor to indicate their contribution to a final grade. For each activity, its weight factor times the numerical score for its letter grade is its assigned score points. To obtain the average grade, find the average score points (sum of the score points divided by the sum of the weight factors) and convert that back to the corresponding letter grade. Suppose a student earned grades as follows:

Activity	Grade (Points)	Weight Factor	Score Points
Test	C(2)	1	2
Test	B( )	1	
Unit test	C(2)	2	4
Quiz average	B( )	1	
Homework.	A( )	1	
Project	A( )	$^1/_2$	
Class participation . . .	B( )		
		Total	Total

Complete the table and find the appropriate letter grade that would be assigned to this students work.

14-12. Suppose that a student had a very low test average which would warrant a grade of F if no other factors were considered. Other factors which might be considered are:

(a) This test average was for the first six-week grading session.

(b) The student tried to complete each homework assignment and usually had about 50 percent of each assignment completed correctly.

(c) The student's attitude about mathematics seemed to be, "I can't get it, but I'll try."

This student is evaluated with an F for this grading period. We could certainly justify this grade in terms of achievement on tests and homework; however, it may do irreparable harm with respect to attitude. The student might think, "I was right. I can't get math so why should I knock myself out trying to get it. An F's an F if I try or not."

Suppose the student is evaluated at D.

1. What effect might this have on his attitude?

2. What does this first six-week grading period have to do with letter-grade assignments?

3. What justification can the teacher use for a grade of D in the light of poor achievement? Relate to a learning assumption as stated in Chapter 2.

4. Which rationale of evaluation is used if grade D is assigned?

14-13. A letter grade assigned to a student for a given course may mean many things. Several philosophies of grading appear below.

(a) The grade should reflect only student achievement of the goals and objectives for the course as measured by teacher made or standardized tests.

(b) Student test achievement is the major contributing factor to a final grade for a course; however, this may be modified one letter grade in either direction by such factors as class participation, citizenship qualities, homework, or attitude.

(c) Same as (b) except factors other than test achievement can only lower the final grade for the course.

(d) The grade for the course is a simple average of the Character Grade, Citizenship Grade, and Subject Matter Competence Grade. (See Fig. 14-1).

1. Which of these philosophies most nearly corresponds with your view of a final grade for a course?

2. What justification might a teacher use for adopting each one of the philosophies listed above?

14-14. Suppose that a student has a C test average, but is capable of doing at least B work. Further, this student turns in a homework paper every day; however, his work shows that little time or effort was expended in completing the assignment. In class this student is not a noisy discipline problem, but rather acts bored and clearly demonstrates the attitude that mathematics is of little interest to him.

If a single grade were to be assigned to this student, a teacher could conceivably justify a D, since homework and attitude in class may contribute a sufficient amount to warrant lowering a C test average to a D overall grade. If on the other hand the evaluation process is used, it may be possible to separate the subject matter competence from the other attributes described for this student.

1. What letter grade (A, B, C, D, or F) would you assign to this student for Character, Citizenship, and Subject Matter Competence?
2. Average the three grades you assigned in (1) to obtain a Total Growth and Performance Grade.
3. If a parent asked you to justify these grades, what would you say?

14-15. Grades for a six-week marking period have just been administered and Johnny X had a C as his mathematics grade on his report card. Shortly after Johnny had received his report card, he rushes up to you and says, "Thank you for giving me a C on my report card." Obviously Johnny did not have a clear understanding of the purpose of evaluation, since the grade is not a gift and thanks are not in order.

1. What might be the teacher's response to Johnny X?
2. Is it possible that this grade is higher than Johnny's test average would warrant? If so, was the purpose substantiated in light of Johnny's comment? Discuss.

14-16. Suppose that a teacher has constructed a test that was thought to be a fair sampling of a specified mathematical content. When the test was administered, it was observed that most of the students did not finish. When the test was scored, the results indicated very low achievement on the part of the students. Several procedures that might be followed are:

  (a) Record the test scores and tell the students you are disappointed in their work and then go on to the next unit.
  (b) Construct a shorter and easier test and administer it in the next class period.
  (c) Return the test and go over it in detail and reteach concepts that were most generally missed. Do not retest.
  (d) Same as (3) but retest at a later date.
  (e) Return the test and ask the students to complete the items they missed as an assignment. Then discuss the test and retest.

 1. Discuss each of the above procedures.
 2. What techniques can the teacher use to combat the apathy that results from failures or poor grades on a test?

14-17. Mathematics teachers pride themselves on being objective in their evaluation of student performance. One view of this, however, is that an objective test is just as subjective as a subjective test. For example, the weights or number of points assigned to each test item is a subjective decision. There are several other types of subjective decisions that are made by the teacher in constructing and grading an objective test.

1. See if you can identify at least four other subjective decisions in objective test construction.
2. Discuss methods which could be used to make these decisions in a fair manner.
3. Debate the question: Does the teacher construct objective tests to substantiate his subjective judgment of students?

14-18. In the evaluation process (Fig. 14-1), direct observation was listed as a method of assessing character traits. State what you would look for if you were observing your roommate and wished to assess cooperation, courtesy, dependability, industriousness, initiative, leadership, motivation, and self-control.

14-19. Teachers are often asked to keep anecdotal records on particular students. Choose some high school student that you don't know and, by observing his behavior, make a case study of him. What inferences would you make about his character and citizenship?

14-20. For a practical classroom guide on how to stimulate and evaluate positive attitudes toward learning, see Mager (1968).

14-21. For a description of the basic principles of evaluation read Hartung (1961). This article defines evaluation and then leads the reader through steps in the evaluation process such as formulating objectives, selecting test situations, recording and analyzing data, and determining changes.

ADDITIONAL SOURCES

Mager, Robert F. *Developing Attitude Toward Learning*. Palo Alto, Calif.: Fearon Publishers, 1968.

Hartung, Maurice L. "Basic Principles of Evaluation," *Evaluation in Mathematics*. Washington, D.C.: National Council of Teachers of Mathematics, 1961, pp. 21–42.

Chapter 15

Teaching as a Profession

Many critical problems face education today, just as many problems confront our society as a whole. The relationships between these two sets of problems is substantial and studies have shown that inadequate education is closely related to such social conditions as unemployment, delinquency, and poverty. Problems which imply such social conditions are the inadequate supply of well-trained teachers, the increasing rate of dropouts in the inner-city schools, inadequacy of teacher pay, overcrowded classrooms and poorly designed or outdated curricular materials. These and many other related problems should be of concern to every teacher. In order to classify teaching as a profession, it is necessary for us to make the solution to such problems our central concern. This implies that professionals in teaching must be vitally concerned with the education of each individual and work effectively toward that end.

One index of how professional you are can be obtained by examining the relationships you have established with your students, fellow teachers, and administration. A second indicator is the extent to which you have prepared and continue your preparation for the teaching profession. Rather than discuss ways in which you can be more professional, the remainder of this introduction will ask a series of questions relating to teaching as a profession. This list is neither exclusive nor exhaustive, but rather should serve as a point of departure for a self-evaluation on the question of how professional you are.

IN THE CLASSROOM

Do I treat each student as an individual?

Do I utilize available information such as ability test scores or personality traits of students in my instruction?

Do I present lessons in a variety of ways to meet individual needs?

Do I evaluate the work of each student in a fair and equitable manner?

Do I provide for sufficient student participation in my instruction?

Do I encourage my students to think?

Do I respect the rights and privileges of students?

Am I concerned about the problems, both personal and academic, of my students?

Am I aware of resources that are available to me in helping students?

Do I point out resources that are available to students for helping themselves?

Am I a warm, friendly person in the classroom?

Do I refrain from actions that would embarrass students?

Do I make mathematics meaningful to the students?

IN THE SCHOOL

Do I seek advice from my colleagues?

Do I share my successful techniques or unsuccessful procedures with other teachers?

Do I commend other teachers for their accomplishments?

Do I utilize other teachers' skills in attempting to resolve instructional problems?

Do I refrain from criticizing a teacher when students or other teachers are present?

Do I refrain from blaming other teachers for my instructional problems?

Do I work effectively with my colleagues in attempting to solve educational problems?

Do I volunteer to help other teachers when they need assistance?

Am I pleasant and friendly with other teachers?

Do I refrain from malicious gossip about students when I am with other teachers?

Do I show other teachers the need for and relevance of mathematics instruction?

Do I work within the policies and decisions of the school administration?

In effecting change or registering complaints, do I begin with the administrator next above me?

Do I offer constructive criticism on school matters upon request?

Do I refrain from criticizing the school administration in public?

Do I honor contractual commitments?

Do I comply with the rules established for operation of the school?

Am I the type of individual with whom administrators can be effective?

IN THE PROFESSION

Do I maintain professional competence by in-service course-work in mathematics or mathematics education?

Do I regularly read professional journals which address themselves to problems of education?

Do I support professional organizations at the local, state, and national level?

Do I seek new and better methods of presenting materials?

Do I encourage small study groups to form and discuss problems of mathematics education?

Do I continue my own education through self-study?

Do I encourage other competent individuals to enter the teaching profession?

Am I willing to expend sufficient time for planning stimulating lessons?

Do I feel that teaching is a worthwhile profession?

Do I accept professional criticism and then modify my behavior accordingly?

Am I professional in my appearance?

The above list of questions is only a beginning to the assessment of how professional teachers are. These questions have all been phrased so that a "yes" answer would indicate a higher degree of professional attributes than a "no" answer. There are, however, a continuum of values between an absolute yes and an absolute no for these questions. It should also be remembered that these questions apply just as readily to experienced teachers as they do to the novice. Through experience, our responses to a list of questions of this sort will change. It is hoped that this change is in the positive direction.

EXERCISES

15-1.   As stated in the textbook, the proposed list of questions was not by any means exhaustive. In fact, only a few of these questions referred explicitly to mathematics.

1. For each category, construct several additional questions that are specifically applicable to mathematics teachers.
2. Augment the list of questions in the introduction with those you have proposed above, and then respond to each question. If you have never taught before, you should form an opinion about how you will feel when you are teaching.
3. Which of the questions do you feel contribute most to the teacher as a professional?
4. Which of the questions do you feel contribute least?

15-2. One of the ways in which teachers can keep up with new developments in teaching is by belonging to professional organizations and reading the professional journals of these organizations. There are a variety of such organizations which are beneficial to teachers in general and mathematics teachers in particular. To be sure, the services rendered and the journals published are applicable to teachers at different levels and areas of instruction.

1. For each organization below determine
   (a) The names of its various publications
   (b) The cost of active membership
   (c) Its services to members
   (d) Its value to mathematics teachers

   American Association for the Advancement of Science
   American Federation of Teachers
   Central Association of Science and Mathematics Teachers
   Local Education Association
   Mathematical Association of America
   National Council of Teachers of Mathematics
   National Education Association
   State Education Association
2. Suppose that as a first-year teacher you have budgeted $35 for dues to professional organizations. To which organizations would you belong and why?

15-3. One view of a philosophy of education is as a statement of idealistic general principles which are to be accomplished by education. Some of these principles might be that (1) education should prepare each individual to function as a responsible citizen; (2) education should serve to perpetuate the good in society and eliminate the bad; or (3) education should function as a transmitter of knowledge. Although these are worthy goals, they do not provide any plans for implementation nor can they be evaluated by observing the behaviors of teachers or students.

A second view of a philosophy of education is more personal and provides a set of principles that will govern the behavior of a teacher in varying educational situations. This view implies that each teacher would have his own unique philosophy of education which is reflected in his teaching. A portion of the philosophy of two teachers relating to treatment of individual differences follows:

Teacher A: I believe there are individual differences among students and to cope with them I give A's, B's, C's, D's, and F's.

Teacher B: To cope with individual differences I let each youngster work through the book at his own rate and I provide individual instruction as necessary.

1. Discuss each of these views and the effectiveness of the stated procedures in dealing with individual differences.
2. What is your own view of individual differences and how they might be handled?

15-4.   In the last exercise we examined a minute portion of a philosophy of education. Note that Teachers A and B were characterized by the manner in which they treated students. If we listen only to words, there are a great number of pseudophilosophies. For example, a teacher may say, if pressed, that homework assignments should not be too long, should reflect varying concepts, should be at different levels for different ability students, should review previously learned concepts and skills, and should only be assigned for properly developed concepts. We cannot, however, accept this as a part of the teacher's philosophy of education until we have observed his practices in the classroom over an extended period of time. Given below are examples of the types of assignments given by various teachers.

Teacher A: Each day he assigns the odd problems over the developed material.

Teacher B: The students work all problems in the textbook.

Teacher C: Each day an assignment of four or five problems over a variety of previously developed concepts is given.

Teacher D: After finishing each lesson, he says, "Oh yes, you need an assignment. Try 5, 7; 8 looks interesting; so do 12 and 15."

Teacher E: Each assignment contains one or two exercises dealing with each concept or skill developed that day.

1. What is the real philosophy relating to homework for each teacher described above? (Note that "real philosophy" is described by behaviors of teachers rather than words.)
2. Rank these teachers on this one aspect of instruction from good to bad.
3. Discuss the effects of each procedure on teaching as a profession.

15-5. A philosophy of education can be construed as a code of ethics which implies how teachers will react to varying problems in the educational setting. As such, it cannot be written completely because of the multitude of situations which confront teachers. For each of the conditions listed below, state your view or feelings pertaining thereto and specify the behavior that would reflect these views. The behaviors, if practiced, would in a sense determine a degree of professionalism for these particular situations.

(a) The importance of mathematics.

(b) Keeping informed about new developments in mathematics education.

(c) The responsibilities of teachers to parents.

(d) Corporal punishment of students.

(e) Making mathematics interesting.

(f) General mathematics.

(g) Teacher strikes.

(h) Teaching children of a race other than your own.

15-6. A method which can be used to gain evidence relating to the effectiveness of your teaching and the learning experiences you provide students is to invite evaluation from students. If you can obtain honest responses from your students, this can be a valuable source of data for you as a teacher. When using student evaluations of this sort, it must be remembered that students are experts at telling us what we want to hear; hence it is essential that the directions clearly state that the results are anonymous and solely for the benefit of improving instruction. Further, students should be urged to be completely honest.

A questionnaire of this type may provide information on instructional techniques, clarity of instruction, personality traits of the teacher, the textbook, assignments, testing techniques, if learning occurred, or the content of the course.

1. Identify several other areas in which student evaluation of teaching and learning would be beneficial.
2. Construct several items which might be given to students to evaluate instruction. For a list of illustrative items for teacher evaluation, see Simpson (1962).

15-7. It is interesting to note the type of student most often discussed by teachers. Many times discussion in the teacher's lounge is centered around the latest episode of one of the school's troublemakers. To be sure, these can be entertaining anecdotes but they seldom go far enough to examine the underlying causes of the behavior or to provide constructive suggestions which, if implemented, might eliminate future incidents.

1. If several teachers are relating the latest on Fred, a low achieving, unmotivated troublemaker, which of the questions asked in the beginning of this chapter are being answered in a negative way?

2. If these teachers went on in the discussion to emphasize reasons why Fred might behave in this fashion and—more important—identify conditions and procedures that they could use to improve Fred's behavior and desire to learn, they would be acting in a more professional manner. What are some causes that might be responsible for Fred's behavior?

3. In the school setting there are several ways to determine if the causes you identified above actually exist. For example, past records of achievement and aptitude are available, some information would be available on his home background, and perhaps some data would be available on his previous behavior. Where might the teachers gather this data? What other information might be available to the teachers?

15-8. As early as possible, the new teacher should become familiar with facilities of the school. In the last exercise mention was made of academic and personal records of the students. This is one facility that is available in each school. To effectively use this information, it is essential that the teacher know.

(a) What information is available.

(b) Where the information is on file.

(c) Who is in charge of the facility.

(d) How to use these resources.

There are a variety of other facilities that are available to some extent in each school. For example, each school would have some duplicating or copying equipment. The extent of this equipment, procedures for its use, and the like can have a substantial influence on the instructional process.

1. Describe how the existence of duplicating facilities can influence your classroom instruction.

Other facilities or services that may be available to teachers are audio-visual equipment, library, health center, supplies, custodial services, and counseling center.

2. How might each of these be used to provide a better educational program in the school?

3. Can you identify any other services which might be available to teachers or students?

15-9. There are a variety of professional issues centered around securing and terminating a teaching position. In seeking a teaching position, it is the responsibility of the teacher to present an accurate description of himself. This is not the time for either boast or modesty; rather, it is the time to be factual in representing your background, attainments, capabilities, and aspirations. Characteristics that are of interest to an employer include scholastic achievement, scholastic honors received, personal attributes, professional outlook, qualities expressed by your references, and interests or hobbies not directly related to your teaching.

1. Write a one-page resume which reflects these characteristics and which you might use to describe yourself. What other qualities do you believe should be included?

In seeking a position, it is also your responsibility to evaluate the school to which you are applying. Topics of interest might include characteristics of the student population which the school services, manners in which discipline problems are handled, facilities available to students and teachers, salary schedule, and academic freedom of teachers.

2. Prepare a list of questions you might ask a representative of a school during a job interview. Remember that you are probably being evaluated on the manner in which you ask these questions.

15-10. Not only does the teacher have a responsibility to the administration but there is also responsibility of the administration to the teacher. Some general questions that relate to the responsibility of an administration to teachers follow:

(a) Does the administration regard teachers as professionals?

(b) Does the administration provide effective channels of communication between teachers and administrators?

(c) Does the administration help teachers when a student is a severe discipline problem?

(d) Does the administration stimulate curriculum reform and implementation?

(e) Does the administration provide opportunities for teacher improvement through meaningful in-service meetings?

(f) Does the administration permit teachers to requisition teaching aids or supplies when these are within the school budget?

There are many more questions which might be asked but these give an indication of several administrative decisions which are influential to the teaching profession.

1. Each of the above questions should be answered yes for good professional relations between administration and teachers. The real questions are "how?" and "to what extent?" are these conditions implemented. Discuss each question above with regard to the possible implementation of the conditions in a school.

2. All of the above questions were general in nature. Write a list of questions relating specifically to the administrator's responsibility to mathematics teachers or the mathematics program. It may be simpler if you phrase the questions in terms of the department chairman's responsibility.

SUGGESTED ACTIVITIES

15-11. The National Education Association proposed a revised code of ethics for educators in March 1968 and adopted this code in July 1968. This code specifies the commitment of teachers to the student, public, and profession. Careful study of this code should provide additional questions that teachers ask of themselves. Read this code of ethics which is reprinted in *NEA Journal* (1968). (Some state education associations provide reprints of this code upon request.)

15-12. Complete a list which identifies personnel (principal, guidance counselor, librarian, custodian, etc.); routines (tardiness, absences, field trips, accidents, illness, etc.); and facilities (see Exercise 15-8) for the school in which you teach.

15-13. To maintain a high level of professionalism, the teacher should be aware of new trends and curriculum projects in mathematics. These should not be restricted to the particular grade level of the teacher but rather should reflect broad coverage of the school mathematics program. To gain a better perspective of the overall mathematics program, read Davis (1967).

15-14. A student journal with which secondary school mathematics teachers should be acquainted is *The Mathematics Student Journal*, published by the National Council of Teachers of Mathematics. Read several back issues of this journal. How might this journal be used to improve instruction in secondary school mathematics?

15-15. Almost all colleges maintain a placement office, and one of the services rendered by this office is to maintain credentials for students and provide leads on prospective positions. Determine what is necessary for you to have your credentials maintained in the placement office, and file the necessary forms.

15-16. A question often raised is the certification requirements for teachers in the various states. It is always possible to obtain a statement of the most recent certification requirements for a state or locality by writing directly to the Teacher Education and Certification Department for the state or locality. Another source which provides a compilation of these requirements is Stinnett (1970).

15-17. Use a good college dictionary to find the definition of a profession and the definition of a vocation. Which of these terms better describes teaching?

ADDITIONAL SOURCES

"Code of Ethics of the Education Profession," *NEA Journal*, March 1968, pp. 42–43.

Davis, Robert B. *The Changing Curriculum: Mathematics*. Association for Supervision and Curriculum Development, NEA, 1967.

Simpson, Roy H., and Jerome M. Seidman, *Student Evaluation of Teaching and Learning*. American Association of Colleges for Teacher Education, 1962.

Stinnett, T. M., and Geraldine E. Pershing. *A Manual on Certification Requirements for School Personnel in the United States.* Washington, D.C.: National Education Association, 1970.

PART II

INTRODUCTION

The remaining chapters of this book deal with specific subjects or mathematics at a particular grade level. As in the previous part of the book, each chapter begins with a relatively brief introduction followed by a variety of exercises. This reflects the views of the authors that a beginning student of mathematics teaching can derive little from merely reading a methods book since he does not have the necessary concrete experience that comes from classroom teaching. It is felt that since the inexperienced person lacks this background, it must be provided. Our way of trying to provide concrete experiences is to have the student encounter many specific situations and gain, little by little, a kind of "secondhand" teaching experience. It does not replace classroom experience or working under the guidance and direction of a master teacher. It is hoped, however, that exposure to examples of various types will enable the student to begin putting pieces together and acquiring teaching methods and strategies that will generalize to new situations and other subject matter.

When examining the remaining chapters, it may seem that the material in any specific chapter does not cover the subject of that chapter deeply enough or comprehensively enough. This is indeed true, and results from the commitment to very specific exercises. It is nearly impossible to cover adequately all aspects of the teaching of a topic. The exercises chosen for any chapter are not intended to give a broad view or even a balanced coverage of the subject. They were selected as being important because of the ideas and suggestions that they contained and which could generate improvement in the teaching of that subject matter.

Chapter 16

Problems in Teaching Seventh- and Eighth-Grade Mathematics

The story of mathematics instruction in the seventh and eighth grades is one of the more fascinating and perplexing episodes in American mathematical education. Spaced between the rather clear-cut mathematics programs of the elementary school and the high school, these two grades are something of a mathematical no-man's land. The mathematics programs of these grades have not been free to establish an identity of their own. More often they reflect some balance of the pressures of getting the student ready for some later course or providing remedial instruction in what he has already encountered.

SEVENTH- AND EIGHTH-GRADE MATHEMATICS CURRICULUM

The mathematics curriculum of the seventh and eighth grades cannot be discussed without the perspective of some history of education in the United States. Secondary schools were not always free nor attended by almost all children as is the practice today. During the latter part of the nineteenth century, most people in the United States attended school for only a few years, and then they left school to go to work. A very small number continued their schooling at their own expense in preparation for college. The curriculum in the common school (public elementary school) was intended to impart basic literacy, and the mathematics consisted mainly of basic rules of computation and mensuration formulas. The mathematics studied by those who prepared for college was determined by college entrance requirements.[1]

---

[1] It is interesting to note the way in which mathematical subjects are compartmentalized, and the order in which they are studied in high schools today. It corresponds exactly to the order in which colleges historically abandoned the teaching of these topics and pushed them down into the high school by requiring them for admission.

Due to many social and economic factors too extensive to be discussed here, more years of free schooling were made possible, and eventually compulsory school attendance laws were passed. By the turn of the century, more and more students remained in school through what is now the seventh and eighth grades. For a majority of students these became the terminal grades of formal education, while those preparing for college remained in high school for four more years before entering higher education. Consequently the mathematics curriculum of the seventh and eighth grades was shaped by those aspects of the subject that would be most practical and useful in the everyday life of the student when he left school. Aside from the review and extension upward of the basic arithmetic found in the elementary school, the major emphasis was devoted to business and social applications of mathematics. Mathematical problems were studied that focused on situations the student would soon encounter in banking, insurance, taxes, handling money, farming, and shopkeeping.

The practice of teaching more social and business applications and less mathematics might not have persisted as long as it did had it not been cemented into the curriculum by a crisis in the goals of teaching mathematics that occurred at about the same time. The study of mathematics was being justified on the basis of mental discipline; that mathematics was especially suited to developing certain reasoning faculties in the mind. It was believed that mathematics trained the general powers of reasoning so well that they would be transferred and used in various contexts even outside mathematics. Studies by psychologists, notably Edward Thorndike, found no evidence of transfer of a general ability from one learned task to another task requiring the same faculty unless some very special and nebulous conditions were present. As a consequence of these findings, the already dying theory of faculty psychology was dealt a crushing blow. In the resulting scramble to defend the teaching of mathematics, educators settled upon the safer utilitarian benefits as the main justification for the study of mathematics. Although there were changes and determined efforts to improve the mathematics offered in these two grades during the first half of this century, it remained until the curriculum reform movements of the late 1950's to finally dislodge the emphasis on social arithmetic.

The "revolution" in school mathematics that began in the 1950's and continued into the next decade brought many fundamental changes to the mathematics curriculum. It was no accident that many of the programs in mathematics dealt with the content in the junior high school, for this was the area where most revision was needed. At a time when a large proportion of students of high school age were completing high school, seventh-and eighth-grade pupils were studying how to budget for a family, buy life insurance, fill out income tax returns, and invest in the stock market. Needless to say, these activities were not uppermost in the minds of students reaching adolescence, students who were several years away from the time when they would be able to use these ideas. The decision of the reformers was to return to the study of mathematics for its own sake and deemphasize social and business applications.

Present programs in seventh and eighth grades reflect two major changes: (1) the addition of new topics and a different treatment of familiar content, and (2) a new spirit that the study of mathematics is intrinsically satisfying to students in the same way that it is to mathematicians. Courses now include sets, logic, finite mathematical systems, numeration systems, equations and inequalities, and nonmetric geometry. Familiar material like percent, ratio and proportion, fractions, decimals, measurement, and negative numbers receive new and exciting treatments. As a result of the second change, emphasis has been placed on the logical structure of mathematics and a more deductive approach to mathematical understanding. While this trend has been interesting and exciting for teachers, it has not been without its concerned critics who feel that this is the wrong approach for adolescents. The critics perform an important function, since they insure that teaching practices and goals are continually reexamined. In this way mathematics programs undergo constant evaluation and improvement and are not allowed to stagnate.

THE PURPOSE OF A MATHEMATICS PROGRAM IN GRADES SEVEN AND EIGHT

If a consensus could be reached as to the intent of a mathematics program in seventh and eighth grades, it would probably be twofold: (1) an extension and deeper understanding of the mathematics already learned, and (2) preliminary exploration and intuitive investigations in broad areas across mathematics. Unfortunately, these two worthy aims are too often interpreted to mean (1) remedial teaching of the arithmetic of elementary school, and (2) adherence to some fixed sequence of content imagined to be essential to "get the student ready for algebra." While some remedial instruction is necessary, it does not replace the kind of instruction that strives to give a broader view or for attainment of a higher level of comprehension.

The belief that the seventh- and eighth-grade mathematics programs are intended to get the students ready for algebra is a particularly misguided one. The content and purpose of every mathematics course must stand on its own merits as worthy of learning and enjoyable to study even if no more mathematics courses are taken. In addition, most students possess all the subject-matter prerequisites necessary to begin the study of algebra; what most of them lack is the mental development and cognitive maturity required for the abstractions of algebra. Mathematics programs for seventh- and eighth-grade students can be devised that are satisfying and worth learning in themselves, provided we do not forget the nature of the students in these grades.

Students in the 12-15 age range are in a period of rapid and turbulent change. They are trying to assert their independence at a time when they are still dependent upon their parents. They are challenging and resisting all forms of authority, dogma, and restrictive rules surrounding their lives. They seek out opportunities to explore, to engage in new experiences, and to challenge accepted assumptions and values in an effort to test themselves and to find out who they are. Most of all, they want to be free to control their own actions and not be the pawns of other people.

A learner in a challenging and independent frame of mind can soon become frustrated and rebellious in a mathematics class. When mathematics is presented as a finished product in which all the questions have clear-cut answers that can be backed up by authority, the student always loses the battle when he ventures a challenge. Each process or principle presented to him to be learned is beyond challenge because it is "true," and because the teacher can state some reason, some authority, that repulses his challenge. The one thing left to challenge or question is which of several ways of doing the problem is better or the all too common rejoinder, "Why do we have to learn this stuff?" Since the student cannot challenge why some fact is true, he must challenge the reason why he should be made to learn it.

A mathematics program for these years should direct student energy toward exploration and questioning in mathematics. He should be encouraged to challenge why we divide fractions the way we do, why a negative times a negative is a positive, why exponents are sometimes added and sometimes multiplied. He should be given the opportunity to explore what would happen if we used different units of measurement; if when adding fractions we added the numerators and denominators; if we allowed division by zero. He should be allowed to use concrete objects, make guesses and conjectures, depend upon his intuition, and engage in inductive activities. Rather than resorting to the authority of the theory and deduction to tell him he is wrong or he is right, he needs to be asked, "Can you show me why you think this is true?" In later mathematics courses the student will be expected to develop proficiency in the specialized skills of algebra and to be able to reproduce the organized knowledge of geometry. The two beginning years of the junior high school is the time for the student to experiment and explore so that a foundation of mathematical experience and maturity is laid.

16-1. It was stated in the Introduction that many familiar topics have received a more rigorous treatment in the newer programs in mathematics. An excellent example is the study of positive and negative numbers. This new treatment is illustrated in the two sample lesson plans found in Appendix D.

1. Review these two lesson plans that develop addition of integers, and notice the dependence of the explanations on the structure of mathematics.
2. Using the same kind of dependence upon the properties of operations used for addition, write an instructional sequence to develop the multiplication of:
   (a) A positive times a positive
   (b) A positive times a negative
   (c) A negative times a positive
   (d) A negative times a negative
3. See Suggested Activity 16-11.

16-2. Review Exercise 11-5. In that exercise you were asked to devise a competitive game that would provide drill on adding integers. A teacher would also want the students to be able to multiply integers quickly. Drill on multiplying integers would be appropriate after the development and assimilation referred to in the previous exercise is completed.

1. Devise a competitive game that could be used to drill students on multiplication of integers.
2. Devise a competitive game that would drill the students on both addition and multiplication of integers.

16-3. Part of the content of grades 7 and 8 requires the development of a deeper understanding of the processes of arithmetic. Interest often can be stirred by considering new and unusual algorithms for the familiar arithmetic processes.

For example, a student may say, "My father said you can multiply a number by 25 if you increase it by adding two zeros and divide by 4. It seems to work out. Why does it work?"

Instead of jumping on the student for saying that adding two zeros to the number increases it, it is a good opportunity to have the student try some examples and help them to derive the mathematical principle:

$$N \cdot 25 = \frac{N \cdot 100}{4}$$

Find the mathematical principles to explain why these algorithms work.

1. To do the problem $\frac{2}{3} \div \frac{1}{2}$, find the least common denominator and rewrite the problem as $\frac{4}{6} \div \frac{3}{6}$. Then the answer is the first numerator divided by the second, i.e., $4/3$.

2. Three is a factor of a number if three is a factor of the sum of its digits. Three is a factor of 291, since $2 + 9 + 1 = 12$ has three as a factor.

3. To multiply a number like 5243 by 11, the last digit of the product will be 3, the next to last 7 (from $3 + 4$), the next 6 (from $4 + 2$), the next 7 (from $2 + 5$), and the first is simple 5. Hence $(11)(5243) = 57673$.

16-4. Gaining a deeper understanding of arithmetic implies learning not only "how to do a procedure" but also why it works. You may be familiar with the procedure of checking a computation by "casting out nines." Example:

$$
\begin{array}{rll}
384 & \text{multiplicand} & \rightarrow 6 \\
47 & \text{multiplier} & \rightarrow 2 \\
\hline
18{,}048 & \text{product} & \rightarrow 3
\end{array}
$$

The digits in the multiplicand are added, and the multiples of nine are "cast out" leaving the remainder 6, to be written at the right. The same procedure is repeated for the multiplier and the product with the results, 2 and 3, respectively. Six is multiplied by 2, and the multiples of nine are cast out, leaving the remainder, 3. Since this remainder equals the remainder of the product, the computation "checks."

1. What is the divisibility rule for determining if a number is divisible by nine? (If you don't know look it up in a seventh- or eighth-grade math book.)
2. Where does the divisibility rule for nine enter into this checking procedure?
3. Where does mod 9 arithmetic enter into the procedure?
4. If the computation checks by casting out nines, the answer may still be in error. Explain why.
5. Suppose we were doing this multiplication problem in a base other than 10, such as base 9. How would you do the checking procedure? What divisibility rule and what modular arithmetic would be involved under these conditions.

16-5. The teacher is often faced with some very hard content questions to explain, even at the seventh- and eighth-grade level. How would you help the student answer the following queries?

1. Isn't mod 5 arithmetic just like base 5?
2. What would happen if we did divide by zero?
3. Why isn't 7 a factor of 12; doesn't $7 \cdot \dfrac{12}{7}$ equal 12?
4. Why isn't 1 a prime number?
5. Why isn't a straight angle considered an angle in our definition?
6. You said $|a| = -a$, but how can the absolute value of a number be negative?
7. I wrote $\pi = \dfrac{22}{7}$ on my paper, and you marked it out. Why?

16-6. The junior high school has traditionally been viewed as a common school, a democratic institution that serves all students regardless of their intellectual abilities and vocational interests. Pride is expressed in the fact that in the United States no early selection is made that determines the vocational destiny or limits the academic future of the students. Presumably the students are free to develop socially in their relations with other pupils of different educational interests and abilities.

A typical practice in junior high school is to group students homogeneously by ability. There are arguments on both sides of this question.

1. List as many advantages of homogeneous grouping as you can find.
2. List as many advantages of heterogeneous grouping as you can find.
3. Take a position with respect to one of the grouping practices, and defend your position in a debate with a classmate who takes the opposite view.
4. Is ability grouping consistent with the concept of a common school?
5. Does ability grouping produce a class of students who have the same intellectual capabilities?
6. How might a junior high school gain some empirical evidence that could help decide the method of grouping best suited to its students and program?

16-7. In the introduction to this chapter it was suggested that the mathematics program for the grades 7 and 8 should be unique. It should have an identity and be noticeably different from the mathematics of the elementary school and of the other four years of high school. One difference would be less emphasis on amassing organized knowledge and perfecting skills, and less concentration on following a sequence dictated by the structure of mathematics. Above all, intuition, induction, and operations with concrete objects would be stressed as much as deduction and logical operations. The rationale for this view is based on four main arguments:

(a) Later courses in high school rely on deduction and abstract thinking which can be better understood if a foundation of inductive experiences and manipulative activities with concrete objects has already been established.

(b) More time can be devoted to attaining process and affective goals of mathematics than will be available in later courses where great amounts of new knowledge must be acquired in the short space of a year.

(c) Younger students are more flexible, more questioning, more restless, and more inclined to explore. They need and learn better from a more active environment.

(d) These two grades are the perfect years since the skills and knowledge necessary to undertake such a program have already been encountered in the elementary school.

Construct an argument against the kind of seventh- and eighth-grade mathematics proposed in this chapter. Try your argument on a classmate.

16-8. Jean Piaget, a developmental psychologist, has studied the way children learn and grow mentally. He has postulated that the mental development of children progresses through identifiable stages. He has described these stages and identified the approximate chronological age of a child entering these stages. Two of the stages relevant to students of junior high school age are summarized below.

Concrete Operations. (7-11).[2] A child is able to logically operate on ideas in his mind provided the ideas refer to real objects that can be known to the senses. The child can imagine how to work with familiar physical objects without actually moving them, but he cannot adequately operate with abstract ideas.

Formal Operations. (11-15). The child begins to develop the capacity for abstract thought using logical arguments rather than arguments based upon imagining physical objects and relationships. He is no longer confined to what is real. He can consider a hypothesis which may or may not be true and work out what would logically follow if it were true.

1. Curriculum reform movements of the 1950's and 1960's placed more emphasis on the logical structure of mathematics and a more deductive approach to mathematics. Does this approach require the kind of mental maturity found in the concrete operations stage or the level of mental maturity indicative of the formal operations stage?
2. In a seventh- or eighth-grade class is it possible that some students will be in one stage and other students in another?
3. What kind of mathematics program seems to be needed for a child whose mental growth is in the concrete operations stage?

---

[2] The lower age indicates when the brightest students might attain that level and the higher number indicates the age of slower students entering that stage. In the case of formal operations, some children may never attain this level of cognitive growth.

16-9. Algebra has become rather firmly established in the ninth grade for most students. Recent changes have seen negative numbers moved down, sometimes several grades. The same is true of using variables such as x and $\square$. In some cases, these ideas are encountered in elementary school. Considering these developments, discuss these questions.

1. Does a beginning seventh-grade student of average ability and achievement in elementary school arithmetic have all the prerequisite knowledge in mathematics needed to begin the study of Algebra I?

2. Why isn't algebra usually taught to students beginning in the seventh grade?

3. In some schools algebra is taught to an elite group of students in the eighth grade. Why can't the other students take algebra rather than the usual eighth-grade course? Many will take algebra in the ninth-grade and do well.

4. Why are some students culled out and never encouraged to take algebra?

5. Why are some students able to do good work in a general mathematics course but are unable to handle algebra?

6. Are mathematics courses such as algebra, geometry, and trigonometry different from the mathematics found in grades 7 and 8 and general mathematics? If your answer is yes, how are these two kinds of mathematics different? If your answer is no, what are the factors that cause the discrepancies cited in questions 1 through 5?

16-10. Bruner proposes that the learning of a topic should progress through three stages of development. As teaching begins, the learner should move from active manipulation of objects (enactive mode), to a pictorial or mental image stage (ikonic) and then on to a symbolic representation and organization of the topic (symbolic). The meshing of this view with the stages of Piaget listed in Exercise 16-8 has many implications for the learning activities of the junior high school. Instruction designed for the attainment of various objectives should progress from activities which permit the students to manipulate concrete objects to activities in which the *student* draws pictures or schematic diagrams and finally to activities which are more abstract and symbolic. It is unfortunate that in much instruction the first two stages are omitted and instruction is provided in only the symbolic mode. [For further information on the three stages listed above, see Bruner (1966).]

Suppose that one topic in the junior high school mathematics program is solution of simple linear equations. Materials which permit manipulation with concrete objects for this topic might include blocks, colored rods, and balances and weights.

1. How might each of these materials be used to provide experiences with concrete objects for teaching the solution of linear equations?
2. Design ikonic stage teaching activities for this topic.
3. Relate the stages defined above to the various modes of instruction described in Chapter 8, i.e., which of the modes would be used predominantly in each stage?

SUGGESTED ACTIVITIES

16-11. The advisibility of having several instructional strategies for the same topic has already been discussed in Chapter 6. Read the excellent illustration of instructional strategies at different levels for the multiplication of negative numbers found in Johnson (1967) p. 34–35.

16-12. In the Introduction it was mentioned that the newer mathematics programs of the late 1950's and 1960's have not been without their critics. This is perhaps an understatement. There has been an increasing chorus of voices in recent years rallying to the side of caution and retreat from the so-called "new math." Of course, many of these people are looking back with the wisdom of hindsight. Perhaps some have over-reacted to the disillusionment they feel as a result of the discrepancy between present practices and their earlier ideals. One who cannot be classed as a Johnny-come-lately critic, however, is Dr. Morris Kline. He has written many articles which question the wisdom of recent curriculum reforms. Read the article by Kline (1966) listed in the Additional Sources.

16-13. The work of Jean Piaget is becoming more and more prominent in explaining how children learn mathematics. Berlyne (1965) describes the stages of mental development identified by Piaget and summarizes his work. Consult this source for a fuller description of the nature and implications of Piaget's work.

ADDITIONAL SOURCES

Berlyne, D. E. "Recent Developments in Piaget's Work," in R. A. Anderson and D. P. Ausubel, *Readings in the Psychology of Cognition.* New York: Holt, Rinehart and Winston, Inc. 1965.

Bruner, Jerome. *Towards a Theory of Instruction.* Belknap Press of Harvard University, 1966.

Johnson, Donovan, and Gerald Rising. *Guidelines for Teaching Mathematics.* Belmont, Calif.: Wadsworth Publishing Company Inc., 1967.

Kline, Morris. "A Proposal for the High School Mathematics Curriculum," *Mathematics Teacher*, 59 (April 1966), pp. 322–330.

Chapter 17

Problems in Teaching General Mathematics

The introduction to the chapter on junior high school mathematics discussed the influence of free education, mass education, and compulsory school attendance upon the mathematics curriculum. This same phenomenon has been largely responsible for the advent of general mathematics.

Free and compulsory education increased the number and changed the nature of the student population attending schools beyond the six years of elementary school. Along with the students who would continue into high school in preparation for college were many other students who would leave the secondary school to enter a vocation. During the time when most students who were not preparing for college would leave school after eight years, the old curriculum of six years of arithmetic, two years of more arithmetic with many social applications, and then four years of college preparatory mathematics, beginning with algebra, survived with few additions and changes. However, the number of students remaining in school beyond eight years increased, as did the length of time they remained in school. With this increasing school population it soon became clear that many students were not interested or were unable to pursue the mathematics being taught to prepare students for college entrance. From this problem arose the practice of establishing a separate track of special mathematics courses called "general mathematics" as alternatives to the usual college preparatory mathematics.

The term *general mathematics* has several meanings not necessarily distinct. One use of the term is to denote a fused course in mathematics that integrates topics from various branches of mathematics such as algebra, geometry, trigonometry, statistics, and number theory. Another meaning is to denote a course that emphasizes the mathematics needed in the general education and daily life of a citizen. We use the term here to refer to the mathematics offered as an alternative to the courses in algebra, geometry, or trigonometry, to include topics from courses that might be called "consumer mathematics," "business mathematics," or "practical mathematics," as well as topics from the various branches of mathematics.

Perhaps no area of mathematics teaching presents more challenges than courses in general mathematics. Certainly the most difficult aspect of teaching general mathematics is the students found in these courses. Classes tend to be very heterogeneous, containing students who are very able and interested in mathematics as well as students who are poor readers, indifferent toward school, inclined to be discipline problems or to dislike mathematics, and many of whom are "slow learners." These are students most in need of inspired and creative teachers. The mathematical instruction of these students is as much or more important than that of their more docile and more able fellow students in algebra, geometry, and trigonometry. Rather than bemoaning the poor quality of the students in these classes we need to look for more effective ways of making progress with them.

There are sources available that offer many excellent suggestions for techniques to improve teaching in general mathematics. Several of these are listed at the end of this chapter. However, the fullest advantage cannot be made of these suggestions until some misconceptions and malpractices surrounding general mathematics are eliminated. In this chapter the main thrust is to identify some obstructions to effective general mathematics teaching and prepare the groundwork for reception of some reforms.

OBSTRUCTIONS TO EFFECTIVE GENERAL MATHEMATICS TEACHING

One malpractice is the assignment of the teaching load in mathematics departments. Staff with the most years of experience or most accomplished as teachers are assigned to teach the most mathematically competent students in the college preparatory courses. Students of intermediate ability are instructed by teachers that stand lower in the departmental "pecking order." The general mathematics classes are reserved for beginning teachers, uncertified teachers, and teachers whose major teaching field is not mathematics. In some departments it is the practice to have some instructors teach only classes in general mathematics rather than distributing the teaching load among all the teachers of the department.

The assignment practices of many mathematics departments reflect two basic misconceptions, (1) general mathematics students are less worthy of nurture and expert attention, and (2) less mathematical knowledge is required to teach general mathematics than college preparatory mathematics. Imagine a hospital where patients with headaches and hangnails are attended by the best physicians and specialists, while those who are seriously ill and need delicate operations requiring skill and expertise are remanded to a student nurse or intern. This corresponds to the situation found in many mathematics departments. The truly outstanding teachers are those who can make mathematics palatable and attainable for the reluctant students. Instead, the fashion is to take pride for outstanding teaching accomplishments with the student who would learn in spite of the teacher.

A second obstruction centers around the misconception that there is a certain amount of fixed content that must be learned. It is inconceivable that such a notion should arise when one knows the history and intent of courses in general mathematics in the high school. Yet this mistaken notion is assumed and used in making curricular decisions. It is manifested in at least three widely practiced forms: (1) we must cover a certain portion of the textbook, (2) the textbook is the curriculum, and (3) all students in a class must study basically the same material. Each of these judgments has been instrumental in contributing to malpractice in mathematics teaching.

In planning any course and making curriculum decisions, mathematics teachers should first study their students, for they are the ones who are to be benefited. More concern needs to be placed upon "uncovering topics" for the students, however long that may require, with less time spent worrying about coverage. The textbook is not sacred and should not be the sole determinant of what is taught in the classroom. Daily lessons that proceed page by page through the book as inevitably as Friday follows Thursday are poor substitutes for planned unit teaching using various supplementary resources and activities developed especially for the students. Textbook authors (present company included) are not the judge of what your class needs. They compile the material in a book, and they have faith that each teacher is wise enough to choose, select, adapt, ignore, or alter that material to fit their situations.

A third obstruction to effective general mathematics teaching is the lack of good materials and books for slow learners. Most materials for general mathematics require and emphasize verbal knowledge not unlike college preparatory mathematics. This is exactly the area in which general mathematics students are weakest and have experienced repeated failures. It seems that a much different approach is necessary to reach these students. Materials that build understanding from numerous concrete experiences, manipulative activities, and realistic application of mathematics would appeal to the strengths of these students. As long as verbal knowledge is the objective, such attempts as trying to teach computational skills in grade 9 that were not learned in the previous eight grades, or organizing courses around vocational interests, practical mathematics, consumer needs, or "easy algebra" seem doomed to failure.

The greatest obstacle is that general mathematics is held in low esteem by everyone. The school and the mathematics department consider such courses as an imposition to teach, not really academic in nature, and outside the real function of the mathematics department. A low estimate of general mathematics is also found among the students. A boy in ninth-grade general mathematics hears his friend who is taking algebra remark about what he is learning, and it sounds "so smart." He wishes he could put his friend in his place, but of course he is only in general math. The students in algebra and geometry look down on their fellow students, the dumb kids in general math. The people who go into mathematics teaching are usually students who came through college preparatory mathematics courses. They have not experienced the feelings of frustration encountered by students in general mathematics, only the intellectual snobbery practiced by the "smart" kids. General mathematics teaching could be improved if we as teachers had more respect for the content and students in these courses.

17-1. You are beginning the school year with a class of ninth-grade general mathematics students. The students generally have a poor record in mathematics and have negative attitudes toward mathematics. They are particularly careless and inaccurate with arithmetic computations. You are planning for the class, and you wonder how to begin the year.

The solution most often chosen in this situation is to start with an intensive study and review of computations with whole numbers, fractions, and decimals. This is material that they should learn, and the teacher believes he is acting in the best interests of the students by concentrating on the "basics." The teacher is extremely naive, however, if he thinks he will be successful where many other teachers before him have failed, since he will not be easing the factors that have contributed to poor achievement. This practice only succeeds in emphasizing the students' past failures, promoting more negative feelings toward mathematics learning, and alerting the students that this year will be a year of drudgery in mathematics.

Discuss the advantages and disadvantages of each of the following possible ways of starting the year in such a class.

(a) Start in the first chapter of their basic textbook.

(b) Administer an inventory test in arithmetic computation.

(c) Ask the students what they wish to study.

(d) Start with a unit on the uses of arithmetic.

(e) Start with a study of hobbies and vocations that use mathematics.

(f) Start with some novel mathematics new to the students, such as modular arithmetic.

17-2. General mathematics classes are not as good as they might be, because they have little prestige. One teacher's remedy for improving the image of the students in the course was to select for study a unit in algebra. The general mathematics students were given an Algebra I book to use. The students could carry their algebra books around and have them noticed. They could hold their heads high in company with their fellow students in the algebra course.

1. Which of the following practices would you recommend as likely to increase the prestige of the general mathematics course?

   (a) Provide students with slide rules to use and carry around with them. How might this help them want to learn about the slide rule?

   (b) Have the teachers with the reputations of being the smartest, ablest mathematics teachers teaching general mathematics.

   (c) Include topics in the course that students in algebra would not know about, such as calculating devices and probability.

   (d) Don't expect students to do homework, and don't hesitate to let them out of class when they want to do something else.

   (e) Have students make interesting objects or undertake projects in mathematics that can be displayed in the school as indicative of the work done in general mathematics.

2. Try to think of some other practices that might be used to increase the prestige of the general mathematics course.

17-3. A great deal could be done to eliminate the four obstructions mentioned in the introduction at the school and departmental level. It should be recognized that the teaching of general mathematics, as well as all mathematics courses, is the function and responsibility of the entire mathematics department and not just the province of one or two teachers. Thus, every teacher should take an active interest and share the responsibility for the instruction in every mathematics course.

One way in which teachers can cooperate in providing a better mathematical education for all students is to exchange classes occasionally for certain units to add some zest to the classes and variety to the teachers' instructional duties.

1. List some other ways that the teaching load in general mathematics could be spread among the mathematics staff to make sure that mathematics instruction is a shared cooperative effort of the department.
2. List some specific ways the departmental meeting could be used effectively to improve the teaching methods in all mathematics classes.
3. List some specific ways the department could work cooperatively to help overcome the lack of good materials for classes in general mathematics.
4. List some specific things the mathematics faculty could do that would increase the prestige and esteem of the students in general mathematics.

17-4. Many students in general mathematics have experienced little positive reinforcement in their work in mathematics. They have not been able to learn mathematics as well as their teachers would expect, and they have encountered years of continued frustration and failure. While failure cannot be eliminated and perhaps should not be, these students need to have the opportunity to experience some success.

Discuss the advantages and disadvantages of some of the following techniques of accenting student achievement.

(a) Give a quiz on material that you are certain they know well and almost all can get 100 percent correct.

(b) Take note of thoughtful comments, and commend good behavior or good work individually.

(c) Display good work on homework and tests by putting them on the bulletin board and praising the students' work in front of the class.

(d) Do not tell the student he is wrong when he gives an incorrect response; rather, ask him to explain how he arrived at his response.

(e) Give frequent short quizzes as a matter of course rather than longer tests, and play down tests and grades.

(f) Tell students that no one in the class can get an A, since if they could, they should be a more advanced class.

(g) Encourage students to express themselves as best they can without criticism or interruption, and ask them to explain problems to students who do not understand, even when it is easier for you to do it.

17-5. Students are classified as "slow learners" on the basis of their lack of ability to learn and retain verbal knowledge as measured by IQ tests, achievement tests, and school grades. We then attempt to instruct them through verbalization with words and symbols. A better avenue to mathematical understanding for these students is a radically different approach that involves using their hands with concrete objects and manipulative devices in structured laboratory situations.

Students are fascinated with adding machines, desk calculators, slide rules, and other computing devices.

1. How could the construction and use of an addition-type slide rule be used to motivate a unit on precision and accuracy in measurement and computation?
2. How could an adding machine or desk calculator be used to stress estimation, round-off errors, and placement of the decimal point in computation?
3. How could an adding machine be used to facilitate the learning of the standard algorithms for adding, subtracting, multiplying, and dividing?
4. How could an adding machine be used to improve students' ability in adding, subtracting, mulitplying, and dividing?
5. How could an adding machine that multiplies but does not take the square root be used to teach a procedure for finding the square root of a number?

17-6. The use of many kinds of instruments in the classroom has never been fully explored. It would seem that a large part of the materials studied in any general mathematics course could be built around activities that ask students to actually use measuring equipment to solve problems using mathematics.

Some sample activities using measuring instruments are provided in this exercise. As you consider these examples, think of ways the students could actually manipulate the devices to solve the problems and identify the mathematical principles they would need to learn to do these problems.

A. 1. How can you determine average speed using only an odometer and a clock?

2. How could you check if an odometer registers mileage accurately by using the attached speedometer?

B. 1. Given only a carpenter's square, decide how you would find the area of a rectangle. A triangle. A parallelogram. A quadrilateral.

2. Given a micrometer and a circular metal rod, how would you find its cross-sectional area?

3. Given a measuring wheel (a rotating wheel with a meter that records the distance traveled) and a right circular cylinder, how could you find its volume?

C. 1. How can you bisect an angle with a carpenter's square?

2. Given a compass and two angles nearly the same in size, how can you determine the larger of the two?

17-7. Evaluation in courses such as industrial arts, home economics, physical education, speech, and science use performance tasks that make the student perform some behavior or construct something to exhibit the skills they have learned. Mathematics teachers should take a cue from these practices, particularly for those students whose weakest area is verbal knowledge. A truer measure of the students' ability could be gained if his behavior were sampled with some performance tasks rather than all paper and pencil items.

Example: Give a group of students each a geoboard, rubber bands, a protractor, and a ruler.

Question:

(a) Make an isosceles triangle that is not an equilateral triangle

(b) Prove to me that your triangle is isosceles.

(c) Prove to me that it is not equilateral.

(d) Make a median of your triangle. Prove to me that it is a median.

(e) Make an altitude of your triangle. Prove to me that it is an attitude.

1. Make a similar question to test knowledge of complementary and supplementary angles.

2. Make a similar question to test knowledge of parallel lines cut by a transversal and the relationship among the angles formed.

3. Make a question to test knowledge of congruent and similar triangles and the relationship of their sides and angles.

17-8. One major criticism of all mathematics teaching is the notion that the textbook is the curriculum. Teachers from other countries are amazed to see how mathematics teachers in this country depend on the textbook for ways to introduce new topics, for classwork and homework exercises, and for tests. Teachers in some countries are given a general course outline and are expected to develop their own course and teaching techniques around this syllabus.

Suppose the basic textbook were eliminated from our mathematics classes, and each teacher was expected to build his own courses around a general list of topics.

1. Would this require people to know more about teaching and mathematics than under the present system?
2. Would this make beginning teachers more insecure?
3. Would this practice eliminate the poor teachers who are unwilling to work and develop new techniques and take no pride in increasing their teaching skills?
4. Would instruction be geared more to the capabilities of the students comprising the class.
5. Would students achieve more or less under this arrangement?
6. Would mathematics department staffs cooperate more in developing ideas, instructional materials, resource units, and tests, or would they shut themselves into their rooms and not communicate?
7. Would instruction in mathematics be less standard from classroom to classroom in the same subjects than it is now?
8. Would this arrangement eliminate some of the bad practices arising from covering a textbook page-by-page in an unselective manner?

17-9. The problems in an applied or general mathematics class should be representative of problems that arise in the real world. As such, each problem should be a means to an end rather than an end in itself. The purpose of these problems is to provide experiences for the student which may be useful to him in later life. To illustrate,this, suppose that the following question had been presented to a business mathematics class:

> A collecting firm which collects payments of money due to other firms has the following charges: They charge 18 percent on the first $300 they collect, 15 percent on the next $200 they collect, and 10 percent on anything beyond this initial amount. If this firm collected $850 for J. P. Brown, what was their charge?

This type of question should be used as more than a routine exercise in an assignment. In fact, questions such as those asked below may be more important than the computation of the charge asked for in the problem.

(a) Why would business firms want to use a collecting firm?

(b) Why would a company have charges stated like this rather than a flat rate?

(c) Is the rate of charge the average of 10 percent, 15 percent, and 18 percent? Why or why not?

1. Classify each of the above questions in terms of the category in Bloom's *Taxonomy* which is being used. (See Chapter 5.)

2. What effect do you think questions of this type might have on the given class?

3. Are there other questions which you, as a teacher, might ask which would give the student a better understanding of the concepts (not necessarily mathematical) involved?

17-10. It has been repeatedly stated that all drill activities need not be dull. Games are especially good modes of instruction to use to sugar-coat a drill pill in general mathematics.

Here is a game that drills plotting of points on a rectangular coordinate system. The axis can be labeled with only positive integers, only positive rationals, both positive and negative integers, or positive and negative rationals. Vertical and horizontal lines are drawn to form a grid, just like rectangular graph paper.

To really get the "feel" of this exercise, you must find a partner, read the directions, and actually play the game. The game described here is set up for adults and may be a little too hard for some classes. For a clear description of how to simplify it and for ideas about how to introduce it to students, look at pp. 1–5 in General Mathematics Writing Project, 1966.

BATTLESHIP

Rules

(a) Each player has a navy of one battleship, one cruiser, and two destroyers.

(b) A battleship consists of four points, a cruiser consists of three points, and a destroyer consists of two points.

(c) The points making up a ship must consist of consecutive points of intersection that may be placed vertically, horizontally, or diagonally.

(d) Each player is given two identical grids. On one grid the player marks the position of his navy and records the shots of his opponent. On the other grid, the player records the shots he fires at his opponent.

(e) Each player begins the game with seven shots to a salvo. The first player calls out the location of seven points. When all the points are selected, his opponent tells him if he has hit any ship, names the ship, but does not disclose the number pair that scored the hit. Each player repeats the process in turn.

(f) A ship is sunk when the opponent has called out all the points on the ship. The player who loses the ship has the number of shots in his future salvos reduced by the number of shots assigned to that ship. The shots assigned to the ships are as follows:

> Destroyer—1 shot
> Cruiser—2 shots
> Battleship—3 shots

(g) First person to sink all of the opponents' ships is the winner.

(h) Keep records by placing a 1 on all the points named in the first salvos, a 2 on all the points named in the second salvo, etc.

17-11. Several exercises in this book have dealt with showing how drill with computations can be accomplished in a game setting or disguised in novel topics such as modular arithmetic, other-number bases, and probability and statistics. Another approach to softening drill is to try and analyze a trick procedure for solving a problem to see why it works. Here is an example suitable for general mathematics.

(a) Choose any two numbers, say 4 and 7.

(b) Add 4 to 7 to obtain 11; then add 7 and 11 to obtain 18; continue in this way until ten numbers have been obtained (4, 7, 11, 18, 29, 47, 76, 123,199, 322).

(c) The sum is 836 and can be found by a trick, using the seventh number in the list.

1. How can the seventh number, 76, be used to get the number 836? Repeat the procedure above with two other numbers and see how the seventh number in the list can be used to get the sum.

2. Generalize the procedure above by letting $\square$ and $\triangle$ represent the two numbers. Generate the list of ten numbers and find their sum. What is the relationship between the sum you found by adding and the seventh expression in the list?

3. How does the relationship you found in answer to question 2 explain the trick you used in question 1 to find 836 from 76?

4. Does this trick for finding the sum of numbers work if the two numbers are 2.3 and 4.7? Does it work if there are only nine numbers being added?

5. What are some of the benefits a general mathematics student might get from being introduced to this problem in the way described above?

6. For more problems of this type see Glenn (1961).

SUGGESTED ACTIVITIES

17-12. For a discussion of some of the alternatives for ninth-grade mathematics students and a good bibliography of sources from a time when general mathematics was receiving more thoughtful attention, see Kinney (1952).

17-13. Some excellent suggestions for improving instruction and handling classroom management in general mathematics classes can be found in Greenholz, (1964, 1968). These would be better remembered and read when you are engaged in teaching general mathematics.

17-14. Examine Sobel (1967). He presents many interesting activities for general mathematics and provides helpful teaching suggestions.

17-15. The NCTM (1966) was instrumental in developing and testing a series of short units in separate booklets that can be used with slow learners. They contain many activities that allow the student to discover mathematical relationships on his own. Examine the appropriateness of the content and reading level of these materials for slow learners.

ADDITIONAL SOURCES

General Mathematics Writing Project. "Formulas, Graphs and Patterns, Unit 1," *Experiences in Mathematical Discovery*. Washington, D.C.: National Council of Teachers of Mathematics, 1966.

Glenn, William H., and Donovan A. Johnson. "Shortcuts in Computing," *Exploring Mathematics on Your Own series.* St. Louis: Webster Publishing Company 1961.

Greenholz, Sarah. "What's New In Teaching Slow Learners In Junior High School?" *Mathematics Teacher* , 57 (December 1964) pp. 522-528.

——. "Reaching Low Achievers In High School." *Today's Education*, Vol. 57 (September 1968), pp. 70-72.

Kinney, Lucien Blair, and C. Richard Prudy. *Teaching Mathematics in the Secondary School.* Holt, Rinehart and Winston Inc., New York: 1952, pp. 268-275.

National Council of Teachers of Mathematics, *Experiences in Mathematical Discovery*. Washington, D.C.: The Council, 1966.

Sobel, Max. *Teaching General Mathematics*. Englewood Cliffs, N. J.: Prentice-Hall, Inc., 1967.

Chapter 18

Problems in Teaching Algebra

The study of algebra presents a radical departure from the preceding study of arithmetic. In algebra the student is confronted with a different if not completely new language, a much higher level of generalization and abstraction, as well as a variety of new skills and concepts. Mastery of these new concepts and procedures is just as essential for students who wish to pursue a career in the sciences as is mastery of arithmetic skills for application to the daily living of all people.

Teaching the skills, rules, and procedures of algebra is an essential phase of instruction. We can, however, teach these in such a manner that the student memorizes a series of steps and, in a rote fashion, applies these steps as a sequence of unrelated manipulations to be performed. On the other hand, we can teach procedures with meaning and for understanding. It should be realized, both by the student and teacher, that every algebraic manipulation can be justified and has a reason. If students are taught the reasons for using certain procedures and for doing certain procedures, they will be better able to learn and remember more mathematics.

STRUCTURE OF ALGEBRA

The philosophy of the above paragraph is evident if current algebra textbooks are examined. These books emphasize teaching algebra as a mathematical system rather than as a set of skills. Within this development there is a great deal of attention devoted to the structure of algebraic systems, an emphasis on basic concepts such as sets, functions, and relations, and a logical and deductive development of concepts. This does not imply that skills are deemphasized; rather, it is felt that an understanding of the basic concepts and structure of algebra will facilitate the acquisition and retention of such skills as factoring and solution of equations. Finally, recent textbooks have placed a greater emphasis on precision of language—that is, the mathematical vocabulary of algebra is more carefully developed and terms are more carefully defined.

Actually, a major portion of the study of algebra is the study of the real-number field. The structure of algebra is the structure of the mathematical system embodied in the real numbers. Early in algebra the students should be exposed to field properties such as the commutative, associative, distributive, identity, and inverse properties, should be able to interpret these properties in a meaningful manner, and be able to apply these properties to the development of new skills or principles. Using these properties, it is possible to give reasons for rules such as

(a) To subtract two numbers, change the sign of the subtrahend and proceed as in addition.
(b) The sign of the product of two negative numbers is positive.
(c) If the product of two numbers is zero, one of the numbers must be zero.
(d) To add like terms, add the coefficients to obtain the coefficient of the sum.

Several exercises will be devoted to deductive developments which can be used to justify some of the techniques and rules used in algebra.

In order to develop such rules and to make them meaningful to the students, it is essential that the meanings of the words used to express the rules are understood. In the past there have been too many instances where we have not defined terms or have attempted to define them only by example. For example, what is meant when we say two things are equal or what is meant by a function. If we define such things by example or if we leave them entirely to chance, students may not be able to understand or apply a rule because they are using an incorrect definition.

The notion of absolute value is one that has often been poorly defined. By example, we say the absolute value of $^-7$ is 7 and of 5 is 5, and then we further go on to say that the absolute value of a number is a number without any sign and, hence, is always positive or zero. This is a very poor and sloppy definition and can lead to an incorrect concept when we are concerned with the absolute values of variable expressions. By giving the definition

$$|a| = \begin{cases} a \text{ if } a \geqslant 0 \\ -a \text{ if } a < 0 \end{cases}$$

we have a precise definition that can be used under any circumstances. The examples given above are certainly necessary to motivate the definition and more examples are needed to illustrate and apply the definition; however, under no circumstances can these examples replace the definition. It should also be noted that this definition emphasizes the field properties, additive inverses, and the consequence that the additive inverse of a negative number is a positive number.

At present there does not seem to be common agreement

about how formal the treatment should be or how much rigor should be included in an introductory course in algebra. There is, however, substantial agreement that the students should be exposed to the properties of the real-number system and that algebra should be developed as a mathematical system which includes undefined terms, axioms, definitions, and propositions to be proved.

WORD PROBLEMS TO MATHEMATICAL SENTENCES

Many teachers have indicated that one of the most difficult units to teach in algebra is that dealing with word problems. You will frequently hear teachers say, "I just can't teach word problems," and just as frequently hear students say, "I just can't solve word problems." The fundamental difficulty in the solution of word problems is that of translating from the physical world language to the language of algebra. Lack of understanding of the physical world language and the problem it presents impedes translation, just as much as lack of understanding the language of algebra. We should stride for meaningful situations and an understanding of both languages.

Perhaps the single most important concept in the study of algebra is that of the variable. Without the use of variables we would not be able to write any generalized expressions which relate properties of subsets of the real numbers. Early in any introductory algebra course variables should be defined as symbols which hold a place for any element of a specified replacement set. Practice should be provided regularly on translating verbal expressions such as "the sum of a number and three" or "the product of two numbers" to their mathematical expressions, $y + 3$ and $r \cdot s$. Practice should also be provided on translation of algebraic expressions such as $2m + 3$ to verbal expressions as "three more than twice a number." After experience in translation of verbal expressions to mathematical expressions involving variables, the next step is to translate sentences which relate two or more expressions. As before, we should not just translate from verbal sentences to algebraic sentences but should also provide practice in the other direction. Procedures of this type strengthen the students' proficiency with the language of algebra as well as with the English language. Perhaps some consideration should be given to this translation process of expressions involving variables each class period.

After an English sentence has been translated to an algebraic sentence, we can apply the techniques and rules of algebra to solve the sentence. Procedures for solving equations and inequalities are used only after translation, and then they yield a solution in the language of algebra. This solution must then be interpreted in the language in which the problem was originally stated. We should note that the procedures just described are identical to the problem solving model discussed in Chapter 1, The Nature of Mathematics.

From this discussion we see that there are a variety of pitfalls in the solution of word problems. When a student in our class says that he cannot solve word problems we need to analyze the situation by obtaining answers to the following questions:

1. Can the student understand the physical situation which the problem portrays?
2. Can the student translate from the language of the problem to the language of algebra?
3. Does the student have sufficient understanding of the algebraic techniques necessary to solve the problem?
4. Can the student interpret and check his solution to the physical problem?

Within each of these questions there are a variety of other questions. For example, an understanding of the problem would include identification of the available information, relationships existing between the given parts, identification of extraneous information, identification of the parts to be found, and the types of results that would be acceptable as solutions. Each of the other main questions could also be subdivided into constituent parts in a similar fashion.

The problem-solving activities involved in the solution of word problems should be an essential phase of any course in algebra. These activities reflect the nature of mathematics and how at least one branch of mathematics can be applied to problems arising in the physical world. To be sure, the teaching and learning of these behaviors is at times difficult; however, the worth of these activities cannot be overemphasized.

THE CONTENT OF ALGEBRA

The preceding sections of this chapter have given some indication of the concepts and skills that should be taught in an introductory course in algebra. It does not seem practical nor reasonable to list additional topics to be taught in a first course in algebra. Rather, the reader is referred to the Table of Contents of any recently published Algebra I textbook. To be sure, from book to book the instructional strategies, the amount of rigor, and the sequential arrangement of topics will vary. Looking at the basic list of concepts to be taught, however, will convince you that all of these textbooks are trying to teach roughly the same content.

The second course in algebra does offer some opportunity for variation. Some selected topics that may be treated in second-year algebra include elementary functions such as polynomial, exponential, and logarithmic; the complex number field; elementary counting techniques; introductory probability; sequences and series; matric algebra; an introduction to abstract algebra; and an extension of the concepts and topics considered in Algebra I. The inclusion of topics such as these reflect the philosophy and goals of the textbook. Again we recommend that the teacher examine several second-year algebra textbooks to gain some perspective on the content to be included.

EXERCISES

18-1. As stated in the introduction to this chapter, the structure of algebra is actually the structure of the real number field. The real numbers form a complete ordered field.

1. State the properties necessary for a number system to be a field.
2. What are several number systems which possess the field properties?
3. *Definition:* If $a, b \in F$, $a - b = c$ if and only if $a = c + b$. Using the stated definition of subtraction, prove "If $a, b \in F$, $a - b = a + {}^-b$."
4. State the properties necessary for a field to be an ordered field.
5. How can we define the order relation, "less than"?
6. In an ordered field, prove, "If $a < b$ and $c < 0$, $ac > bc$."

18-2. There are a variety of ways in which to justify the rule of signs for multiplication of integers. If the basic structure of the integers is assumed, then the procedures for multiplication of integers can be derived in a deductive manner. The teacher should realize that this technique is based upon several assumptions. First, students will readily agree that a positive integer times a positive integer is a positive integer. This is rarely, if ever, justified because it seems too obvious, and in fact it is, if one realizes that the positive integers act just like the natural numbers. Mathematically we would say that the system of natural numbers is isomorphic to the system of positive integers.

To establish the rule that a positive integer times a negative integer is a negative integer, we may use the following procedure. Let a, b, be positive integers. Then

1. $b + {}^-b = 0$ Additive inverse property
2. $a(b + {}^-b) = a \cdot 0$ Multiplication property
3. $ab + a \cdot {}^-b = a \cdot 0$ Distributive property
4. $ab + a \cdot {}^-b = 0$ Multiplication by 0
5. $ab + {}^-(ab) = 0$ Additive inverse property
6. $ab + a \cdot {}^-b = ab + {}^-(ab)$ Transitive property of equals
7. $a \cdot {}^-b = {}^-(ab)$ Subtraction property
8. ${}^-(ab)$ is a negative integer   The additive inverse of a positive
                                      integer is negative

Note that the above derivation does more than establish the sign of the product. It actually provides the algorithm for multiplying a positive integer times a negative integer. State this algorithm. Assuming the above derivation, how would you establish the procedure for (1) multiplying a negative integer by a positive integer; (2) a negative integer by a negative integer?

18-3. Another deductive procedure for justifying the statement, $a \cdot b = {}^-a \cdot {}^-b$ is as follows. Let a, b be integers.

1. $a \cdot b + {}^-a \cdot b + {}^-a \cdot {}^-b = a \cdot b + {}^-a \cdot b + {}^-a \cdot {}^-b$
2. $(a \cdot b + {}^-a \cdot b) + {}^-a \cdot {}^-b = a \cdot b + ({}^-a \cdot b + {}^-a \cdot {}^-b)$
3. $(a + {}^-a) \cdot b + {}^-a \cdot {}^-b = a \cdot b + {}^-a \cdot (b + {}^-b)$
4. $0 \cdot b + {}^-a \cdot {}^-b = a \cdot b + {}^-a \cdot 0$
5. $0 + {}^-a \cdot {}^-b = a \cdot b + 0$
6. ${}^-a \cdot {}^-b = a \cdot b$

1. Fill in the justifications for each step in the above development in the system of integers. These are the properties upon which the development is based.

   When using a derivation of this type a good procedure to follow is:

   (a) Before beginning, make sure the class knows the goal of the procedure.

   (b) Be concerned with details, omit no steps in the derivation, and explain each step as the work progresses.

   (c) After completing the derivation, summarize the work that has been done and interpret the result.

2. To illustrate the manner in which the statement, $a \cdot b = {}^-a \cdot {}^-b$ might be interpreted, substitute several integers for a, b.

3. What does this statement tell you if a is negative and b is positive?

4. What does this statement tell you if a is negative and b is negative?

18-4. The preceding two exercises provided a deductive procedure which justifies the rules that are used to multiply two integers. From a mathematical point of view, these procedures explain why we use a particular algorithm. It is presumed that if a student understands the mathematical derivation, he will be better able to use and remember the procedure that was developed. Many times, however, the abstract mathematical development is not sufficient and students should be provided with illustrations of the concept from the physical world. Within the past several years, a number of ingenius ideas to teach multiplication of integers has been developed.

See if you can develop a physical model that could be used to teach multiplication of integers. If you have difficulty, read:

Warren H. Hill, Jr., "A Physical Model for Teaching Multiplication of Integers."

Robert B. Davis, *Discovery in Mathematics*, pp. 21-25.

18-5. In algebra, there are many instances in which a series of manipulations are performed to obtain some result to be used as an intelligent guess. For example, the procedures that we follow in solution of equations are for the purpose of making intelligent guesses. Consider the following:

$$3x + 5 = 9$$
$$3x = 4$$
$$x = 4/3$$

We were given the equation $3x + 5 = 9$ to solve and following a series of manipulations, we obtained $x = 4/3$. This procedure has given us an intelligent guess for the solution of $3x + 5 = 9$, namely 4/3.

1. If we were given

$$\frac{60}{x^2 - 36} + 1 = \frac{5}{x - 6}$$

to solve, what would be intelligent guesses for solutions to this equation? Are your intelligent guesses solutions to the given equation?

In each of these instances you were given an equation which might be symbolized by $f(x) = c$ and obtained one or more statements of the form $x = a_i$. The manipulations which were performed established the statement, "If $f(x) = c$, then $x = a_i$" for each a_i. We cannot infer from this that a_i is a solution to $f(x) = c$. We know, however, that a_i is a solution to $x = a_i$ so if we could prove the statement, "If $x = a_i$, then $f(x) = c$," then we would know that a_i is a solution to $f(x) = c$.

2. Prove: If $x = 4/3$, then $3x + 5 = 9$. (*Note*: This proves that 4/3 is a solution to $3x + 5 = 9$.)

3. State why you can't prove,

$$\text{If } x = 6, \text{ then } \frac{60}{x^2 - 36} + 1 = \frac{5}{x - 6}$$

18-6. In the preceding exercise we said that 4/3 was a solution to the equation $3x + 5 = 9$. From this statement we know that there is at least one solution to the equation. The teacher should also be prepared to show that this is the only solution. One method that can be used to show the uniqueness of a solution to a linear equation is by an indirect proof. Assume that there are two different solutions to $3x + 5 = 9$, and show that this leads to a contradiction.

1. What concepts can be emphasized when constructing this proof?

Another procedure that could be used is to note that if $3x + 5 = 9$, then $x = 4/3$ is a true implication. Hence a necessary condition for $3x + 5 = 9$ is $x = 4/3$. Since there is obviously only one value for x for which x is 4/3, there is at most one value of x for which $3x + 5 = 9$.

2. Show how this method could be used to show that there are at most two solutions for the equation

$$\frac{60}{x^2 - 36} + 1 = \frac{5}{x - 6}$$

18-7. When attempting to solve fractional equations [equations that have variable expression(s) in the denominator(s)], it is necessary to multiply both sides of the equation by an expression containing one or more variables. This procedure may yield a derived equation which is not equivalent to the original equation.

1. Under what conditions will the derived equation and the original equation have different solution sets?
2. How can this be explained in the classroom?

Another situation that sometimes arises in the classroom concerns division of both sides of an equation by an expression containing a variable. For example, in the equation $4x = 6x^3 + x^2$, information is lost if both sides of this equation are divided by x. If a student does this, it may be possible to correct his error by a series of questions such as:

(a) Is $4x = 6x^3 + x^2$ equivalent to $x(6x^2 + x - 4) = 0$?
(b) What is one solution to $x(6x^2 + x - 4) = 0$?
(c) If $x = 0$, can we divide both sides of the equation by x?

3. This line of questioning could also lead to a discussion about the number of roots of a polynomial equation. Explain how this might be done.

18-8. A series of algebraic manipulations may sometimes be performed to obtain an equivalent equation for further analysis. This might occur when the quadratic function, $y = ax^2 + bx + c$, is being investigated. Thus, the following development might be used:

$$y = ax^2 + bx + c$$

$$y = a\left(x^2 + \frac{bx}{a} + \frac{c}{a}\right)$$

$$y = a\left(x^2 + \frac{bx}{a} + \frac{b^2}{4a^2} + \frac{c}{a} - \frac{b^2}{4a^2}\right)$$

$$y = a\left[\left(x + \frac{b}{2a}\right)^2 + \left(\frac{c}{a} - \frac{b^2}{4a^2}\right)\right] \qquad \text{(i)}$$

An introduction to this development might state, "We are interested in properties of the graph of $y = ax^2 + bx + c$ and we wish to see what happens to the y values as x varies. Unfortunately it is not obvious how y changes as x varies when the function is in the given form. Hence, we must transform the given expressions to an equivalent expression by algebraic manipulation."

Following this derivation, the graph of the equivalent expression (i) is investigated by asking and answering questions such as:

(a) What values may $\left(x + \frac{b}{2a}\right)^2$ assume?

(b) Since $\left(x + \frac{b}{2a}\right)^2 \geq 0$ for what value of x is it 0?

(c) What is the minimum value for the expression inside the brackets in (i)?

(d) If $a > 0$, does y have a minimum or a maximum?

(e) Can $a = 0$? Why or why not?

(f) If $a < 0$, does y have a minimum or maximum?

(g) What is the minimum or maximum value of y?

(h) For what values of x does y assume a minimum or a maximum?

1. Answer each of the above questions.

2. Devise a series of questions which analyze (i) to show that the graph is symmetrical about $x = \frac{-b}{2a}$.

3. Use (i) to indicate the effect that the magnitude of $|a|$ has on the graph.

18-9. In Chapter 1, The Nature of Mathematics, we saw the importance of translation from the language of the physical world to the language of mathematics. One of the most important and powerful concepts in the study of algebra is that of the variable. Lack of understanding of this concept impedes, if not prohibits, translation from the language in which the problem arises to the language of mathematics. For example, we have all heard and you as a teacher shall soon hear, "I understand it when you write it with numbers but not when you use letters." This comment implies a lack of understanding of the variable concept and the inability to translate from one language to another.

One manner in which the concept, the variable might be introduced is to provide a variety of examples of variables before defining them formally. This might be done using sentences as:

Bob plays on the basketball team.

He is president of the United States.

She sails beautifully.

She is of the female sex.

1. What are the variables in each of the sentences above?
2. From what sets can we choose elements to replace the variable?
3. If we choose some elements, will we get a false sentence?
4. Are there different replacement sets that could be specified for the variables?
5. Are any of the statements true as they are stated?

By considering questions of this type we can begin to teach the variable concept. This experience should be followed by statements in mathematics such as:

For any natural numbers a, b, $a + b$ is a natural number.

$x + 5 = 7$.

If x is an integer, $x + 5 < 7$.

6. Answer each of the above questions for these mathematical sentences.

18-10. By considering questions such as those asked in the previous exercise, we should be able to generate a precise definition of variable. This is essential so that the students do not make a false generalization from the examples that have previously been given.

1. Define *variable*.
2. Does your definition include those symbols you designated as variables above?
3. Does your definition specify the need for a replacement set (a set of elements any of which could be substituted for the variable?)

18-11. Algebra has sometimes been defined as generalized arithmetic because one general statement is used to express an entire class of specific statements. Thus, according to this definition, $a + b = b + a$ is an algebraic statement used to express statements such as $1.7 + {}^-3.5 = {}^-3.5 + 1.7$, $2/3 + 3/4 = 3/4 + 2/3$ and the like. This definition also implies that the variable concept is one of the cornerstones in the study of algebra.

In the teaching of algebra, we should remember that one way to motivate a generalization is to examine many specific cases. For example, to motivate the theorem, "If $a \cdot b = 0$, then $a = 0$ or $b = 0$," the students must have a considerable amount of experience with problems such as $5 \cdot 0 = 0$, $0 \cdot \sqrt{9} = 0$, $2/3 \cdot 0 = 0$, etc. We should also emphasize that manipulations with algebraic expressions are manipulations with any numbers from the replacement sets for the variables. This can be used to provide a check for a variety of problems, to help students translate algebraic statements to numerical statements, and perhaps to provide the student with a better understanding of variables.

1. To illustrate this, divide $x^4 - 5x^3 + 3x - 7$ by $x - 2$.
2. Show that your work is correct when $x = 5$.
3. Can you show your work is correct for $x = 2$? Why or why not?

18-12. Another troublesome topic is that of like terms and then the combining of like terms. In many instances the idea is troublesome because we have never really defined what we mean.

1. See if you can give a definition for "like terms." Remember that it is handy to give examples such as $5x$ and $3x$ are like terms but this does not constitute a definition.

2. Using your definition, are terms such as $7ab$ and $^-3\,ab$ like terms?

3. Are $7x^2$ and $6x$ like terms? Why or why not?

Once this definition is accepted and students can identify like terms and terms that are not like, it is easy to teach the skill "combining like terms" by using the distributive property of multiplication over addition.

4. Show how this property can be used to add

   (a) $7ab + 3ab$

   (b) $4(a + x)^2 \cdot c - 9\,(a + x)^2 \cdot c$

18-13. Factoring trinomials is actually an extended application of the distributive and associative properties. It may be beneficial to begin instruction in factoring by considering problems such as:

$$a^2 + 3a + 4a + 12$$

which can then be grouped as

$$(a^2 + 3a) + (4a + 12)$$

and by using the distributive property, we have

$$a(a + 3) + 4(a + 3)$$

and, finally,

$$(a + 4)\,(a + 3)$$

When factoring the expressions $a^2 + 7a + 12$, the first step is to rewrite the $7a$ as $3a + 4a$ and apply the above procedure.

1. If, for example we wish to factor $x^2 + x - 6$ using this procedure, the first step would be to replace x by what sum?
2. What clues are available to find the two coefficients of x in this sum?
3. How would you try to explain to a student a procedure, other than trial and error, for determining these coefficients?

18-14. There are a number of terms that mathematics has used from our everyday language which may cause some confusion in mathematics classrooms. These terms may imply one concept in everyday usage and other contradictory usage in mathematics. It behooves the teacher to avoid these terms wherever possible and if impossible, to make certain that the mathematical usage of the term is clearly understood. One such term that we use is reduce, which in one sense means make smaller, while in the mathematical sense means to write another name for the same number.

1. For each of the words below, identify the possible confusion that might result in the mathematics classroom when using the word, and identify ways in which these words might be avoided.
   (a) Cancel
   (b) Extraneous root
   (c) Imaginary number
   (d) Complex
2. Can you think of other words that may imply a false concept in algebra from the ordinary usage of the word?

18-15. Some rather interesting psuedoproofs can be used to stimulate discussion and interest in mathematics. They are called psuedoproofs because the conclusion is obviously false. Hence, there must be at least one incorrect or nonjustifiable step in the proof. An example of a proof of this type appears below. They would serve nicely as a problem on a bulletin board under the title, "Can you find the error?"

$$1 = \sqrt{1}$$
$$\sqrt{1} = \sqrt{(-1)(-1)}$$
$$\sqrt{(-1)(-1)} = \sqrt{-1}\sqrt{-1}$$
$$\sqrt{-1}\sqrt{-1} = i \cdot i$$
$$i \cdot i = -1$$
$$1 = -1$$

1. Fill in reasons for the above proof and find the error.
2. Another common step used to prove a contradictory result is division by zero. See if you can derive a psuedoproof showing that $1 = 2$ using division by zero somewhere in your work.
3. When might arguments of this type be used in algebra class?

18-16. For many situations there are two or more ways in which the situation may be solved. Some people argue that this should not be done because if two different ways are taught to do the same thing, it will confuse the students, and as a result they will not remember either technique. Alternatively, there are those who argue that several techniques should be taught so that if a student is unable to apply one technique he has a second technique which he may be able to apply. Both of these views avoid the main issue of having a variety of techniques which are applicable to a problem and from which one can choose the most efficient procedure.

A particular example might be the solution of quadratic equations. Procedures that are applicable to this type problem are trial and error, graphing, factoring, completing the square, and the quadratic formula. By teaching each of these techniques, we provide the student with a variety of procedures from which he may choose to solve any quadratic equation. To be sure, the trial-and-error method is rarely an efficient way to solve an equation and graphing rarely yields an exact solution. We should recognize, however, that important mathematical concepts are emphasized by consideration of these techniques. For example, trial-and-error solution emphasizes true and false mathematical sentences, the meaning of solution, and the need for more refined techniques.

1. What mathematical concepts can be illustrated when teaching the solution of quadratic equation by the graphical method?

Suppose that the five methods for solving quadratic equations had been taught and you wish to emphasize the using of the most efficient technique available. The three examples to be used are:

(a) $3x^2 - 5x + 3 = 0$
(b) $3x^2 + 4x - 32 = 0$
(c) $x^2 - 5x = 0$

2. Which technique should be used for each equation?
3. Which techniques are not applicable for each equation and why?

18-17. One of the objectives of algebra courses is, "The students should be able to solve word problems." If solution of word problems is relegated to one portion of the course, it is generally very difficult to teach and teaching efforts usually meet with little success. If the above objective is to be attained, efforts at solving problems of this type should be integrated throughout the course.

At the very earliest time verbal problems which require translation, application and analysis skills should be considered and assigned. In fact, one good procedure to follow is to put at least one word problem on each assignment. This necessitates that the teacher must accumulate a good supply of problems which require the application of a variety of skills. Several problems of this type appear below. Solve each of these problems and then identify the skills and concepts necessary to successfully solve them.

(a) Two engineers are hired by an engineering consultant firm. Mr. Clark is to be paid $10,500 with a raise of $1,000 per year. Mr. Smith is to be paid half yearly, starting with $5,000 and rising $500 per half year. Which has made the better bargain if they each work for the firm for five years?

(b) Three men play a game in which only one man can lose on each trial and the loser doubles the money of each of the other two. After three trials each man has lost exactly once and each man finishes with $24. How much money did each man have at the start?

(c) A traveler notices that six times the number of telephone poles he passes per minute equals his speed in miles per hour. Find the distance between poles. (Assume he is traveling at a uniform rate.)

SUGGESTED ACTIVITIES

18-18. The last exercise implied that teachers should accrue a supply of problems illustrating and using a variety of concepts. Several sources for problems are:

Yearly Mathematics Examination sponsored by the Mathematical Association of America, the Society of Actuaries, and Mu Alpha Theta. The Problem Section of *The Mathematics Student Journal*. Books such as Jerome S. Meyer, *Fun With Mathematics*, and The NCTM's *Mathematical Challenges*.

Excluding textbooks, find three other good sources which contain problems that might be used in algebra classes.

18-19. One method suggested for generating teaching strategies (see Chapter 6) was to look at other textbooks which presented the same content. Another reason for using other textbooks is to obtain a greater variety of exercises that illustrate particular topics. Select two recently published Algebra I textbooks. Compare and contrast:

(a) The content presented in these books
(b) The instructional strategies for one or more selected topics
(c) The exercises that students are to complete for these topics

18-20. Follow the instructions in Activity 18-19 for two Algebra II books. It is likely that there is a greater divergence of mathematical content in books at this level than there is at the Algebra I level.

18-21. One of the tasks which confronts all mathematics teachers is to teach problem solving. A plan that can be used to solve many problems is presented in Polya (1957). How might you teach a plan such as this to students who are solving mathematical problems? It is also interesting to compare the phases of this plan to the activities of a teacher in preparing a lesson.

18-22. A completely different approach to the solution of verbal problems is presented by Dahmas (1970). In fact, Dahmas states that implementation of his method is difficult if the students have previously been subjected to other methods. Compare and contrast this approach to Polya (1957).

ADDITIONAL SOURCES

Charosh, Mannis, ed. *Mathematical Challenges*. Washington, D.C.: National Council of Teachers of Mathematics, 1965.

Dahmas, Maurice E. "How to Teach Verbal Problems," *School Science and Mathematics*, Vol. 50 (February 1970), pp. 121–138.

Davis, Robert B. *Discovery in Mathematics*. Reading, Mass. Addison-Wesley Publishing Company, 1964.

Hill, Warren H., Jr. "A physical Model for Teaching Multiplication of Integers," *The Arithmetic Teacher*, Vol. 15 (October 1968), pp. 525-528.

Meyer, Jerome S. *Fun With Mathematics*. Greenwich, Conn.: Fawcett Publications, Inc., 1957.

Polya, G. *How to Solve It*. Garden City, N. Y.: Doubleday Anchor Books, 1957.

Chapter 19

Problems in Teaching Geometry

The discussion and exercises in this chapter are confined solely to illustrating strategies in three aspects of teaching geometry. The areas examined are:

1. Teaching for comprehension and application of the geometric content found in the postulates, theorems, and definitions.
2. Teaching students to discover and write logical arguments and formal proofs.
3. Teaching students to make and test conjectures and to construct definitions.

These areas of geometry teaching can be thought of as successively higher levels in a hierarchy. A lower-level area can be achieved without attaining a higher-level one, but achievement of a higher-level task depends upon the accomplishment of the lower-level ones.

TEACHING FOR COMPREHENSION OF GEOMETRIC CONTENT

Imagine a textbook in geometry that consists entirely of a careful listing of all the postulates, theorems, definitions, and exercises commonly found in a high school geometry book. Assume the book contains no proofs, no figures, no examples, and no explanations—just a long list of statements about geometry. This catalog or listing would include most of the *geometric content* or information to be learned from high school geometry. The proofs, figures, examples, and explanations do not in general add new information to the storehouse of geometric knowledge; they only verify the validity, make the meaning clearer, or show applications of the statements.

It should be clear that a geometry course could be taught in which the only goal would be to make clear to the students the meaning and applications of the content found in the postulates, theorems, and definitions. All the instructional strategies would be directed toward explanation and interpretation of what the statements say, and getting students to comprehend the full meaning of each assertation. While this one-goal approach to teaching geometry is certainly not advocated, teaching the meaning of the statements is an important function and is sometimes lightly stressed or overlooked in favor of other goals.

Comprehension of the statements of geometry is necessary before students can do proofs. The proof of any theorem is based upon postulates, definitions, and previously proven theorems. The totality of such statements can be considered as a storehouse that contains the items needed for a proof of the theorem at hand. When a student is confronted with a theorem to prove, he will be extremely handicapped if he cannot mentally picture the list of available statements and readily recall those that appear promising in the situation he faces. Asking the student to memorize verbatim all postulates, theorems, and definitions is useless to him in doing proofs even if he could be compelled to do such a distasteful chore. Other methods of learning the statements so that they can be recalled and used when needed are available, and some are suggested in the Exercises.

TEACHING "PROOF MAKING"

A separate aspect of geometry teaching is teaching the student that the statements of geometry (as with other branches of mathematics) can be organized as a deductive system in which some ststements are chosen as basic assumptions and used to verify the remaining ones on the basis of logical reasoning. As explained in Chapter 1, proof is essential in mathematics since it is the only method available to determine if statements are valid or non-contradictory.

The ultimate goal in teaching proof is for the student to be able to discover and write proofs. Yet many intermediate objectives can be stressed that will aid the student toward the goal of developing original proofs himself. The exercises on "proof making" illustrate various techniques that can be used in getting students to do proofs.

Some teachers, who desire their students to learn to do proofs, require them to memorize proofs of specific theorems and ask them to reproduce them on tests. There are benefits to be derived from memorizing and being able to reproduce proofs of specific theorems. No criticism is intended of this practice; in the cases of famous theorems it is highly desirable. The point here is that test items that require reproduction of memorized proofs do not measure the students' proof-making ability. They measure the ability to recall previously learned material. To test a student's ability to discover and write proofs, he must be asked to produce a proof in a situation not completely known or familiar to him.

TEACHING STUDENTS TO MAKE AND TEST CONJECTURES

Knowing the statements of geometry and being able to prove them is not all that should be expected of students if they are to get the full benefit of studying mathematics. They need to be led one step higher and presented with situations where they can produce conjectures and test them. Pupils become accustomed to always seeing precise definitions and having statements written before them that they know will be true before a proof is given. They do not often have the opportunity to see how a definition evolves or how a finished theorem begins as a conjecture or hunch whose validity is uncertain. If a student never encounters false statements that need to be refuted or doubtful conjectures that require the test of a logical argument to support their validity, he certainly cannot fully appreciate the need for or the role of deductive proof in mathematics.

Teaching students to make and test conjectures, whether in geometry or any other branch of mathematics, should give the student the opportunity to:

1. Make a list of guesses and conjectures, both correct and incorrect.
2. Draw figures and try examples to test his guesses and either strengthen his confidence in his conjectures or provide counterexamples.
3. Select the order in which the proofs of the conjectures will be attempted and to revise the order when it becomes apparent that certain theorems must be proved before others.
4. Devise an informal argument to justify the conjectures orally.
5. Write a formal proof with reasons only after the student has an idea for a proof and can give an informal argument.
6. Determine if the theorems hold for special cases or special figures.
7. Determine if any of the theorems hold for more general cases or figures or identify those steps in proofs that will be true for the more general cases or figures and those that will fail to hold.
8. Make conjectures, verify them, and write formal proofs for new but similar situations with little guidance from the teacher.

Reference List of Statements For
Use in Exercises 19-1–19-3

Definition 1 A line, L, is the perpendicular bisector of $\overline{AB}$ in plane N if and only if L is perpendicular to $\overline{AB}$ and L intersects $\overline{AB}$ at its midpoint.

Theorem 1 Any line segment has at least one perpendicular bisector.

Theorem 2 There is at most one perpendicular bisector of a line segment in any given plane.

Lemma 1   If L is the perpendicular bisector of $\overline{AB}$ in plane N and P is any point on L, then $PA = PB$.

Lemma 2   If L is the perpendicular bisector of $\overline{AB}$ in plane N and P is any point in N such that $PA = PB$, then $P \in L$.

Theorem 3   If L is the perpendicular bisector of $\overline{AB}$ in plane N, then $L = \{P \mid PA = PB, P \in N\}$.

Corollary 1 Let line L and $\overline{AB}$ be in plane N and C, D two distinct points of L. If $AC = CB$ and $AD = DB$, then L is the perpendicular bisector of $\overline{AB}$.

19-1. Students learning the content of theorems, definitions, and postulates need to be able to restate them in several ways. The more ways they can restate them, the better they will come to know and use them.

A. A useful technique to use is to try to find several ways of expressing the same statement.

1. Theorem 2 is a uniqueness theorem and can be stated in several ways:
    (a) If a line is the perpendicular bisector of a segment, then it is the only one in that plane.
    (b) If two lines are perpendicular bisectors of the same segment in the same plane, then they are equal.
2. Find two or more restatements of these theorems:
    (a) A line segment has at most one midpoint.
    (b) There is only one plane on three noncolinear points.
    (c) Corollary 1.

B. Another technique is to translate statements from words to symbols, or vice versa.

1. Translate from words to symbols:
    (a) Theorem 1.
    (b) Theorem 2 and the restatements shown above.
    (c) Definition 1.
2. Translate from symbols to words:
    (a) Lemma 1.
    (b) Lemma 2.
    (c) Theorem 3.

19-2. Suppose it were desired that students learn the statements in the reference list at the beginning of the exercises. The samples below illustrate types of activities that a teacher could use to help the student learn the statements.

A. Studying individual statements:

1. What is the antecedent of Lemma 2? Theorem 1?
2. What is the consequent of Lemma 2? Theorem 1?
3. What is the contrapositive of Lemma 1? Is it true?
4. What do the words "if and only if" mean in the definition?
5. What is the converse of Lemma 1? Is it true?
6. What is a lemma? A corollary?
7. Which statement tells what a perpendicular bisector is?
8. Which statement(s) tells how many perpendicular bisectors a line segment has?
9. Draw a figure that corresponds to the "if" part of Corollary 1.

B. Comparing and contrasting statements:

1. Tell how the "if" parts of the Definition, Lemma 1, Lemma 2, and Theorem 3 are alike and how they are different.
2. Which statements assume you have a perpendicular bisector? Which ones conclude you have one?
3. Name two implications with the same conclusion.
4. Which statements have a conclusion that two sets are equal?
5. Which theorems are existence theorems?
6. Which theorems are uniqueness theorems?
7. Draw a figure to illustrate the given of Lemma 1 and another for the given of Lemma 2. How do they differ?

19-3. To help students use theorems in problems and proofs, there are activities that the teacher can design like those illustrated below.

A. One-step applications of the theorems:

1. Suppose you were told that L is the perpendicular bisector of $\overline{AB}$ in plane N. State what conclusion you can make, if any, from (a) Definition 1, (b) Theorem 2, (c) Lemma 1, (d) Theorem 3.

2. Suppose you were told that $\triangle ABC$ is isosceles with $AB = AC$. Indicate which of the statements in the reference list would you use to conclude that

   (a) A is on the perpendicular bisector of $\overline{BC}$.

   (b) The median from A to $\overline{BC}$ is the perpendicular bisector of $\overline{BC}$.

B. Working backwards:

1. Suppose you wished to conclude that a line K is the perpendicular bisector of a segment $\overline{GH}$ in a plane N. State what you would have to know first, if you used (a) Definition 1, (b) Theorem 2, (c) Corollary 1.

2. Suppose you are to conclude that a line L is a perpendicular bisector of segment $\overline{AB}$ in plane N. Indicate which statement you would be using if you tried to first show that

   (a) $AE = EB$ and $AF = FB$ where E and F are two points on L.

   (b) $L \perp \overline{AB}$ and L intersects $\overline{AB}$ at its midpoint.

19-4. The following theorem will be used in this and later exercises to illustrate some techniques that can be used to guide students toward making their own proofs.

Theorem: In $\triangle GHK$, $GK = HK$ and M is between G and H such that $\angle GKM \cong \angle HKM$, then M is the midpoint of $\overline{GH}$.

A. One common practice is to provide information such as the following for the students:

Given: $\triangle GHK, GK = HK$

         M between G and H, $\angle GKM \cong \angle HKM$

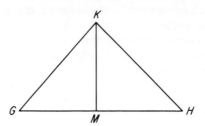

Conclusion: M is the midpoint of $\overline{GH}$.

Proof

Statements	Reasons
1. $GK = HK$	(1)
2. $\angle GKM \cong \angle HKM$	Given
3. _____(2)_____	Identity
4. $\triangle GKM \cong$ ____(3)____	(4)
5. _____(5)_____	(6)
6. _____(7)_____	Definition of midpoint

The directions to the student might be to indicate in the figure the information given and the conclusion. Secondly, he would be expected to fill in the blanks to make a proof of the theorem. Do the work expected of the student.

B. The proof given above depends on the presence of the figure. That GHK is a triangle and that M is between G and H is not used in the statements of the proof. Write a proof for the theorem that does not depend upon referring to a figure.

19-5. The technique shown in the previous exercise requires the following proof-making type reasoning:

(a) Give reasons for statements (blanks 1 and 4).

(b) Give a statement using a reason as a clue (blank 2).

(c) Give a statement that logically follows from a previous statement (blanks 3 and 5).

(d) Give a statement by knowing it is the conclusion (blank 7).

(e) Give a statement by working backwards from a conclusion and its reason (blank 5 can be filled in by working backwards from 7 and its reason).

A. Examine the following two techniques and identify instances of proof-making type reasoning that these techniques can foster in the student.

1. Using the theorem in the previous exercise as an example, the teacher would write everything except the reasons for the statements. The student would be expected to provide the correct reasons.

2. With each new theorem, definition, or postulate, the teacher makes the students use each new statement in a two-step proof. For example: Using the figure, if $\triangle GMK \cong \triangle HMK$, then show that M is the midpoint of GH.

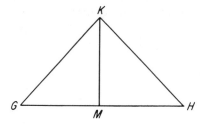

B. In what order should the two techniques from this exercise and the one technique of 19-4 be introduced to the students?

19-6. The technique described in Exercise 19-4 does not help the student on some aspects required to do a proof of an original theorem. The student does not have to:

(a) Produce on his own a strategy or plan for approaching the proof.

(b) Consider whether the statements and reasons are in a correct logical order.

(c) Decide which statements should be included and which statements can be omitted.

(d) Consider alternate approaches to proving the theorem.

A. Consider the advantages and disadvantages of these three techniques with respect to correcting the objections listed above.

1. On a sheet of paper write out the theorem and proof including all statements and reasons, but do not number the statements and reasons. Cut the lines of the proof apart, leaving the statements and reasons intact. Put the pieces of the proof in an envelope along with the statement of the theorem and figure, and them ask the students to arrange the pieces into an order that provides a proof of the theorem. How many acceptable ways could the lines in the proof in Exercise 19-4 be ordered?

2. A modification is to separate the statements and reasons by cutting them apart so that the student must order both the statements and the reasons.

3. Another modification is to include extra statements and reasons in the envelope packet that can logically follow from the needed statements but that are unnecessary for the proof.

B. Devise other modifications of this scheme that would require that the student move more and more toward devising his own proofs.

19-7. Eventually the student has to start devising his own proofs for theorems, but he should be introduced to it gradually. He can start with very short two- or three-step proofs and keep expanding to longer and longer proofs. Exercises such as the following can be helpful in learning how longer proofs chain together shorter implications.

A. Using the figure, write a proof for each theorem and compare it to the previous one.

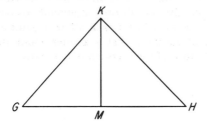

1. *Given:* In $\triangle GKH$, $\triangle GMK \cong \triangle HMK$
   Prove: $GM = MH$
2. *Given:* In $\triangle GKH$, $\triangle GMK \cong \triangle HMK$
   Prove: M is the midpoint of $\overline{GH}$.
3. *Given:* In $\triangle GKH$, M is between G and H. $\angle GKM \cong \angle HKM$ and $GK = HK$
   Prove: M is the midpoint of $\overline{GH}$.
4. *Given:* $\triangle GKH$ is isosceles, M is between G and H, and $\angle GKM \cong \angle HKM$
   Prove: M is the midpoint of $\overline{GH}$.
5. *Given:* $\triangle GKH$ is isosceles where $\overrightarrow{KM}$ is the angle bisector of $\angle GKH$ and M is between G and H.
   Prove: M is the midpoint of $\overline{GH}$.

B. In what ways would an exercise such as this help a geometry student?

19-8. One important step in developing the ability to do proofs is for the student to concentrate on figuring out an argument before he writes down any part of a formal proof. He should write the statements and reasons of a formal proof only after he has an idea about the way the proof might proceed. One way to get the student to develop this skill is to have him practice giving informal arguments orally and not requiring him to write down the details. When he can give the entire argument, then he can be asked to write down his statements in a logical order and supply the supporting reasons.

1. Draw a figure and give an informal argument to show the validity of the statement: If $\overline{AR}$ and $\overline{BH}$ bisect each other at point F, then $\overline{AB} \cong \overline{HR}$.

2. Construct a list of questions that a teacher could use to guide a student through an oral proof of the theorem in (1) above.

19-9. A very worthwhile technique for students and teacher to learn in getting ideas for proofs is to work backward from the conclusion. This procedure is called an *analysis*, and an example of it is given in the conversation below for the theorem in Exercise 19-4.

Teacher: Let's write down the "given."

Now, skip some space and let's write the conclusion. That is, M is the midpoint of $\overline{GH}$. What must first be true before we can say that M is the midpoint of $\overline{GH}$?

Student: We need to know that $GM = MH$.

Teacher: Fine, let's write that on the line before our conclusion. Now, continuing to work backward, how might we show that $GM = MH$?

Student: If we knew that $\triangle GMK \cong \triangle HMK$, then GM and MH would be corresponding parts.

Teacher: Good. Then let's write on the line above: $GM = MH$, if $\triangle GMK \cong \triangle HMK$.

What do we need, to know in order to get $\triangle GMK \cong \triangle HMK$?

Student: We need SSS, SAS, or ASA. We know $GK = HK$ and $\angle GKM \cong \angle HKM$ from the given.

Teacher: What else do we need to know to get $\triangle GMK$ congruent to $\triangle HMK$?

Student: Another side or $\angle KGM \cong \angle KHM$. We can get another side, since $KM = KM$ so we can get the triangles congruent.

Teacher: Will you start at the given now and tell me how to get, step by step, to the conclusion?

1. Read through the conversation, and write the analysis exactly the way the teacher wrote it.
2. Do an analysis for the theorem: In $\triangle ABC$, where $AB = AC$, the angle bisector of $\angle BAC$ is the perpendicular bisector of $\overline{BC}$.

19-10. In this exercise you are to learn what a gib is by answering each question "yes" or "no" and then checking your answer on the next line.

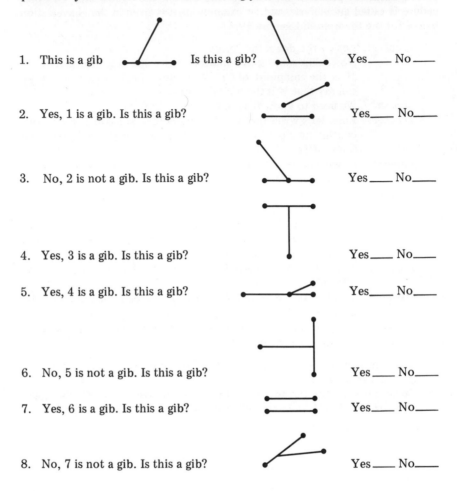

1. This is a gib   Is this a gib?   Yes___ No ___

2. Yes, 1 is a gib. Is this a gib?   Yes___ No___

3. No, 2 is not a gib. Is this a gib?   Yes ___ No___

4. Yes, 3 is a gib. Is this a gib?   Yes___ No___

5. Yes, 4 is a gib. Is this a gib?   Yes___ No___

6. No, 5 is not a gib. Is this a gib?   Yes ___ No___

7. Yes, 6 is a gib. Is this a gib?   Yes___ No___

8. No, 7 is not a gib. Is this a gib?   Yes ___ No___

9. Yes 8 is a gib.

If this instructional sequence has been successful, there has developed in your mind an idea of what a gib is that is similar to what the authors think it is. Your knowledge could be tested by giving you more examples to try and compare your responses to that of the authors. Instead, your knowledge will be tested by asking you to write a definition of a gib. Write your definition so that another person reading it who does not know what a gib is could use your definition to determine whether something placed in front of him is a gib or not.

19-11. A definition must be precise, not ambiguous. When confronted with an example, you should be able to use the definition to decide whether or not the example is an instance of the concept defined.

1. Use only the statement of the definition you wrote in the previous exercise, no other knowledge learned about a gib, decide if the following examples are gibs.

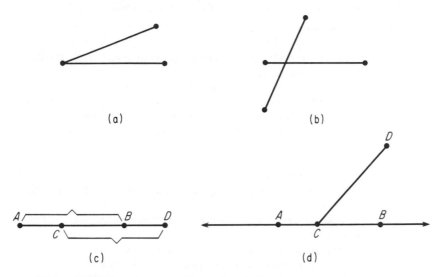

If the definition you wrote is precise, then for each of these examples it will clearly indicate whether each of these examples are gibs or not.

2. Another feature of a definition is that it be worded so that it includes all examples that are intended to be gibs and excludes all examples that are not intended to be gibs. In the authors' conception of what a gib is, example (b) above is a gib, but examples (a), (c), and (d) are not gibs. Did your definition include (b) as a gib and exclude (a), (c), and (d)? If it did not, then what you are defining as a gib is different from what was intended. The questions in the previous exercises were purposely made to mislead you so that you might see the point: that a definition is made to conform to some concept in the mind and its only function is to precisely and exactly convey that concept.

3. Rewrite your definition of a gib so that example (a), (c), and (d) above are excluded, but that example (b) is included.

19-12. Referring to the two previous exercises about a gib, perhaps you would have learned all about the concept of gib much better and more quickly by merely being presented with the entire precise definition of a gib at the outset:

> A gib is the set of points in the union of two distinct congruent line segments which intersect in exactly one point such that the point is an interior point of at least one of the line segments.

Answer these questions:

1. How was the concept of gib taught?
2. Would a learner "know" the concept of gib if he could write the definition given above from memory?
3. Is the concept of gib an important piece of knowledge?
4. Assuming it is of no value to learn what a gib is, did you learn anything of value to you from the experience of learning this concept?
5. Which of the following objectives do you think could be accomplished in a geometry course?

The student should be able to:

(a) Read and interpret new definitions.
(b) Recognize that there is more to "knowing" a concept than memorizing its definition.
(c) Recognize that more than one written definition can be given for the same concept.
(d) Recognize the need for precision in a definition.
(e) Describe why definitions are not proved like theorems.
(f) Describe what is meant by the statement, "A definition is an agreement."
(g) Describe what is meant by a definition being inclusive and exclusive.
(h) Describe what is meant by the statement, "A definition is reversible."
(i) Recognize that agreement on the definition and the word for a concept is necessary to facilitate communication of a concept between people and to avoid misunderstandings.

6. Which of the objectives listed above are important goals for everyone to achieve, even if they are not going on in mathematics?

19-13. Assume that the students in a geometry class have learned the definition of a quadrilateral and they are ready to learn the definitions of special quadrilaterals. As the teacher you decide that rather than telling them the definition for each special quadrilateral, you will make this an exercise in definition-making so that they will learn some of the items listed in question 5 of the previous exercise.

Outline a way of teaching simultaneously the concepts of trapezoid, parallelogram, rectangle, rhombus, and square so that all the work is done by the student, not by the teacher's showing and telling. Devise the outline so that the student will have the opportunity to:

  (a) Develop a system of categories and to decide if a figure is a member of a particular category.
  (b) Make up names for each of the categories.
  (c) Write a precise, inclusive, and exclusive definition for the concept corresponding to each category.

19-14. Getting students to make and test conjectures is not easy since they are not familiar with this type of activity. Theorems about special quadrilaterals are good candidates to teach making and testing conjectures.

Suppose you desired to concentrate on theorems about parallelograms and you wanted the students to make conjectures, both correct and incorrect. It may be necessary to show them a special parallelogram such as the rhombus shown in the accompanying figure. Using the example for a parallelogram, some conjectures might be made that could be refuted by a counterexample. Outline a way of teaching the theorems about parallelograms that requires the student to go through all of the steps for teaching students to make and test conjectures listed in the introduction to this chapter.

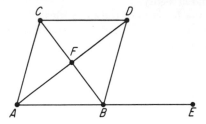

SUGGESTED ACTIVITIES

19-15. There is often confusion as to what is being proven when a proof of an implication is given. A careful discussion of this point can be found in Smith (1968).

19-16. Most teachers can benefit from more knowledge of logic, particularly symbolic logic. A particularly hard question to answer without some knowledge of logic is: Why do you use the "given" as true when proving a theorem but have to show it is true when using the theorem after it is proven? An excellent as well as an enjoyable workbook-type source on logic is Brant (1962).

19-17. Students often confuse a proof with an analysis. An analysis is merely getting an idea or a plan for writing a proof, usually by working backward from the conclusion. A useful analogy that may be helpful in distinguishing between an analysis and a proof can be found in Johnson (1967), p. 78.

19-18. An excellent article detailing a procedure that a high school geometry teacher successfully used when teaching a unit on parallelograms is Avers (1964). This article describes a way to encourage the making and testing of conjectures by students.

ADDITIONAL SOURCES

Avers, Paul W. "A Unit in High School Geometry Without the Textbook," *Mathematics Teacher*, March 1964, pp. 139-142.

Brant, Vincent, and Mervin L. Keedy. *Elementary Logic for Secondary Schools*. New York: Holt, Rinehart and Winston, Inc., 1962.

Johnson, Donovan, and Gerald Rising. *Guidelines for Teaching Mathematics*. Belmont, Calif.: Wadsworth Publishing Company, 1967.

Smith, Stanley A. "What Does a Proof Really Prove?" *Mathematics Teacher*, May 1968, pp. 483-484.

Chapter 20

Problems in Teaching
Advanced Mathematics

Within the past several years the nature of the college and high school mathematics curricula has been shifting. In the not too distant past the college preparatory mathematics curriculum in the last four years of most high schools consisted of two years of algebra, a year of plane geometry, one-half year of solid geometry, and one-half year of plane trigonometry. Following this preparation, the first two years of college mathematics contained a sequence of five courses: college algebra, trigonometry, analytic geometry, differential calculus, and integral calculus. Many colleges are now moving toward a curriculum for students majoring in mathematics and related areas in which the first year contains a unified course in analytic geometry and the calculus of one real variable. The second year may consist of matrix algebra and multivariate calculus for the most able students, or more calculus of one real variable and differential equations for other students.

Changes in the college curriculum have obvious implications for the secondary school mathematics curriculum. It is essential for some students entering college to have the prerequisite mathematical training necessary for beginning college mathematics at the analytic geometry-calculus level. To achieve this, many high schools have fused plane and solid geometry into one course and the second year of algebra may contain some trigonometry. Thus two years of algebra and a year of geometry is a usual common core in college preparatory mathematics for grades 9 through 11. Many schools, however, are beginning algebra in grade 8 for the best students, which leaves two years rather than one year available for the study of mathematics beyond the common core of algebra and geometry. It is the mathematics beyond this common core that we will call advanced mathematics, and we will include trigonometry in this category.

ALTERNATIVES FOR ADVANCED MATHEMATICS

There are several schools of thought concerning the selection of content for advanced mathematics. One view is that of "getting the student ready for college" at the level of analytic geometry-calculus. When only one year is available for advanced mathematics, a customary offering is a precalculus course integrating topics from trigonometry, analytic geometry, and content found formerly in college algebra. The intent of such a course is a review, extension, and deepening of material learned previously. Other patterns used for this same purpose are portions of the year devoted to two or more subjects such as analytic geometry, college algebra, trigonometry, or elementary functions.

Another view of mathematics in high school is that of "advanced placement." When two years of additional time for teaching mathematics are available, the second year may be devoted to teaching analytic geometry-calculus. This is intended as an accelerated program. If a student does well in a program of this type he may be able to receive college credit for his high school course and begin his college mathematics at an advanced level.

A third view stresses "broadening of mathematical horizons." Instead of forcing the student on a narrow track which leads him to and through calculus faster, the student is exposed to new areas of study intended to give him breadth and maturity in mathematics. The proponents of this view advocate a course that provides one or more units on several mathematical topics. Some of the topics for consideration in a program of this type are probability, statistics, algebraic systems, linear algebra, non-Euclidean geometries, logic, set theory, and number theory. The extent of coverage for any one of these topics may range from a unit to a course.

It is well to remember that there are a lot of students who will enter college programs that do not require calculus. They probably will only need geometry and algebra with some trigonometry for college entrance in their field. They will usually be required to take mathematics in college, but the mathematics courses they need will be different from the calculus sequence. Hence they may not need the same advanced course in high school as their fellow students preparing for mathematics-related fields. Yet there should be a suitable advanced course in mathematics available to them to get them ready for college mathematics or possibly even advanced placement.

Because of the wide diversity of career choices of students and differences among high schools, the mathematical content to be included in advanced mathematics is continually debated. There have been many suggestions and recommendations for courses or units to be taught at this level. We cannot deal with all of the possible suggested courses here. Rather, we will discuss briefly the teaching of trigonometry and then only make some general observations about the teaching of other advanced topics. We believe this is defensible, since advanced topics are seldom taught by new or inexperienced teachers.

TRIGONOMETRY

Historically, trigonometry was used almost exclusively as a device to make indirect measurements. More recently it has been viewed as a supporting course for analytic geometry, calculus, and the sciences. Using this view, trigonometry is now studied as a set of functions which have interesting and important properties that can be applied in many areas. Application to measurement problems is only one part of this study.

The shift in purpose of trigonometry from measurement to an analytic study of functions has quite often resulted in the deletion of a course entitled Trigonometry in the secondary school curriculum. This is a consequence of the views of many curriculum study groups which have recommended that the study of algebra and trigonometry be fused together to form one integrated course. It seems quite natural to do this since both of the courses rely quite heavily on the functional approach and this has resulted in a course which is often entitled Elementary Functions. The treatment of trigonometry in a course such as this emphasizes the analytic aspect of trigonometry and relates the study of trigonometry to both algebra and geometry. Almost all of the content that was in a traditional course is still included in the treatment given to trigonometry, although there has been a vast reorganization of the topics as well as a change in emphasis. Thus in more recent treatments the trigonometric functions are defined as a function on the set of real numbers. This general definition is then modified for applications in which we need a function of a particular angle measured in degrees. After the trigonometric functions have been defined in general, the student studies and verifies the fundamental identities which relate the various trigonometric functions. This can be a very challenging aspect of the curriculum because it is possible for the students to use inductive reasoning to generate these identities. The student should be encouraged to draw pictures using the unit circle and to identify lengths associated with each of the six trigonometric functions for a given arc length. Experimentation with pictures of this type can also be used to discover formulas for functions such as $\sin (\alpha + \beta)$ or $\sin (\alpha - \beta)$. Once formulas of this type are discovered and the students have an intuitive feeling for their validity they should be encouraged to prove them in an algebraic manner.

Graphing trigonometric functions is an aspect that receives strong emphasis in current approaches to trigonometry. Students should be encouraged to investigate systematically the resulting changes in the graph of a trigonometric function such as $y = \sin x$ when it is changed to $y = 2 \sin x$ or $y = \sin 2x$ or $y = \sin (x + \pi /2)$. With content of this type it is quite easy to use a heuristic method of instruction which permits the student to independently develop some of the important notions relating to trigonometric functions.

Solution of triangles and indirect measurement are not ignored in the current approach to trigonometry; rather, these topics are considered as applications of trigonometry. Problems in surveying, determination of distances that cannot be measured directly, solution of vector problems arising in navigation, or in solution of vector problems arising when weights slide down an inclined plane can all be used as meaningful field applications of trigonometry. One very useful activity to illustrate the applications of trigonometry is to have the students learn to use surveying instruments and to apply the trigonometry they have learned. If this is done, procedures recommended for use with a laboratory lesson should be followed—that is, careful thought should be given to planning the lesson, the problem for the students should be clearly and precisely stated, instruments to be used should be available, and instructions for proper use of the instruments provided for students to read. To be sure, an observer may think that there is a lot of unnecessary student activity and motion in a lesson of this type, but there is also a great deal of learning taking place which applies mathematical skills to problems arising in the physical world. These lessons can be most beneficial if they are planned carefully and the students know what is expected of them.

One topic that is often neglected in the application of trigonometric functions to problems arising in the physical world is that of computation with approximate numbers. This is an excellent place to review or teach topics such as greatest possible error in measurement, relative error in measurement, and the implications of these topics for computation. For example, if we are interested in finding the height of a flagpole and measure its shadow correct to the nearest foot, can we honestly report the height of the flagpole correct to the nearest hundredth of a foot? When asked in this manner, the answer to this question is obviously no. Actually, it is not meaningful to report the height of an unknown quantity to a degree which is more precise than the measurements that were used to find this value.

ADVANCED TOPICS

Regardless of the content that is to be taught in advanced topics, the instructional emphasis should be placed on teaching basic processes of the content, rather than on mechanical procedures for solving problems. If, for example, calculus is to be taught in the secondary schools, it is preferable to develop a good intuitive idea of the limit process and apply this process to develop an understanding of derivatives and integrals. An intuitive understanding of basic ideas from the calculus is in contrast to a very formal approach which might present the delta-epsilon definition of a limit. It is doubtful if this type of formal approach is advantageous until there is a basic understanding of the process involved.

A second emphasis for each of these topics should be the applications that they have both for future mathematical study and for problems in the physical world. An indication of the usefulness of a unit in statistics is found by reading the selected goals for a unit of this type in Appendix A. There are a multitude of practical examples for the calculus. The obvious ones here are velocity, acceleration, area, and volume. A course in linear algebra would also have many applications to problems arising in physics such as force and velocity.

Finally, the instructor teaching advanced mathematics should be a good teacher with a high level of preparation in mathematics. Just as with general mathematics, advanced mathematics should not be entrusted to the inexperienced teacher, the inept instructor, or the person lacking a strong background in mathematics. People teaching mathematics at this level should have a depth of preparation possibly equivalent to a master's degree in mathematics as well as several years of successful teaching experience.

EXERCISES[1]

20-1. Like many words in mathematics, *function* is a term with a less precise and possibly confusing everyday English meaning. One everday use of the noun form of the word is that of the performance of an act or the serving of a purpose. For example, we would say our stomach has the function of digesting food. Another English usage closer to the mathematical one is that of dependence or causality. For example, we might say human growth is a function of hereditary factors—i.e., growth depends upon hereditary factors.

In mathematics, the term function is defined in different ways. Two definitions for the term as it is used in mathematics are

(a) A function from a set A to a set B is a rule of association that assigns to each element of A exactly one element in B

(b) A function from a set A to a set B is a set of ordered pairs, (a subset of $A \times B$, the Cartesian product of A and B) where each element of A occurs as a first element in some ordered pair having a second element from B, and no ordered pair contains two different second elements for the same first element.

In definition (a) a function is defined as a rule, while in (b) a function is a set of ordered pairs. It should be noted that these definitions are equivalent (see 4 and 5 below).

1. Which definition corresponds more closely to your "intuitive" feeling of a function?

2. Which definition seems more "intuitively" appealing when you are looking at a graph and trying to decide if it is a graph of a function?

3. Using definition (b) which of the following would be functions from the real numbers into the real numbers? Why? (x is any real number.)

$$(i) \quad f(x) = x^2 \qquad (iii) \quad \{(x, y) \mid y = x^2\}$$
$$(ii) \quad \{(x, x^2)\} \qquad (iv) \quad y = x^2$$

4. Would every rule of association of the type described in definition (a) produce a set of ordered pairs like that described in definition (b)?

5. For every set of ordered pairs of the type described in definition (b) could a rule of association of the type described in definition (a) be found that would relate the first and second elements in the ordered pairs?

[1] The exercises in this chapter relate almost exclusively to the teaching of trigonometry. Those not dealing explicitly with trigonometry may be included in an advanced mathematics course designed to teach a variety of mathematical topics. This decision was made due to the diversity of twelfth-grade mathematics courses.

20-2. The following responses were obtained when a class was asked to define the concept, function.

(a) A function is a process of association of two or more elements—that is, one's magnitude affects the other's value.

(b) Function is a correspondence that exists between variables.

(c) A function is a set of ordered pairs, (x,y), such that no two second elements possess the same first element.

(d) The process by which a value is acted upon to give another value.

(e) Function—characterized by a graph no two points of which lie in the same vertical plane.

(f) A function is a relationship between two variables (x,y) such that for any value of x there is only one corresponding value of y.

1. Compare each of these statements to the two definitions given in the previous exercise. Indicate if the statement clearly and precisely defines a function. If no, which parts are ambiguous?

2. Distinguish between acceptable and unacceptable statements listed above. Defend your choice.

20-3. Suppose that the students in trigonometry have had experience with algebraic functions and are beginning a study of the trigonometric functions. One method of defining these functions is to introduce a "wrapping function." To describe a wrapping function, we might think of a wire being wrapped around the edges of a square piece of cardboard, both in a clockwise and a counterclockwise manner. Each point of the wire covers exactly one point on the edge of the cardboard square. This is then a model of a function from the set of points of the wire to the set of points on the edge of the cardboard.

If this physical model is now abstracted by letting the wire be a line and the edge of the cardboard be a simple closed curve, we have a more general description of a wrapping function. If the line is coordinatized and the simple closed curve lies in a coordinate plane, then this procedure could define a function of the set of real numbers to a set of ordered pairs of real numbers.

1. On a coordinate plane, draw a square having vertices $A = (1,1)$; $B = (^-1,1)$; $C = (^-1,^-1)$; and $D = (1,^-1)$. On this same graph, draw the line $x = 1$ and label the point $(1,2)$, E and the point $(1, ^-2)$, F.

2. Wrap ray AE around square $ABCD$ in a counterclockwise direction and ray DF around the square in a clockwise direction. Does this wrapping procedure define a function of the points on the line $x = 1$ to the set of points on the square?

3. Using the y coordinates on the line $x = 1$, the wrapping function contains $((0,(1,0)), (^-1,(1, ^-1)), (3,(^-1,1)),$ and $(^-4^1/_2, (^-1, ^1/_2)$. Verify that these points are in the wrapping function and then list at least five other points in this wrapping function.

4. Draw in your figure the line segment that represents each number in $(^-3/2,(\frac{1}{2}, ^-1))$.

5. Suppose $(a,(b,c))$ is an element of the wrapping function. If $a = 7$, find (b,c). If $a = ^-12$, find (b,c).

20-4. As stated in the last exercise, a wrapping function can be defined for any simple closed curve and a wrapping line. When the simple closed curve is a circle, a wrapping function important to the study of trigonometry is defined.

1. Carry out the directions below to define a wrapping function. Draw a unit circle on a coordinate plane; then draw a tangent line to this circle at (1,0). This is the line $x = 1$. Coordinatize this line by using its y coordinates. Now imagine the positive part of the line wrapped around the circle in a counterclockwise direction and the negative part of the line wrapped in the clockwise direction.

2. Since the line is infinite, how many times will the line wrap around the circle?

3. What are several ordered pairs contained in this function? (Remember the second member of each ordered pair is an ordered pair.)

4. Find all values of u for which $(u,(0,1))$ belongs to the wrapping function.

5. For each value of u, in the table below, find the ordered pair (x,y) so that $(u,(x,y))$ is an element of the wrapping function.

u	$\pi/6$	$7\pi/6$	$13\pi/6$	$19\pi/6$	$25\pi/6$	$31\pi/6$
(x,y)						

6. Are wrapping functions periodic? Discuss.

20-5. The wrapping function that was defined in Exercise 20-4, can be used to define the trigonometric functions. If, for example, the ordered pairs of the wrapping function are $(u,(x, y))$ where u is a real number and (x, y) are the coordinates of a point on the unit circle, with center at the origin, then the set of ordered pairs (u, x) and the set of ordered pairs (u, y) define two of the trigonometric functions—i.e., the sine function and the cosine functions.

1. Under these conditions which function does the set of ordered pairs (u, x) define? Which does the set of ordered pairs (u, y) define?

2. The remaining four trigonometric functions can then be defined in terms of the two that we already have. Using the same notation as above supply the correct names for each function below:

   (a) The set of ordered pairs $\left(u, \dfrac{y}{x} \right) x \neq 0$

   (b) The set of ordered pairs $\left(u, \dfrac{x}{y} \right) y \neq 0$

   (c) The set of ordered pairs $\left(u, \dfrac{1}{x} \right) x \neq 0$

   (d) The set of ordered pairs $\left(u, \dfrac{1}{y} \right) y \neq 0$

20-6. There are a variety of advantages to be accrued by using the method described in Exercises 20-4 and 20-5 as an introduction to the trigonometric functions. This model defines the sine and cosine functions that have the real numbers as the domain. This is preferable to defining the sine and cosine for acute angles in a right triangle and then trying to modify and extend this definition for angles with measure greater than 90°. A second advantage of the wrapping function is that it clearly shows that the trigonometric functions are periodic and how the sine and cosine functions are related to a circle. Finally, this procedure describes a model which is fairly easy to construct with materials that are easily and cheaply obtainable.

1. Describe how the wrapping function approach to the trigonometric functions relates to the more conventional approach that defines these functions for central angles and angles of rotation.
2. Which approach do you think is preferable and why?

20-7. One way to generate trigonometric identities is to begin with any one of the simple identities that are given in the textbook and then to transform this identity to some other equivalent form. As an example, suppose we start with $\sin^2 x + \cos^2 x = 1$ and go through the following steps:

$$\sin^2 x + \cos^2 x = 1$$
$$\sin^3 x + \sin x \cos^2 x = \sin x$$
$$\tan x\,(1 - \cos^2 x) + {}^1\!/_2 \sin 2x = \tan x$$
$$\tan x\,(2 - 2\cos^2 x) + \sin 2x = 2 \tan x$$

1. Justify each step in the above derivation.
2. Any of the equivalent forms above could be given as an identity for students to prove, that is, the three steps each yielded a different valid identity. For each identity given below, generate three different identities which students could be asked to prove.
   (a) $1 + \tan^2 x = \sec^2 x$
   (b) $\sin 3x = 3 \sin x - 4 \sin^3 x$
   (c) $\cos (x - y) = \cos x \cos y + \sin x \sin y$

20-8. An interesting student question arose in a trigonometry class when the half angle formulas for the tangent were being considered. The textbook [Vanatta (1965), p. 137] listed two of these formulas as follows:

$$\tan\frac{\alpha}{2} = \pm\sqrt{\frac{1 - \cos\alpha}{1 + \cos\alpha}}$$

$$\tan\frac{\alpha}{2} = \frac{1 - \cos\alpha}{\sin\alpha}$$

It further continued that the plus or minus sign is not used in the second formula. The student readily agreed that the two formulas are related with the exception of this sign problem.

1. How would you justify to a trigonometry class that the minus sign is never needed in the second formula?
2. What picture would you draw to supplement your verbal justification given in 1?

20-9. Learning to graph trigonometric functions consists basically of knowing two things: (a) the general shape of the graph of each basic function and its amplitude, period and x-intercepts, and (b) the effect on the graph when the basic function is changed by such processes as adding or multiplying the independent variable by a constant. It was mentioned in the introduction that much of the development of initial understanding of these graphing notions can be accomplished by allowing the students to discover them. After these ideas have been learned, there remains a quite different instructional problem. The students must become skillful in graphing all kinds of trigonometric functions quickly and correctly. One useful technique is illustrated below.

Example: Sketch the graph of the function $y = \sin 3t$. All sine functions have essentially the same shaped graph as $y = \sin \square$ where $\square$ represents the independent variable. The graph of $y = \sin \square$ goes through one cycle of its shape as $\square$ goes from 0 to 2π and it has intercepts at the endpoints and middle of the interval. Using these notions we can solve the problem.

Let $3t = \square$. Then $y = \sin \boxed{3t}$ goes through one cycle for $0 \leqslant \boxed{3t} \leqslant 2\pi$ or solving t, it goes through one cycle for t between 0 and $2\pi/3$. Hence, the intercepts are 0, $\pi/3$, and $2\pi/3$ and its period is $2\pi/3$, the length of the interval. Now, we have the information necessary for sketching the graph.

1. Sketch the graph of $y = \cos 4t$ using the procedure described above.
2. Using the same procedure given above, find the period and t-intercepts for the graph of the function $y = \sin (t + \pi/2.)$ Notice this is the case where a constant is *added* to the independent variable.
3. Repeat question 2 for the function $y = \sin (2t + \pi/3)$.
4. Repeat question 2 for the function $y = A \sin (Bt + C)$ for $B > 0$. Also find the y-intercept and the amplitude.

20-10. After students have learned to solve for the missing parts in a triangle it is time for an application lesson which uses these skills to solve problems arising in the physical world. As indicated in the introduction to this chapter, a surveying application with surveying instruments can be a real learning experience. Even if these tools are not available, meaningful problems can be generated.

One example of an outdoor activity that can be used is to determine various lengths without actually measuring them. Although this may seem to be contrived, it has the advantage of permitting a direct measurement check of values obtained indirectly. Suppose you wished to use this activity with your class. The first thing you should do is to determine the distance that the students are to find—i.e., find two suitable landmarks which span a reasonable distance. Then it is necessary to formulate a statement of the problem which clearly delineates the conditions under which the problem is to be solved, identify and obtain the necessary supplies and conditions, and determine ways in which you can help students who are having trouble.

If the distance you want measured is from the base of a tree in the school yard to the base of a tree across a busy street:

(a) How would you state this problem for the students?

(b) What conditions would you stipulate for its solution?

(c) What materials would the students need?

(d) What are several strategies for solution of this problem?

(e) How could the students check their work and what equipment would they need for this?

20-11. Whenever we make a measurement such as measuring a line segment or an angle, we select some unit of measure and try to find the integral number of units in the object we are measuring. The number we obtain is not the true or exact measure of the line segment or angle, but only an approximation. For example, if we say $\overline{AB}$ is 12.9 in., we mean the length is closer to 12.9 in. than to 12.8 in. or 13.0 in. A more precise way of saying that our approximation is 12.9 in. is to say that the true measure of $\overline{AB}$ (denoted $m(\overline{AB})$ is between 12.85 in. and 12.95 in., or using symbolism, $12.85'' \leqslant m(\overline{AB}) < 12.95''$. This interval in which the true measure lies is called the *interval of error*. The greatest possible error (GPE) for a linear or angle measure is one-half its interval of error. In our example, the GPE of the measure of $\overline{AB}$ is 0.05''.

Refer to right triangle ABC in answering questions below.

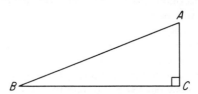

1. An approximation to $\overline{BC}$ is reported as $10^{1}/_{2}$ inches. Since this is reported to the nearest half inch, the unit of measurement is one-half inch. Write the interval of error and the GPE for this measurement.
2. If the interval of error for side $\overline{AB}$ is $14.5'' \leqslant m(\overline{AC}) < 15.5''$, find the unit of measure and the GPE.
3. If $\angle B$ is $49°$ correct to the nearest $2°$, find the interval of error, the unit of measure, and the GPE.
4. Using the information in the previous question, find an approximation to $\angle A$, and report the GPE of your approximation.

20-12. When two or more approximations are added or multiplied, the GPE of their sum or product is greater than for either of the individual approximations. Since errors may increase when computing with approximate numbers, the final result should give some indication of the error involved.

Suppose the intervals of error and GPE's for $\overline{CD}$ and $\overline{EF}$ are

$$\overline{AB}: \quad 12^1/2'' \leqslant m\,(\overline{AB}) < 13^1/2'' \quad \text{GPE} = {}^1/_2 \text{ inch}$$

$$\overline{CD}: \quad 8^1/4'' \leqslant m\,(\overline{CD}) < 8^3/4'' \quad \text{GPE} = {}^1/_4 \text{ inch}$$

If we added the reported measures of $\overline{AB}$ and $\overline{CD}$ (13 in. and $8^1/2$ in.), we would get an approximation of $21^1/2$ in. for the sum of $\overline{AB}$ and $\overline{CD}$. However, the sum of their true measures could be as small as $20^3/4$ in. or as large as $22^1/4$ in. Hence, the interval of error of their sum is $20^3/4'' \leqslant m(\overline{AB}) + m(\overline{CD}) < 22^1/4''$. It can be computed by adding the lower endpoints and the upper endpoints of the intervals of error of the individual measures. The GPE of the sum is one-half the interval of error and for this example, it is $3/4$ of an inch.

The GPE and the interval of error for the product is found in an analogous way. The lower endpoints and the upper endpoints are multiplied to obtain the interval for the product. The GPE for a product is found by taking the differences of the product and endpoints of the interval. The difference with the larger absolute value is the GPE. In the example, the interval of error of the product is $103^1/8'' \leqslant m(\overline{AB}) \cdot m(\overline{CD}) < 118^1/8''$ and the GPE is $7^5/8''$.

1. In right triangle ABC with right angle at C, $\angle A$ is $49°$ correct to the nearest degree. Find the interval of error and the GPE for $\angle A, \angle B, \angle C$, and the sum of the three angles.

2. In the triangle in 1, side $\overline{AB}$ is $10.1''$ correct to $0.1''$. We can find $\overline{BC}$ by multiplying the measure of $\overline{AB}$ times the sine of $\angle A$. Find an approximation to the length of $\overline{BC}$. Find the GPE and the interval of error for $\overline{BC}$.

3. How should the length of $\overline{BC}$ be reported accurately to another person? (i.e., to the nearest inch, to the nearest $0.1''$ or what?)

4. Is there any need to use four place sine tables when working with data of this sort?

5. In problems of this type, if a student reports his answer to the nearest thousandth, what should you tell him? What is the rule of thumb usually used with computations with approximate numbers?

20-13. There are a variety of opportunities to teach the limit concept prior to its formal introduction in a course in the calculus. Listed below are several cases which may arise somewhere in the secondary school curriculum.

(a) When we repeatedly flip a coin we would expect the number of heads divided by the total number of tosses to be near 1/2.

(b) $1/2 + 1/4 + 1/8 + \ldots = 1$

(c) $1/3 = .333 \ldots$

(d) As x approaches $\pi/2$ the function $\tan x$ gets large without bound.

(e) The graph of a hyperbola approaches its asymptotes.

(f) Between any two rational numbers there is another rational number.

1. Rewrite (a)-(d) above using the limit notation.

2. List several more examples in which the limit concept is used in secondary school mathematics concepts.

3. If situations such as those listed above are considered in the curriculum, they can be used to provide students with a foundation for, and an insight into, the limit concept. How might each of them be treated in the classroom so that the student gains a deeper understanding of the limit concept?

20-14. An interesting technique that can be used when advanced students are studying analytic geometry is to generate conic sections by paper folding.

1. Take a rectangular piece of wax paper with size approximately 5 in. × 6 in. Draw a horizontal line about 1 in. from the bottom of the paper and put a point about 1/2 in. above the line and near the center of the paper. Now begin folding the paper so that a point of the line you drew coincides with the point just above the line. Continue folding until a familiar shape emerges.

2. See if you can identify the focus, directrix, and axis of symmetry for this figure.

3. By varying the distance between the point and the line a variety of different parabolas can be obtained. Why does the shape change? Use a fresh piece of wax paper for each parabola.

4. Other conic sections can be generated by replacing the line by a circle. What figure do you obtain if the point is inside the circle? What figure do you obtain if the point is outside the circle?

This procedure and further information on paper folding can be found in the NCTM publication by Johnson (1957).

20-15. Presuming that the equivalent of two years of algebra, a year of geometry, and a half-year of trigonometry have been completed by the end of the eleventh year, there are two main views pertaining to the content of a senior mathematics course. Should the twelfth-year mathematics program be devoted to advanced placement or to broaden the mathematical background of the students? By advanced placement we would mean a course in analytic geometry and the calculus which may permit the student to begin his college mathematics training at an advanced level. On the other hand, there are a variety of courses such as modern algebra, probability and statistics, or matrix algebra that could be used to broaden mathematical background.

Many conditions should be considered before deciding on one course or the other. Such factors as availability of qualified teachers and capability and needs of students should be considered before any final decision on a course can be made.

1. What other factors or conditions should be considered in deciding the twelfth-year curriculum?
2. Select one of the two views (advanced placement or broadening) and give an argument which could be used to justify your position to a fellow teacher, your department chairman, or your principal.

20-16. In the introductory portion of this chapter, it was stated that in the teaching of advanced topics, emphasis should be placed on the practical applications of the mathematical content. There were several indications of this in that calculus has applications to velocity, acceleration, centroids, and moments; vectors can be applied to force or velocity type problems; and statistics is applicable to the interpretation of much data which arises in the physical world. For each of the topics listed below, find one or more real applications from the physical world.

(a) Solution of a system of linear inequalities.

(b) The algebraic structure, group.

(c) Matrices.

(d) Bayes' theorem in probability.

(e) Exponential functions.

(f) Conic sections.

SUGGESTED ACTIVITIES

20-17. For a brief overview of several twelfth-grade mathematics programs, read Woodby (1965). This report also provides brief descriptions of emerging courses and summarizes some features of these courses that the author feels are important. The "Conclusions and Recommendations" section, pp. 34–37, provides an indication relating to the lack of agreement on the content of twelfth-grade mathematics and methods for studying this problem.

20-18. One report that outlines a possible secondary school mathematics curriculum of the future is the Cambridge Report (1963). Read the outline of the curriculum for grades 7–12, pp. 42ff. Do you think that you could teach a curriculum of this type with the training that you currently have? Do you think this is a realistic curriculum for secondary school students?

20-19. An indication of several applications of the functions $y = a \sin (bx - c)$ and $y = a \cos (bx - c)$ is found in Wylie (1955), pp. 100–101. If a trigonometry teacher knows that there are applications of these functions in physics, perhaps several students with a background in physics could build a model to illustrate these applications. This also provides an excellent opportunity for cooperation between the mathematics teacher and the physics teacher.

20-20. Textbooks on a variety of mathematical contents have been written especially for use in the secondary schools. At the present time there are textbooks for courses in probability and statistics, linear algebra, matrix algebra, analytic geometry, and textbooks that have a selection from these topics. Calculus textbooks are usually selected from those designed to be used with college freshmen. Find one or more mathematics textbooks designed for advanced students and scan it. What prerequisites are expected of students who are to study from this textbook?

20-21. There have been many debates for and against accelerated mathematics as well as for and against enrichment or broadening mathematics courses. One of these views is thoroughly examined in Grossman (1962) as he questions the concept of advanced placement in high school mathematics.

20-22. Good teachers should continually search for new and better ways to teach topics, particularly if the topic is particularly difficult for students to learn. One such topic is solving inequalities. Frandsen (1969) provides a technique that can be used effectively for teaching this topic. This is only one example of the many helpful and practical suggestions that are available in professional journals.

ADDITIONAL SOURCES

Frandsen, Henry. "The Last Word on Solving Inequalities," *Mathematics Teacher*, October 1969, pp. 439-441.

Grossman, George. "Advanced Placement Mathematics—For Whom?" *Mathematics Teacher*, November 1962 pp. 560-566.

Johnson, Donovan A. *Paper Folding for the Mathematics Class*. Washington, D.C.: National Council of Teachers of Mathematics 1957.

Report of the Cambridge Conference on School Mathematics. *Goals for School Mathematics*. Boston: Houghton Mifflin Company, 1963.

Vannatta, Glen D., Walter H. Carnahan, and Harold P. Fawcett. *Advanced High School Mathematics*. Columbus, Ohio: Charles E. Merrill Books, Inc., 1965.

Woodby, Lauren G. *Emerging Twelfth-Grade Mathematics Programs*. Washington, D.C.: Government Printing Office, 1965.

Wylie, C. R. Jr. *Plane Trigonometry*. New York: McGraw-Hill Book Company, 1955.

APPENDIXES

Selected Goals of a Unit on Statistics

The list below contains, in a scrambled order, some of the content goals, process goals, and affective goals that might be stated by a teacher for a unit on statistics.

1. Appreciation of the usefulness and necessity of statistics to a modern society.
2. Skill in computing summary statistics from ungrouped data.
3. Ability to critically analyze, draw valid inferences, and make predictions based upon the data.
4. Ability to apply statistical terms and techniques in the utilitarian, recreational, and cultural aspects of the learner's life.
5. Display a reasonable amount of trust and belief in results based upon sound statistical procedures.
6. Show a healthy skepticism and cautiousness before accepting any results based upon statistical techniques.
7. Capability to identify situations that can be approached by statistical methods and formulate procedures that could be applied to collect, summarize, and present data that will yield predictions and conclusions.
8. Knowledge and understanding of statistical terms and sampling techniques.
9. Display a receptiveness and willingness to encounter statistical terms and concepts that might arise in the student's life.
10. Organize, summarize, and present data using graphical representations and descriptive statistics.
11. Ability to critically analyze the use of statistical techniques and concepts by other people to insure that the results and conclusions are supported by data that are appropriate and unbiased.

12. Find enjoyment and excitement in knowing that humans can, by exerting their reasoning powers, bring order to and make predictions about events that seem to be unpredictable and uncertain.
13. Read and understand findings and results based upon simple statistical techniques and graphical representations.

Selected Objectives of a Unit on Statistics

The list below contains some of the specific objectives that give more concrete expression to some of the broad, general goals of a unit on statistics that were listed in the previous Appendix. The student should be able to

1. State descriptions of the terms population, sample, representative sample, biased sample, random sample, parameter, statistic, mean, median, mode, prediction, conclusion, bar graph, line graph, and circle graph.
2. Construct a line graph, bar graph, or a circle graph when given data to be represented graphically.
3. Calculate the mean, median, and mode when given a set of ungrouped numbers.
4. Distinguish between population or sample values that are exact and values that are estimates or approximations.
5. Identify conditions of sampling from a population that would bias the drawing of a representative sample with respect to some given population characteristic.
6. Describe procedures for drawing a representative sample with respect to some population characteristic when the population is given.
7. Describe and demonstrate procedures for obtaining estimates of population characteristics or parameters by sampling from the population.
8. Order several estimates of a population parameter from more reliable to least reliable on the basis of a criterion such as size of the sample or number of independent samples that the estimate is based upon.
9. Distinguish among conclusions or predictions based solely upon given data, based partially on given data, and contrary to the given data.

10. Distinguish among conclusions or predictions that follow directly from given data, require an interpolation from the given data, and those that are derived by an extrapolation from the given data.

11. Construct predictions or conclusions on the basis of graphical data, summary data, or sample statistics.

12. Search for bias in statistical presentations by trying to identify the relationship between the choice of summary statistics or graphical representation presented and the motives of the presenter.

13. Search for bias in sampling techniques by trying to identify the relationship between results based upon the sample and the motives of the person selecting the sample.

14. Given a choice between alternative courses of action that require the student to make evaluative judgments, he will choose an alternative consistent with given data rather than an alternative inconsistent with given data.

15. Given the choice between a course of action based upon no statistical data or objective information and a course of action based upon data, the student will select a course of action based upon the statistical data.

16. Given the choice between a course of action based upon estimates from a representative sample and a course of action based upon conjecture and guessing, the student will select the course of action based upon sample estimates.

17. Read and attend to statistical information presented in books, newspapers, radio, television, magazines, and in conversation more than he did prior to the study of the unit on statistics.

18. Choose to read articles on the extent to which statistics helps people do things in their occupations that could not be done without statistics more often than before the study of the unit on statistics.

Sample Lesson Plan: Statistics

Topic: Statistics

Date:

Class: General Mathematics
Ninth Grade

Objectives: The student should be able to
(Determining the objectives for this lesson is Exercise 11-6 in Chapter 11.)

Content and Procedure[1]	Feedback	Materials, Equipment, Notes
I. 1. 1 millimeter = .03937 inch How long is a millimeter to the nearest (a) thousandth of an inch? (b) hundredth of an inch? (c) tenth of an inch?	Walk around the room as they are working to check their answers and see who needs help.	Have the 3 questions on the chalkboard or overhead when they come into the room. Have answers ready on overhead or board to show them after five minutes and let them check their papers.
2. What percent is 3 of 10?		
3. There are 33 pupils in a class of which 30 percent are girls. How many boys are there in the class? Look carefully at your answer.		

[1] This plan is read horizontally across columns for each grouping of sentences.

Content and Procedure	Feedback	Materials, Equipment, Notes
II.		Make the students put all their books and papers off of their desks except one clean sheet of paper and a pencil.
1. YESTERDAY WE LEARNED ABOUT THE MEAN, MEDIAN, AND MODE AND HOW TO COMPUTE EACH OF THESE FROM A SET OF NUMBERS. [2]	1. IF I TOLD YOU THE MIDDLE SCORE, WOULD THAT BE THE MEAN, MEDIAN OR MODE?	
	2. HOW DO YOU COMPUTE THE MEAN OF SEVERAL NUMBERS?	
	3. WHAT IS THE MODE OF A SET OF NUMBERS?	
2. TODAY, WE ARE GOING TO SEE HOW TO INTERPRET DATA USING THE MEAN, MEDIAN, AND MODE. BEFORE WE DO, HAVE ANY OF YOU SEEN IN THE NEWS OR ON TV WHERE SOMEONE PREDICTED WHO WOULD WIN AN ELECTION BEFORE PEOPLE ACTUALLY VOTED? WAS THE PREDICTION CORRECT? WE'RE GOING TO BEGIN TO LEARN THE WAY THIS IS DONE AND WHY THE PREDICTIONS ARE SOMETIMES WRONG.		

III. Indicate the bucket to the class and tell them it contains marbles of different colors. Don't tell how many marbles or how many different colors.

Have a large bucket containing different numbers (known only to you) of red, black, white, and blue marbles in the front of the room.

Have prepared on the chalkboard, but hidden from the class's view a copy of the following chart:

color	number	percent

1. SUPPOSE I WISHED TO KNOW ABOUT HOW MANY RED MARBLES ARE IN THE BUCKET. HOW WOULD YOU DE-CIDE ABOUT HOW MANY RED MAR-BLES THERE ARE? List all their sug-gestions on the board without comment or judgment. Get them to suggest guessing and counting all of the marbles.

2. WHICH OF THE WAYS SUGGESTED DO YOU THINK WOULD RESULT IN THE MOST PRECISE ANSWER? THE LEAST PRECISE ANSWER?

3. LET'S TRY TO FIND OUT HOW MANY RED MARBLES ARE IN THE BUCKET. SINCE I'M TOO LAZY TO COUNT THEM *ALL* AND GUESSING IS TOO IMPRE-CISE, HOW MIGHT I TRY TO GET A REASONABLY GOOD ESTIMATE? (When emphasizing that you won't count *all*, imply that you might count some.) Tell them that when you select part of the total, that is called a sample. Relate to soil sam-ple, water sample, sample of yard goods, or a sample of cake.

---

[2] Notice that words spoken by the teacher to the class are written in capital letters.

Content and Procedure	Feedback	Materials, Equipment, Notes
4. WE'LL DRAW A SAMPLE FROM THE BUCKET AND USE IT TO GET AN ESTIMATE OF THE NUMBER OF RED MARBLES IN THE BUCKET. (Select two students, one to draw a sample of ten marbles and the other to record the results in the chart on the board except for the column headed percent.)	Walk about the room as the students are computing the percent column.	Ask each student at his seat to copy the chart from the board, fill in the results of the drawing, and compute the percentage of occurrence of each color in the sample.
5. LOOKING AT THE RESULTS OF OUR SAMPLE, WHAT ARE SOME THINGS WE CAN ESTIMATE ABOUT THE MARBLES IN THE BUCKET THAT WE DIDN'T KNOW BEFORE? Number of different colors and percent of each.		Call upon students in the class to tell the recorder at the chalkboard the numbers to put in the percent column of the chart.
6. DOES THE SAMPLE TELL YOU THE TOTAL NUMBER OF MARBLES IN THE BUCKET? THE TOTAL NUMBER OF RED MARBLES? No.		
7. IF I TOLD YOU THAT I PUT 250 MARBLES IN THE BUCKET, WOULD THAT TELL YOU THE NUMBER OF RED MARBLES? AN ESTIMATE?	Ask a student to explain at the chalkboard the method of getting the estimate.	Give each student time to think and work through this to figure out an estimate of red marbles.
8. IS ____ RED MARBLES THE EXACT NUMBER OF RED MARBLES IN THE BUCKET? IS ____ RED MARBLES THE		

EXACT NUMBER OF RED MARBLES IN OUR SAMPLE? Make the distinction that the number of red marbles in the sample is exact, the number we say is in the bucket is an estimate based on the sample.

WHAT IS THE WORD USED TO DESCRIBE A PART OF THE TOTAL? HOW DO YOU THINK PEOPLE ESTIMATE HOW AN ENTIRE STATE WILL VOTE DURING AN ELECTION? WHY ARE THEIR PREDICTIONS SOMETIMES WRONG?

Tell them the exact number of red marbles in bucket if they are curious as well as the number of each of the other colors.

IV. TODAY WE LEARNED HOW TO GET AN ESTIMATE FROM A LARGE NUMBER OF OBJECTS WITHOUT EXAMINING EACH ONE.

TOMORROW, WE ARE GOING TO LEARN HOW TO GET ESTIMATES FROM SEVERAL SAMPLES THAT ARE MORE PRECISE THAN THE ONE WE FOUND TODAY. ALSO, WE'LL LOOK AT THE WAYS IN WHICH THE SAMPLE IS DRAWN AND HOW THIS AFFECTS THE PRECISION OF OUR ESTIMATES.

Content and Procedure	Feedback	Materials, Equipment, Notes
V. PUT AWAY ALL OF YOUR PAPERS AND KEEP YOUR PENCIL. WHEN I TELL YOU, GET INTO YOUR REGULAR GROUPS OF THREE. I WILL HAND EACH OF YOU AN EXERCISE SHEET. EACH GROUP WILL DISCUSS EACH QUESTION AND MARK THEIR ANSWER. TOMORROW, BRING YOUR COMPLETED EXERCISE SHEET TO CLASS AND EACH GROUP WILL BE ASKED TO REPORT ON ONE OR MORE OF THEIR ANSWERS. MOVE QUIETLY INTO YOUR GROUPS. [3]	Move from one group to another. Do not answer any questions directly. Always turn the question back to the student with another question. Make notes of those that are disagreed upon and arrange to have some of them reported by those that disagree.	Hand each student the exercise sheet on mean, median, and mode that is on the next page. Have a key already made out for the exercise sheet as well as likely alternative answers.

VI. Assignment: (Constructing a homework assignment for this lesson is Exercise 11-14 in Chapter 11.)

[3] The class exercise sheet referred to here is on the next page.

Mean, Median, and Mode

Data: The Chamber of Commerce of a town located along the ocean recorded the amount of rainfall per 24 hour period during a 31 day month in the summer. The measurements were recorded to the nearest hundredth of an inch. The following figures for the "average" amount of rainfall per 24-hour period were found:

Mean = .85 in.
Median = .01 in.
Mode = 0 in.

I. In this exercise you are to see how well you can make correct interpretations from the data given above. After each statement listed below you are to place a check mark in one of the five columns according to the following rules. You should check the column headed:
1. if the statement can be shown to be true from the data given,
2. if the statement is probably true, but cannot be shown true from the data alone,
3. if the data is insufficient and no other experiences suggest whether the statement is probably true or probably false,
4. if the statement is probably false, but cannot be shown false from the data alone,
5. if the statement can be shown to be false from the data given.

	1	2	3	4	5
(a) All the rainfall occurred in 16 consecutive 24-hour periods.					
(b) The most frequent reading occurring during this month was no rain.					
(c) Less than 25 inches of rain fell during the entire month.					
(d) This was a wet month for this area.					
(e) There were more days that it rained than days in which no rain fell.					
(f) Not all the rainfall during the month occurred at night.					
(g) Almost half of the days of the month were sunny.					
(h) Either many 24-hour periods were rainy or there was a deluge during several 24-hour periods.					
(i) At least nine 24-hour periods had no measurable rainfall.					

II. Sometimes an average is reported and no indication is given whether it is the mean, median, or mode. People who do not know the difference or do not question what other people tell them can be misled.

Suppose the Chamber of Commerce wanted to publish some information advertising the town to promote its growth and their business. They decide to include the "average" daily rainfall. State which "average" (mean, median, mode) would be most helpful for use in their advertising if they wanted to

____   1. attract tourists to vacation at their beach
____   2. attract industry to move into their town
____   3. attract men willing to build and maintain a golfing resort area
____   4. encourage the growing of a delicate agricultural crop that cannot survive an extreme cloudburst.

Sample Lesson Plans: The Integers Under Addition

THE INTEGERS UNDER ADDITION

Class: Junior High   Date: Day 1

I. Objectives: The student should be able to:
  1. Distinguish between the numeral for an integer and a numeral for a whole number.
  2. Distinguish between the symbol "+" and "-" used as an operation symbol and used as a part of a numeral for an integer.
  3. Identify and state the additive inverse of any given integer.
  4. Demonstrate that two integers are additive inverses by adding them together to determine if their sum is zero.

II. Materials: Colored chalk.

III. Activities:
  1. For each property listed, place a check mark in the column if the number system possesses the property named.

	Whole Numbers	Mod 5
Closure for addition Closure for subtraction Commutative for addition Associative for addition Identity element for addition Additive inverses		

  Have the activity above on the chalkboard or overhead to be started when the bell rings. Discuss as they finish.

  2. Preview: WE HAVE SEEN THAT SUBTRACTION IS ALWAYS POSSIBLE IN MOD 5 ARITHMETIC, YET IN THE WHOLE NUMBERS WE CAN ONLY SUBTRACT WHEN THE SMALLER NUMBER IS SUBTRACTED FROM THE LARGER NUMBER. TODAY, WE WILL CONSIDER WHAT IS REQUIRED TO HAVE CLOSURE FOR SUBTRACTION IN A SYSTEM LIKE THE WHOLE NUMBERS.

417

3. LAST NIGHT FOR HOMEWORK YOU WERE REVIEW-
ING THE USE OF THE DEFINITION OF SUBTRAC-
TION, HOW WOULD THIS PROBLEM BE DONE?

$$7 - 3 = \square$$

Have a student tell how to write 7 - 3 = □ as

$$3 + \square = 7 \text{ and, hence, } \square = 4$$

TRY THE DEFINITION OF SUBTRACTION ON THIS
PROBLEM.

$$3 - 7 = \square$$

Have a student tell how to write 3 - 7 = □ as 7 + □ = 3.
CAN YOU THINK OF A WHOLE NUMBER THAT
ADDED TO 7 WILL YIELD 3? ALTHOUGH THERE IS
NO SUCH WHOLE NUMBER, LET'S LOOK AT THIS
EXAMPLE A LITTLE LONGER TO GET AN IDEA OF
WHAT IS LACKING IN THE WHOLE NUMBERS THAT
PROHIBITS ANSWERING THIS PROBLEM. WHAT
WOULD BOX HAVE TO REPRESENT IF WE WISHED
TO GET AN ANSWER TO OUR PROBLEM? (If they say
"minus three," ask how could I have 7 plus minus 3. That
would mean add and then subtract 3. If I did that, I would
get 0 and, hence, I would have 7 = 3. Impossible!).

Rewrite 7 as (3 + 4) so that the problem now looks like

$$(3 + 4) + \square = 3$$

DOES THAT HELP YOU TO DECIDE WHAT □ WOULD
HAVE TO BE?
Rewrite the expression as

$$3 + (4 + \square) = 3$$

Accent the (4 + □) by underlining it with colored chalk.

WHAT NUMBER MUST THE EXPRESSION IN THE
PARENTHESES NAME?

Give them plenty of time to see this. SINCE 4 + □ = 0,
WE HAVE TWO NUMBERS THAT WHEN ADDED
HAVE THE IDENTITY AS AN ANSWER. HOW IS THE
NUMBER REPRESENTED BY □ AND 4 RELATED?
HENCE, WE COULD DO THIS SUBTRACTION PROB-
LEM IF THE WHOLE NUMBERS HAD ADDITIVE IN-
VERSES. HOW DOES THIS CONCLUSION COMPARE
WITH WHAT WE KNOW ABOUT MOD 5 ARITHMETIC?
FOUR DOES NOT HAVE AN ADDITIVE INVERSE IN
THE WHOLE NUMBERS. WE ARE GOING TO MAKE UP
A NEW NUMBER SYSTEM IN WHICH FOUR AND
OTHER WHOLE NUMBERS WILL HAVE ADDITIVE IN-
VERSES. LOOK AT THIS NUMBER RAY WITH THE

WHOLE NUMBERS SHOWN ON IT. Have number ray on board and numerals labeled with colored chalk.

THE NEW NUMBER SYSTEM WE ARE GOING TO MAKE UP WILL BE CALLED THE INTEGERS. SINCE ALL WE WANT IS ADDITIVE INVERSES FOR NUMBERS LIKE THE WHOLE NUMBERS, WE WILL MAKE UP PART OF THE INTEGERS TO ACT JUST LIKE THE WHOLE NUMBERS. Start writing above each whole number, using a different colored chalk, the corresponding positive integer.

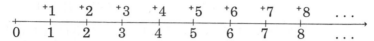

THESE INTEGERS THAT I'M WRITING THAT ARE TO ACT JUST LIKE THE WHOLE NUMBERS WE WILL CALL THE POSITIVE INTEGERS. THE NUMERAL FOR A POSITIVE INTEGER HAS TWO PARTS: (1) A POSITIVE SIGN, AND (2) A NUMERAL FOR A WHOLE NUMBER. Write this on the chalkboard.

$^+2$ IS READ AS "POSITIVE TWO"

HOW WOULD $^+8$ BE READ? THE SYMBOL "$^+$" USED HERE HAS NOTHING TO DO WITH THE OPERATION OF ADDITION. ALTHOUGH A PLUS SIGN AND A POSITIVE SIGN LOOK ALIKE, NOTICE THAT THE POSITIVE SIGN IS RAISED HIGHER THAN A PLUS SIGN FOR ADDITION SO THAT THEY WILL NOT BE CONFUSED.

AN ADDITION PROBLEM WITH POSITIVE INTEGERS WOULD LOOK LIKE:

$^+2 + {}^+3 =$

WHICH "$+$" SYMBOL IS PART OF A NUMERAL? WHICH "$+$" SYMBOL INDICATES THE OPERATION OF ADDITION? HOW WOULD THIS PROBLEM BE READ OR SPOKEN ORALLY?

FOR EACH POSITIVE INTEGER WE ARE GOING TO INVENT ANOTHER INTEGER TO GO WITH IT, AND WE ARE GOING TO SAY THAT THEY ARE ADDITIVE INVERSES. FOR THE INTEGER $^+1$, WE WILL MAKE UP $^-1$ AND SAY THAT $^-1$ IS THE ADDITIVE INVERSE FOR $^+1$. IF WE ADD THEM, WHAT MUST WE THEN GET AS AN ANSWER? WE'LL DO THE SAME FOR $^+2$, $^+3$, ETC.

Write the additive inverse of each integer on the number

line during this discussion and indicate each time that their sum would be zero.

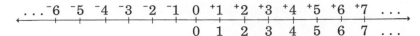

THESE INTEGERS THAT WE ARE MAKING UP TO BE THE ADDITIVE INVERSES OF THE POSITIVE INTEGERS WILL BE CALLED NEGATIVE INTEGERS. THE NUMERAL FOR A NEGATIVE INTEGER CONSISTS OF TWO PARTS: 1) A NEGATIVE SYMBOL, 2) A NUMERAL FOR A WHOLE NUMBER. Write this on the chalkboard.

⁻3 IS READ "NEGATIVE THREE"

ALTHOUGH A NEGATIVE SIGN AND A MINUS SIGN LOOK ALIKE, NOTICE THAT THE NEGATIVE SIGN IS RAISED HIGHER THAN A MINUS SIGN FOR SUBTRACTION SO THAT THEY WILL NOT BE CONFUSED. A SUBTRACTION PROBLEM WITH NEGATIVE INTEGERS WOULD LOOK LIKE

$$^{-}2 - {}^{-}3 =$$

HOW WOULD THIS PROBLEM BE READ OR SPOKEN ORALLY?

5. LET'S LOOK BACK AT WHAT WE HAVE DONE. IN ORDER TO HAVE SUBTRACTION CLOSED, WE DECIDED THAT WE NEEDED INVERSES FOR ADDITION. WE INVENTED A NEW NUMBER SYSTEM.

   (a) WHAT ARE THE NEW NUMBERS CALLED?
   (b) WHAT ARE THE NUMBERS TO THE LEFT OF 0 CALLED? TO THE RIGHT OF 0?
   (c) WHY ARE THERE POSITIVE AND NEGATIVE INTEGERS?
   (d) WHICH INTEGERS ACT EXACTLY LIKE THE WHOLE NUMBERS?
   (e) WHAT DOES THE NUMERAL FOR AN INTEGER LOOK LIKE?
   (f) HOW CAN YOU TELL A NUMERAL THAT NAMES A WHOLE NUMBER FROM ONE THAT NAMES AN INTEGER?
   (g) WHAT IS THE DIFFERENCE BETWEEN A PLUS SIGN AND A POSITIVE SIGN?
   (h) WHAT IS THE ANSWER TO ⁻3 + ⁺3? ⁺5 + ⁻5?

6. HERE ARE SOME PROBLEMS FOR YOU TO TRY IN THE INTEGERS. WORKING ON THESE SHOULD HELP YOU GET A BETTER GRASP OF TODAY'S WORK AND ALSO HELP YOU WHEN WE BEGIN TO ADD INTEGERS TOMORROW. Help students as they are working.

Class Exercise

A. Place a circle around the symbols that represent operations and a triangle around the symbols that are part of a numeral for an integer.

1. $^+2 + {}^+3$ 4. $^+1 \cdot {}^-2$
2. $^-3 + {}^-2$ 5. $^-2 \div {}^-3$
3. $^-3 - {}^-2$ 6. $^+2 - {}^-3$

B. For each problem in part A, translate the problem completely into words. For example, $^+2 - {}^+3$ would be "positive two minus positive three."

C. Write the additive inverse of each of the following integers.

1. $^+3$ 6. $^-(4 - 1)$
2. 0 7. $^-({}^+4)$
3. $^-15$ 8. $^-({}^-6)$
4. $^+(3 \cdot 6)$ 9. ^-a
5. $^-(4 + 1)$

D. Pairs of expressions are given below. Determine for each pair if they are additive inverses. Be prepared to explain your answer.

1. $^+3$ $; {}^-({}^-3)$ 4. ^-a $; {}^-({}^-a)$
2. $^+(1 + 2); {}^-(1 \cdot 3)$ 5. $^+15 + {}^+5; {}^-5 + {}^-15$
3. $^-(2 + 2); {}^+(1 \cdot 3)$ 6. $^+14 + {}^+2; {}^+2 + {}^+14$
                                  7. $^+14 + {}^-2; {}^+2 + {}^-14$

Have answers ready on the overhead or another sheet so that they can check their work.

IV. *Assignment:* (All problems in book from previously studied chapters.)

Three problems in dividing fractions.

One multiplication problem with decimals.

One problem in finding the greatest common factor and least common multiple of two numbers.

One word problem on distance-rate-time.

V. *Summary:* WE BEGAN THE LESSON BY TRYING TO FIND OUT WHAT WAS LACKING IN THE WHOLE NUMBERS SINCE THEY WERE NOT CLOSED TO SUBTRACTION. BECAUSE WE HAD STUDIED MODULAR ARITHMETIC, WE RECOGNIZED THAT INVERSES FOR ADDITION WERE NEEDED. WE MADE A NEW NUMBER SYSTEM, THE INTEGERS, WHERE EVERY NUMBER HAS AN ADDITIVE INVERSE. YOU WILL HEAR A GREAT DEAL MORE ABOUT INTEGERS IN YOUR FUTURE YEARS, BOTH IN MATHEMATICS AND IN YOUR EVERYDAY LIFE.

THE INTEGERS UNDER ADDITION

Class: Junior High   Date: Day 2

I. Objectives: The student should be able to:

1. Demonstrate and describe a procedure for adding any two

integers based upon the requirement to preserve the properties of the whole numbers and assuming the properties
of an additive group.

2. Construct and demonstrate shortcut rules for adding any
   two integers.
3. Describe why the shortcut rules work basing the explanation on the procedure described in objective 1.

II. Materials: No special materials.
III. Activities:
1. Check homework by calling upon students to give their
   answers. Walk around the room and look at homework
   papers as they are answering.
2. Call upon different students to recall and recount to the
   class what they remember of the main points covered in
   the previous day's developmental lesson.
3. Preview: TODAY, WE ARE TO LEARN HOW TO ADD
   ANY TWO OF THESE NEW NUMBERS CALLED INTE-
   GERS. NOTICE THAT WE TRY NOT TO LOSE ANY OF
   THE PROPERTIES OF OUR OLD NUMBER SYSTEM,
   SINCE THAT WOULD DEFEAT OUR PURPOSE. THUS
   WE WILL DEFINE ADDITION OF INTEGERS SO THAT
   THEY WILL HAVE ALL THE PROPERTIES OF THE
   WHOLE NUMBERS AND ALSO GAIN A NEW PROP-
   ERTY FOR ADDITION.
4. LET'S START BY ADDING TWO POSITIVE INTEGERS.
   SINCE THE POSITIVE INTEGERS ARE TO BEHAVE
   LIKE THE WHOLE NUMBERS, WHAT SEEMS TO BE A
   REASONABLE WAY TO ADD:

$$^+6 + {}^+5 =$$
$$^+4 + {}^+8 =$$

WHO CAN DESCRIBE, IN GENERAL, HOW TO ADD
TWO POSITIVE INTEGERS? (Write the general description on the chalkboard for reference.)

5. WE NOW KNOW HOW TO ADD TWO POSITIVES AND
   AN INTEGER AND ITS ADDITIVE INVERSE. LET US
   TURN NOW TO THE PROBLEM OF ADDING TWO
   NEGATIVE INTEGERS, SAY

$$^-5 + {}^-3 = \square$$

WE DON'T KNOW HOW TO ADD $^-5$ to $^-3$. WHAT IS AN
INTEGER YOU DO KNOW HOW TO ADD TO $^-3$? LET'S
ADD THAT.

$$(^-5 + {}^-3) + {}^+3 = \square + {}^+3$$
$$^-5 = \square + {}^+3$$

WHAT INTEGER DO YOU KNOW HOW TO ADD TO $^-5$?
LET'S ADD IT.

$$^-5 + {}^+5 = (\square + {}^+3) + {}^+5$$

$$= \square + (^+3 + ^+5)$$

$$0 = \square + ^+8$$

SINCE $0 = \square + ^+8$, WHAT INTEGER MUST $\square$ REPRE-SENT? THE RESULT OF ADDING NEGATIVE FIVE TO NEGATIVE THREE MUST BE NEGATIVE EIGHT. Ask them to repeat the same procedure to find the sum of negative two and negative four. Let them continue until they can carry out the procedure.

(If anyone thinks that the answer to $^-5 + ^-3$ should be $^+8$ then say) WE KNOW THAT $^+5 + ^+3 = ^+8$. IF $^-5 + ^-3 = ^+8$, THEN THEY BOTH NAME $^+8$, THEIR SUM WOULD BE $^+16$, LIKE THIS:

$$(^-5 + ^-3) + (^+5 + ^+3) = ^+16$$

AND

$$0 = ^+16$$

6. LET'S LOOK AT ADDING A POSITIVE AND A NEGA-TIVE INTEGER, SAY

$$^+5 + ^-3 = \square$$

WE DON'T KNOW HOW TO ADD $^+5$ TO $^-3$. WHAT INTE-GERS DO WE KNOW HOW TO ADD TO $^-3$? DO YOU SEE WHERE WE MIGHT GET A $^+3$ TO ADD TO $^-3$?[1]

$$(^+2 + ^+3) + ^-3 = \square$$

$$^+2 + (^+3 + ^-3) = \square$$

$$^+2 + 0 = \square$$

$$^+2 = \square$$

THUS THE SUM OF POSITIVE FIVE AND NEGATIVE THREE IS POSITIVE TWO. Ask them to do the following in the same manner as the one above.

$$^+8 + ^-5 = \square$$

$$^+3 + ^-7 = \square$$

Go around the room helping any student needing help. When they are able to follow the procedure, start them on the following exercises.

7. Assimilation exercises on the procedures for adding inte-gers introduced in the activities above. (Constructing as-similation activities for this lesson is Exercise 11-8 in Chapter 11.

---

[1] The student may suggest here a procedure like that used in adding $^-5 + ^-3$. That is, starting with $^+5 + ^-3 = \square$, adding first $^+3$ and then $^-5$ to get $0 = \square + (^+3 + ^-5)$. From this they could infer that $\square = ^-3 + ^+5$, but that is all, since they don't know how to add $^-3 + ^+5$. If they suggest this, let them go down this blind alley and let them think about it long enough to realize that it is a dead end.

IV. *Assignment:* Two problems in dividing with decimal numerals.

One problem in changing a numeral from one base to another base.

One word problem on simple interest.

Two problems in adding fractions.

V. *Summary:* Call upon a student to state in one sentence what the day's lesson was about. WHO CAN THINK OF TIMES IN YOUR OWN LIFE WHEN YOU HAVE ALREADY HAD OCCASION TO ADD OTHER THAN POSITIVE INTEGERS? Among other things they might suggest would be temperature, football yardage, and monetary losses.

Appendix **E**

Planning Checklist

PLAN AHEAD

Planning is:

1. Writing out a lesson plan before the class in order to remember what to do and to do it effectively and efficiently.
2. Putting a difficult figure on the chalkboard or on a chart before class begins.
3. Practicing drawing figures and learning the spelling of words used in the lesson.
4. Not erasing the previous example that you need in a later development or exercise.
5. Thinking of effective uses of colored chalk to accent certain aspects of the development.
6. Thinking of which aspects of the development should be written on the chalkboard or overhead and the way they are to be organized.
7. Preparing audio-visual aids and instructional materials that will help a student to learn difficult concepts.
8. Looking ahead for several weeks in order to schedule films, speakers, filmstrips, field trips, and the like.
9. Knowing the subject matter and its development so well that it is automatic and you can concentrate on the students and your teaching techniques.
10. Preparing a short drill, puzzle, or some other activity to have on the chalkboard for the class to work on when the bell rings.
11. Preparing short drills on previously learned material to enhance retention and maintain skills.
12. Making short drills SHORT and frequent and providing opportunities for the students to check their own work quickly.
13. Preparing a short warm-up on old concepts that must be recalled and used in understanding the development of the new material.

14. Providing a preview of what is to occur during the instructional period.
15. Looking ahead in order to indicate to the students how present learning tasks fit into the entire course and where he will encounter them later.
16. Looking in other sources for different instructional strategies for the same topic.
17. Having available an instructional strategy at a higher level and at a lower level to help overcome individual differences.
18. Knowing a different instructional strategy at the same level as the one used in the development for use in a review lesson, or to use with those students who did not understand the first approach and must be retaught.
19. Devising examples and illustrations that are better, clearer, or more interesting than those used in the textbook.
20. Anticipating the places where students will have difficulties and designing activities to help overcome them.
21. Preparing key questions to ask the students during the development to determine if they are comprehending the development.
22. Having counterexamples ready to refute a student's wrong conjecture.
23. Making use of patterns, charts to be filled in, guessing, analogies, and other inductive techniques in the development.
24. Choosing examples that progress from simple to complex.
25. Choosing examples that illustrate a wide range of variations and extreme cases, rather than minimal variety.
26. Providing motivation and experiences that suggest the statements of and reasonableness of axioms, definitions, and theorems.
27. Preparing activities that show the need for precision in notation, symbolism, and language.
28. Looking for strategies in the present topic that are common to all mathematics that the student should generalize.
29. Looking for examples in the topic where deductive techniques at some level of rigor could be used.
30. Preparing activities that involve the student whenever possible.
31. Designing activities that use several modes of instruction during any class period.
32. Looking several days ahead to determine activities intended for assimilation, maintenance, and transfer.
33. Preparing a summary or review at the end of each lesson to clinch the main points.
34. Working out the homework problems in advance before they are assigned.
35. Choosing homework problems that review or drill material that has been developed and assimilated.

36. Choosing homework problems that will provide recall of material needed in an upcoming developmental lesson.
37. Having a word problem in every homework assignment rather than the one time they are studied in the course.
38. Giving different homework assignments to different individuals based upon their needs and abilities.
39. Choosing homework assignments that are short and worthwhile rather than mere busywork or drudgery.
40. Reading in other sources to obtain interesting historical notes, relevant stories, and possible applications.
41. Getting information on your students to help you determine their mathematical abilities and anticipate and forestall problems that may arise.
42. Caring for, having compassion for, and showing a professional affection for your students.

Index